A TENDER B

PETER PELZ

After studying and graduating from Cambridge University in 1969, Peter Pelz worked as a teacher and organizer of arts festivals. He is a writer and an artist who has exhibited throughout Europe. He speaks German, Russian and French as well as English. He was a consultant on the Urban Ministry Project and has been instrumental in establishing the Soul of Europe.

He provided the illustrations to Jim Cotter's *Prayer for the Day*.

DONALD REEVES

After being ordained in 1963 he served as Chaplain to the Bishop of Southwark where he learnt about the problems for the Church in an urban area and how important it was for a priest to understand what makes our cities work. In 1970 he went as vicar to a parish in South London, a large housing estate with 40,000 people. There he established a training centre for young clergy to help them in their ministry in cities – the Urban Ministry Project. In 1980 he was appointed Rector of St James's Church, Piccadilly, an elegant historic church designed by Sir Christopher Wren. But there was only a small congregation and financially it was bankrupt. In eighteen years he established a ministry of 'good practice' which was an inspiration to churches throughout the United Kingdom and mainland Europe. Many visited from all over the world to learn from this ministry, and it was these 'visits' which led him to establish the Soul of Europe when he left St James's in 1998. He is a well-known writer and broadcaster.

Books published include *Church and State*, Hodder (1981), *For God's Sake*, Fontana (1984), *Making Sense of Religion*, BBC (1989) and *Down to Earth*, Mowbray (1996).

A TENDER BRIDGE

A JOURNEY TO ANOTHER EUROPE

PETER PELZ &
DONALD REEVES

CAIRNS PUBLICATIONS
SHEFFIELD
2001

British Library Cataloguing in Publication Data

A record for this book is available from the British Library

ISBN 1 870652 34 7

CAIRNS PUBLICATIONS
47 Firth Park Avenue, Sheffield S5 6HF

www.cottercairns.co.uk
office@cottercairns.co.uk – orders
jim@cottercairns.co.uk – editorial

Typeset in Monotype Baskerville by
Strathmore Publishing Services, London N7

Printed in Great Britain by
Biddles of Guildford and Kings Lynn

I dedicate this book to my aunt,
Jutta Bergt,
who survived Auschwitz
and taught me how to face human wickedness.

I mix up life and death – who are joined by a tender bridge

SENGHOR

CONTENTS

FOREWORD

This journal is a mixture of a detailed travelogue and the birth and refinement of an idea. It charts the deep concern at the loss of faith in Europe in the realm of the Spirit – its Soul – to an engagement with a particular country and its communities and people. In a real sense the Soul of Europe through its officers, Donald Reeves and Peter Pelz, has been led to that region of Europe where the Spirit has been and continues to be, most savagely crucified. It ends in Bosnia and the particular communities of Banja Luka and Bihac and their people. It is here that the Soul of Europe has come to focus its energies. For those associated with the it, the realm of the Spirit is inseparable from how we, as human beings, as Europeans, live together. But the journal also carries a message. It is not only that forgiveness is fundamental to the future of Bosnia, it is fundamental to the future of Europe too. Europe itself needs forgiveness for the part it has played in the history of the Balkans and in the betrayals of the conflicts of the 1990s. Forgiveness implies the acknowledgment of responsibility at both a personal and national level. It is critical for Europe's soul and its very future. That is why Europe must not forget or ignore Bosnia. The Soul of Europe is privileged to be engaged with these profoundly important issues through its work in Banja Luka and Bihac

JOHN AUSTIN
Bishop of Aston
Birmingham, September 2001

PREFACE

A Tender Bridge – a Journey to another Europe charts the progress of the Soul of Europe from the birth of a vision in 1998 to the establishing of projects in Bosnia in 2001.

After each journey two reports were written: one for the Advisory Council who monitored our progress, and one for those who had given donations, so they could see how their money had been spent. These reports were written by Donald Reeves. Then there were reports of a more detailed and personal nature, in the form of a diary written by Peter Pelz, which became the basis of this book.

Our initial plan was to complete our journeys throughout Europe before deciding on particular projects, but our visit to Serbia brought that objective forward more quickly than we anticipated.

PETER PELZ

DONALD REEVES

Crediton, September 2001

ACKNOWLEDGMENTS

Chief among these are Donald Reeves without whom this book would never have been written and Jim Cotter who painstakingly edited my script. I also want to thank Lazar Markovic for organizing our first visit to Serbia and so changing my life. Acknowledgments must also be made to Igor Solunac, Adnan Jabucar, and Teuvo Laitila who corrected mistakes in the manuscript. And thanks to all the people I met on my travels around Europe who appear in this book and who inspired it.

I also wish to thank Nadir Dinshaw and my father, Dr Werner Pelz, for their constant encouragement and support.

MAPS

The map of Europe on the left-hand page shows places where the initial visit has resulted in an organization becoming a partner in the Soul of Europe.

The larger scale map on the right-hand page shows locations visited on the tour to Serbia and Bosnia.

Locations of partners of the Soul of Europe

Locations visited on the journey to Serbia and Bosnia

PROLOGUE

PETER PELZ AND DONALD REEVES

Far to the West of Europe, in North Wales, high on a hill overlooking Tremadoc Bay stands Llandecwyn, a simple nineteenth-century church built on medieval foundations. One thousand five hundred years ago a party of missionary monks sailed up the Irish Sea from Brittany and one of them chose to settle here. The view from the churchyard, which has been a burial place from pre-Christian times, embraces a wide panorama from Harlech Castle on the left, over the Llyn Peninsula with its scattered farms and homesteads, the small town of Porthmadog and the village of Portmeirion built in the Italian style and famous for its setting of the Seventies cult TV series, *The Prisoner*, across the estuary of the Afon Dwyryd and to the right, the majestic Mount Snowdon. Sheep populate the slopes around the church, their bleating mingling with the trilling of larks and the twittering of swallows who nest in the eaves of the porch. The church is not used much, and so Jim Cotter, a priest from Sheffield, comes in the temperate summer months to keep the place open every day for prayer and meditation. Whoever passes is welcome. People come from all over to join him. Often he prays alone. Sometimes at night's approaching, by himself or in company, he watches before evening prayer the sun set over the Llyn Peninsula while necklaces of lights begin to twinkle around the estuary. On clear nights, the moon rises furtively over the remote mountains behind Harlech Castle. Then it can be light enough for a walk up Snowdon to wait for the next morning's sunrise. The church is occasionally used for weddings and traditional services, but mostly it is a place of meditation and quiet reflection. In winter, unheated and too far from the main road, it remains empty, the winds blowing fiercely from the sea.

Far to the South and East of Europe in a remote region of North Western Bosnia, in the village of Martin Brod, another small church nestles in a valley between high, thickly forested hills, turquoise waters falling over majestic waterfalls into the calm wide River Una which flows between flower filled meadows through Bosnia, along the border with Croatia and across Serbia before joining the Danube and moving eastward to the Black Sea. A thousand years ago Orthodox monks established the Rmanj Monastery here. For centuries the communities of these three countries fought, killing one another, destroying homes, churches and mosques, right to the present day. The monastery no longer exists, but the small church survives. Brothers Sophronje, Seraphim and Serghei, three young monks, have chosen to return. They live in borrowed accommodation, and worship daily in the church. Recently a Canadian army officer managed to defuse a carefully laid mine intended to blow them up with the building. As regularly as he can, Bishop Chrysostom of Bihac Petrovac crosses the mountains from Shipovo, two hours' ride away, to join in their prayers. People are gradually returning to the area, fearfully but wanting to settle in their old homes. A few attend Sunday Service. Mostly the monks are alone, faithfully celebrating the ancient traditional Orthodox liturgies. Outside, the cherry trees blossom, and people till the land and fish the waters of the River Una.

The Soul of Europe visited both these churches in June/July 2000 and is creating a link between them, at either end of Europe, remote and neglected places where a few dedicated souls manage to keep the fragile flame of prayer alight. A poem by Heine expresses the yearning for a relationship across a seemingly unbridgeable continental divide:

In the North, a pine tree
Stands alone on a bleak mountain;
It slumbers, wrapped
In a white cover of snow and ice.

It dreams of a palm tree
Far away in the East

Solitary and silently grieving
On a burning rock face.

In Bosnia, in the town of Banja Luka lives a mufti who has nowhere to worship. Every mosque was destroyed in the most recent war. His community fears to return and the authorities block his appeals to rebuild the Ferhadija Mosque, a jewel of the Ottoman Empire. Meanwhile the Orthodox bishop in Banja Luka is allowed to build extravagant new churches. In the town of Bihac, several hours' drive to the west, the Orthodox bishop there has nowhere to worship either. The unfinished walls are daubed with graffiti and the wind whistles through the empty windows. Meanwhile shiny new mosques bristle in the surrounding countryside. We visited both places and hope that our modest efforts will help these separate communities to learn to tolerate one another.

We travelled to Northern Europe, visiting Finland, Sweden and Denmark. There the churches stand smart and undisturbed and, with notable exceptions, few people come to worship. We met with church leaders, politicians, and people of influence, who listened to us attentively, if often bemused and doubtful about the precise nature of our objectives. They preferred to have concrete proposals, projects that can be seen and quantified. They would assist us once we had something definite on paper. The situation in the Balkans is recognizably desperate; so our projects there attract attention and interest. However, the situation in the rest of Europe, though not as dramatic and tragically extreme, is not so different, in the sense that all communities have difficulties living together. Europe remains a sharply divided part of the world. It is hard to consider Bosnia and the rest of the Balkans as part of the same continent. The Soul of Europe is attempting to help the process of healing these divisions, to bring people together from every corner, to link those fragile flames and make them more vigorous.

The fundamental vision of the Soul of Europe has remained steadfast throughout the first year of its existence, though the nature of the project has changed as a result of the first journeys throughout Europe. This was to be expected. Our intentions were to be open-eyed, open-minded and open-hearted on all our travels. This book traces the development of these changes, starting with Donald Reeves's sermon at Grace Cathedral in San Francisco where the idea of the project first took shape. At each step of the way we recorded meetings and ideas, and submitted reports, and through them it becomes clear how the Soul of Europe progressed. Meanwhile I have been writing a more elaborate diary of events and experiences, observing people, places and encounters with both a more objective and subjective eye – objective in that I try not to impose a particular project-based perspective on what happened, letting the facts speak for themselves, subjective in that as an artist I am only too aware of the importance of the personal viewpoint, because it is shared emotion that elicits the most powerful and therefore most productive response.

Donald's eighteen-year ministry between 1980 and 1998 at St James's Church, Piccadilly, in the centre of London, attracted visitors from all over the world, particularly priests from other countries. They wanted to learn how to build successful, lively, open-minded and reflective ministries in a world that is turning mostly secular, or where people are turning to exclusive and extreme forms of fundamentalism. Donald did not retire from St James's: he wanted to devote his time to exploring ways of networking these new ministries throughout Europe, so that people could learn from one another and be in active contact. Before St James's he established an equally vibrant ministry in the housing estate parish of St Helier on the outskirts of London. Here he established the Urban Ministry Project where clergy, social workers, teachers and whoever was interested could improve their work methods, widen their vision, and create effective working links with the community. The experience of these two ministries over more than thirty years has given Donald the particular skills needed to establish the networks of communities and ministries that are now the Soul of Europe.

Alan Jones, Dean of Grace Cathedral, St Francisco, invited Donald to preach a sermon there a few months after he left St James's. Donald works occasionally as a consultant for the mining company Rio Tinto, advising them on their community affairs policy, and he visited one of their mining operations in California before preaching the sermon. The unlikely and unexpected perspective of this different kind of work inspired him. Donald preaches without a script. The preparation is strenuous, sermons are written out, learnt, discarded, and written again. The texts then become so familiar that he can share asides, jokes, and images with the congregation, moving about between them rather than standing aloof in a pulpit, holding eye contact and so preserving a high quality of concentration. Here is a reworking of the sermon which led to the birth of the Soul of Europe. It was given on 17 January 1999.

I have just returned from the Mojave Desert visiting US Borax – a mining operation owned by Rio Tinto. This is an Anglo Australian company; I work there as part-time consultant on community relations and ethical matters.

Before that I was in San Juan Capistrano at a Conference Centre together with twenty-five pastors, mostly evangelical and involved in church 'planting'. There my task was to help the clergy look at their work – what they felt about it and what they could do differently or better.

These visits were for me, and I hope for the many I worked with, an exercise in the use of the imagination. 'Everything begins in the imagination,' said the English poet, William Blake. Imagination is God's gift to us – it is the ability to see the world differently, to see it as it might be, as it could be. The imagination invites the dismantling or at least the relinquishing of the familiar. Unless our ideals 'catch the imagination' they will die. The imagination disturbs, disrupts and destabilises familiar and fixed ways of understanding experience and through symbols, metaphors, images and stories suggests alternative worlds. It is the crucial agent for change.

So in the mining industry moral questions are stacking up. If the construction of a mine means jobs in an area of great poverty, is that price worth paying for the loss of a variety of species which have provided people with a livelihood of sorts? Is it right for exploration to take place on land regarded as sacred by those whose ancestors are buried there? Should a company like Rio Tinto, which has endorsed the United Nations Declaration of Human Rights, operate in a region where basic human rights are ignored? The answers to these difficult questions ultimately invite new understandings of the place of business in the community. And that is a task for the imagination. (There are now so many questions being asked of business that an unhurried, imaginative approach to business is required. However, institutions of every sort co-opt the imagination: it then becomes difficult to 'think the unthinkable'.)

So for the clergy, I invited them to describe the social and economic context in which they lived and worked, and then – for that description was often a dismal process – to suggest in pictures, images, and metaphor what their world could be like: thinking the unthinkable, what could their parish be? Their imagination became the means for transformation and without fail it encouraged, refreshed, and inspired. ('Means for transformation' implies more than lighting on an image. It means analysis, prayer, reflection, hard work and so on.)

The imagination may seem to some a little fanciful. But consider the Gospels. Story after story invites the reader to see herself and the world as it could be. For example in St Luke, Chapter 13, Jesus comes upon a woman who has been crippled for eighteen years. He invites her to stand up straight. He lays his hands on her. Later, Jesus addresses her as 'a daughter of Abraham', one in whose body the promises of God are powerfully at work. The world sees her differently: crippled, dysfunctional, worthless. Moreover she had accepted that debilitating condition as the way her life was. Jesus contradicts this. He renames her. He imagines her otherwise. She accepts. And as the story says: 'she stood up straight and began praising God.' The power of Jesus lies in part in this ancient Abrahamic text, 'daughter of Abraham', to which he appeals in a context where that text had long ago been domesticated, flattened and dismissed.

This has been a long prologue to what I want to speak about this morning: something about which I have never yet spoken in public and which for the first time I feel it is right to address in this place, in this most cosmopolitan of cities, far from London.

For many years in the United Kingdom, there has been a debate: it has taken place in the narrowest of circles among politicians and business people. It has been about the future of Europe, and the place of the United Kingdom in Europe. The debate centres round the loss of the pound sterling and joining the single currency – when the time is ripe. But is there nothing more to be said? Is building a new Europe just a political and economic exercise? Is there not a spiritual and ethical dimension demanding our attention? Given the diversity of peoples in our cities, are there not urgent questions about justice to be answered? How can our imagination be put to work? My strictures about the market should not be misconstrued. I believe in a 'market economy'. I wish it could be more humane and collaborative in its operation and more regulated. My objections to the market are when consumerism becomes an addiction, when what is essentially a transaction is turned into a pseudo-religion, demanding our allegiance and rendering us powerless. This is idolatry and it weakens true religion, which is to love God and our neighbour as ourselves.

So other voices need to be brought swiftly, urgently into this debate – vulnerable minorities, the broken and the poor, those who speak on behalf of the environment, the voices of women, poets, philosophers and artists, the voices of all religious communities, Christian, Muslim and Jewish. The debate (it can hardly be called that, so uninterested are ninety-five per cent of the British public) must be widened, extended, deepened and thickened. All of us living in European cities have to find a way to live together; discovering a politics, a citizenship, where difference and diversity are welcomed and celebrated. It is a task for the imagination.

It is the imagination that has given me the vision of a network of European churches who with many others will help to bring to birth a new Europe, well beyond the agenda of economists and politicians, important as they are. I long for the day when the 'Soul of Europe' can be affirmed and celebrated, when the dignity of each and every person, of every living soul, is recognized, and everyone and everything flourishes. That is the best I can do to describe the Kingdom of God – never to be fully realized on this earth!

Such a vision has to be ecumenical – Orthodox, Protestant and Catholic – Eastern as well as Western Europe. It will be rooted in local communities. For many years there have been gatherings of academics, theologians, church leaders and church representatives on matters European, but now here is an opportunity for local communities already working in this process of transformation to learn from one another, powerfully support one another and share their stories of best practice. Already I hear of unusual liturgies in Oslo and Cardiff; I am learning of Catholic and Muslim communities in Marseilles working together. They should know what is going on in Bradford, England. I know of many Orthodox churches in St Petersburg and Moscow trying to be places of sanity in situations of grave danger.

Notice how the vision of the 'Soul of Europe' – big words – is brought down to earth in the strivings of local communities. As these stories are brought to light on a wider stage, so the debate about Europe will change, and at the same time church communities across regions and countries will discover a new solidarity and a new fellowship together.

Such a project is not for Christians alone. Over the last six months I have listened to politicians, journalists, artists, business-people responding to what I am saying. Many ask: "What about the other religions, particularly Judaism?" In Russia and parts of Germany there is still much anti-Semitism. And what about Islam? There is a long history of prejudice in Christian Europe against Muslim communities. So in every city where this project is based there needs to be an ongoing forum of the major religious traditions who through thick and thin will meet together, hasten to respect and learn from one another and work for peace and reconciliation, each tradition drawing out its very best for the common good.

These words are easier said than done because we have betrayed a whole generation in whose hands our future lies. Recently I was invited to undertake a mission to University College, Dublin, a Catholic University on the edge of that great city. Each lunchtime and early evening I spoke to some three hundred people on Christianity and its relationship to the formidable problems facing the planet. You will no doubt guess the subjects I spoke about. In the evenings I visited the common rooms and there I received almost total contempt for what I had said in my lectures. For them, Christianity was like an ageing, near extinct dinosaur. For them, the irrelevance of the churches was the kindest thing they had to say. I was thrown by the vehemence of their comments. But over the years, in many places and in many countries, I have met this sense of betrayal. We are experiencing a dark night in which Christ has withdrawn from the Church. It is as if we have been abandoned by God, forgotten by God – as if we have been deserted. And there is a real urgency to acknowledge this abandonment and to discover some sense and practice of corporate repentance as we move forward in developing and working out the vision I have shared with you today.

The image of the dark night comes from St John of the Cross, but it is also an image pregnant with hope because it is at the darkest place where God's absence is experienced – in despair and in nothingness – that the light slowly dawns. Then we can embrace our vocation for justice, for the soul of each and every person. And this work of justice, establishing right relations, is a continuous process. It is the incarnation of God's unconditional love.

I have said that this is the first time I have spoken publicly about this vision, which I feel called upon to realize. I rest in the promises of God. The Bible confesses more than it understands: it claims more than can ever be explained. For ancient Israel, so often the Bible tells stories of God who makes promises and keeps them, promises given in the most difficult situations (think of Abraham and Sarah – so old she could not bear children, and yet…). I rest in amazement and wonder at these promises. Or as St Paul puts it, reflecting on that very story in Romans, chapter 4, this God in whom Israel believes "gives life to the dead and calls into existence the things that do not exist" (verse 17).

So here is my dream, for myself, for us all, and for Europe:

> Bread. A clear sky. Active peace.
> A woman's voice singing somewhere.
> The army disbanded.
> The harvest abundant. The wound healed.
> The child wanted. The prisoner freed.
> The body's integrity honoured.
> The lover returned. The labour equal,
> Fair and valued.
> Delight in the challenge for the consensus
> To solve problems. No hand raised
> In any gesture but greeting.
> Secure interiors of heart, home, land.
> So firm as to make
> Secure borders irrelevant at last.
> A humble earthly paradise.

Amen. So be it. Let it be so.

CHARTRES, PARIS AND BRUSSELS

April 1999

DIARY – PETER PELZ

During that visit to San Francisco, Alan Jones invited Donald to his wedding in Chartres Cathedral. We attended the ceremony before travelling to Brussels on a fundraising mission for our European Churches Network – as we then called the Soul of Europe. The purpose of the visit was to meet Members of the European Parliament who might become our allies and then to gain access to the inner sanctum of Commissioners (mostly disgraced after recent charges of corruption, but still operating) because they have their hands on the pursestrings. Just as Rio Tinto plc provided the unexpected inspiration for the sermon at Grace Cathedral, so the wedding in Chartres became an important part of the development of the Soul of Europe .

CHARTRES

There was nothing straightforward about this wedding. The bride and groom were both divorced, each with a family of grown-up children. Alan Jones is Anglican. His bishop, an Episcopalian, had agreed to perform the ceremony in the Catholic cathedral at Chartres. Apparently the bride, Cricket, had fallen in love with Chartres and throwing caution to the winds had simply asked the dean of Chartres whether their marriage could be quietly blessed there – suggesting using the crypt – and he agreed without hesitation, while insisting that the ceremony should be in the Great Choir. It seems that similar ecumenical cross-church celebrations happen occasionally. The Catholic hierarchy in Paris frowns on such liberalism and it is forbidden. But grassroots activity like this forges ahead and will eventually change the rigid pattern of demoninationalism in Europe.

Donald had originally been asked to play the organ, but in the event, the organist of Grace Cathedral came over specially.

Donald then found himself standing in for Robert Runcie, the former Archbishop of Canterbury, who had been invited to celebrate the Eucharist at the wedding but was unwell and couldn't come.

We met Jim Cotter, the priest from Sheffield who spends the summer months in the quiet church overlooking Tremadoc Bay in North Wales, and discussed with him the purpose of the Soul of Europe. We tried to establish the cause of the universal malaise, particularly with religion and the church, at the end of the millennium. Jim came up with a potent image of the old traditions in tatters and us now being left to spin fresh thread for future generations to weave new cloth. We contemplated the splendour of the cathedral that represented ancient traditional religious certainties and wondered what the human imagination might produce in the next thousand years to match this confident and transcendent vision.

I offered to turn the pages for the organist. The organ in Chartres Cathedral is reached by a secret spiral staircase. The doors have to be kept locked at all times, probably for reasons apart from the privacy of the organist. It can be dangerous up there with no banister along the high corridor and it would be easy to fall eighty foot below (or push someone). Two of the rooms on the way to the organ are full of the most priceless sculptures that have been removed from their original places in the cathedral. Possibly they had been mutilated in the Revolution, or had been replaced. I ran my hand wonderingly over the beautifully polished features of Madonnas and saints and speculated how easy it would be to fit one under my jacket and take it home. The organ loft is not for those suffering from vertigo. It perches high above the cathedral floor and every creak makes the heart beat faster. But the view is sensational. One can see close up the windows of the upper storeys and they are different from the ones below. Those more familiar stained glass masterpieces teem with detail and narrative, all the incidents wrapped in bold swirling decorative patterns. The upper windows are portraits of warrior knights and bishops, larger than life, many of whom had been on crusades, and having slaughtered Muslims there, brought back the inspiration of Islam that permeates the cathedral. The warriors look ferocious, eyes blazing with psychotic conviction of their righteous task, legs apart and weapons grasped firmly in large hands. The portraits also manage to convey, subtly through fractured structure and the use of muddy brown colours interrupted by gashes of blazing crimson, the toughness of their times and the squalor of their lives. The colours are even more vivid and uncontrolled than in the great windows below where the famous Chartres blue predominates, the heavenly blue of Mary who gives the cathedral her name. Here angry reds splash over the portraits like blood and wine. Looking too long at these portraits can be oppressive, but they moved me unexpectedly. They provided a final balance to my overall impression of this ever-surprising cathedral. Even the bishops held weapons, but their faces did not stare with the violent intensity of the warriors, rather melting with fear and compassion.

The young organist of Chartres Cathedral was showing the wedding organist how to work the instrument. The difficulty apparently is judging the volume of sound. Since the pipes surround the player it requires imagination to judge the amount of sound desired, because only the people below can hear it. A television screen and an intercom help the organist coordinate with the priests celebrating Mass way out of sight and reach. Later in the vestry Donald and the other invited clergy tried on vestments, the dean sitting on a throne-like chair and ordering his handsome, harassed but ever polite and kindly verger (one of only two who look after the cathedral and keep it clean) to display a multitude of sumptuous robes. Ancient and elaborately jewelled chalices were chosen as were also golden croziers for the bishop to carry. Bishop Swing of San Francisco looked decidedly embarrassed. The message seemed to be that since the ceremony flouted the rules anyway, it might as well be celebrated with pomp and style.

At the wedding ceremony, standing in the organ loft gave me a spectacular view of the famous Chartres labyrinth in the middle of the nave. The chairs had been moved specially and I watched one of the American women guests, carefully and thoughtfully wending her way along the elaborate curves until she reached the centre, a moment that comes unexpectedly after a long walk and she stood still in a state of shock. In ancient rites the priest would have led the congregation in a dance towards this focal spot which is also the epicentre of the cathedral. At a time when there was no furniture in the building, the worshippers would have experienced the awe-inspiring sensation of being pivotal in this spectacular edifice built to the glory of God. For that moment each person would have felt both the intimacy of their relationship with God as well as an awareness of the infinite and eternal. Outside the cathedral, life is bounded by the certainties of death and the Day of Judgement. Inside, human beings had attempted to convey the wonder and mystery of paradise, the abode of God, through the scale of the building and the splendour of the stained glass. Yet it is specifically at the centre of the pagan symbol of a labyrinth that each person can most intensely experience oneness with God.

From the organ I got the best view of the procession because the dean ordered the west door to be opened and light flooded in from below, creating an unexpected contrast to the rose window and the three great windows below it. With the doors closed the windows dominate the dark interior with their shifting schemes of light and colour. People are insignificant. But when light floods in through the door, suddenly people become important and are framed by the radiant windows all round. The dean, bishops, and priests moved like a forest of Christmas trees in solemn procession to greet the bride and groom, who then walked down the aisle. The doors closed behind, shutting out the sunlight and rendering the people insignificant again.

PARIS

We had contacted a number of journalists scattered over Europe who contribute regularly to *The Tablet*, a Catholic weekly in England. It is read and admired by all denominations for its open-minded opinions and high standard of reporting, and has always encouraged and helped Donald, regularly inviting him to write articles. This might seem odd considering that Donald is an Anglican, but the Anglican newspaper, the *Church Times*, treats him with suspicion and cautiously restricts his contributions, if accepted, to the letter pages, where the paper can be seen to be fair without appearing to support his views. Most of *The Tablet* journalists replied to our letter which tried to describe as clearly as possible the as yet tentative proposals for setting up a network of lively churches and communities throughout Europe. We told them our objectives: establishing contact with those who attend to matters of justice and peace, are concerned with social and environmental issues, supportive of minorities, and developing imaginative ministries. They may be experiencing difficulties with their hierarchies, and feeling vulnerable, in need of encouragement because they operate on the edge of traditional religious practice. The purpose of such a European network would be to challenge and provide an alternative to the narrow interests of the European Union, an alliance of the richest and most powerful countries of the continent locked in their obsessions with money, business and politics to the exclusion of other more human and pressing issues. We hoped that a few journalists might understand the gist of our objectives and help us locate interesting and exciting communities and churches, perhaps even introduce us to relevant people and set up meetings.

Robert Kelly, who reports on French church matters for *The Tablet*, replied from Paris, so we decided to stop there on our way to Brussels. We engaged in our first serious discussion about the project with a sympathetic stranger.

Robert Kelly met us outside the metro station at Montparnasse. He reminded me of my father, wiry and trim with an intellectual's shaggy beard, kindly, open-minded and thoughtful. He spoke with a broad Glaswegian accent and fed us much information and advice about people and places to contact.

He first took us to a chapel situated next to the Gare Montparnasse, a part of Paris with few striking historical monuments and no palaces, just high rise and featureless buildings, constant traffic and crowds of office workers rushing past the beggars crouching outside the station. The Gare Montparnasse contains a gigantic subway connecting metro lines where people are reduced to swarms of ants moving ceaselessly like the set of Fritz Lang's futurist film fantasy, *Metropolis*. The exterior of the chapel looked unpromising, with a dispiriting, tapering, and rusty metal cross pinned on the outside and a couple of tramps loitering at the entrance. The interior opened into a roomy, pleasantly furnished and decorated lounge area, a cool, clean haven from the heat and bustle outside.

We sat down on spacious metal chairs which cupped the body in such a way as to make it hard to get up again, and from this embarrassingly prone position wasted no time on introductory pleasantries but began to discuss the project. Robert Kelly had prepared a long list of likely groups to contact and I found myself scribbling lists, hardly able to follow the speeding conversation and certainly unable to join in. He told us about the Lazaristes, known also as the Vincentian Fathers, committed to working for the poorest, who have a mother house in Paris where the network might be able to hold international meetings (they provide instantaneous translations as well) and which, perhaps because of the monastic standards of accommodation, is classically underused. He told us about St Gervais near the Pompidou Centre where a Catholic charismatic community have an interesting liturgy, orthodox in style but prayerful.

Robert Kelly advised us on the way the Soul of Europe network might operate in concentric rings, with committed churches at the centre of the organization and interested others circling on the edge. He also told us to concentrate on those traditional orders like the Franciscans and Dominicans who keep close to founding principles. The latter have a popular ministry in Amsterdam where I remember attending morning service on a Sunday – immediately it ended the whole congregation sat back with a sigh of relief and lit cigarettes, smoke suddenly rising from several hundred upturned faces and creating a nauseating cloud that filled the church. In Paris the Dominicans are apparently more academic. The Jesuits are open, engaged, and activist in

Paris: we should go to St Ignace where pastoral and academic concerns run in parallel. Present day Jesuits are no longer the ogres of history and mythology who converted colonies with swords, guns, and threats of hellfire, or involved themselves in corrupt power politics. I remember one particular Jesuit priest from Central America who visited Donald at St James's and ever since has carried a reproduction of the Seven Lamps triptych I painted for the church on his travels across the region where he attends to the poor and sick. The picture when opened is a dream of heaven on earth, an attempt to depict the opening lines of those parables of Jesus which begin with the words: "The Kingdom of God is like unto...", followed by an often perplexing story, ambivalent in its message and flaunting accepted worldly principles of moral justice which stipulate that only success in life is rewarded. The story shows how the promise of heaven is open even and especially to those who feel they have failed and who are lost. The picture also tries to convey the hope and wonder of those passages in the Bible which describe impossible and contradictory images of peace and coexistence, lions lying down with lambs, children with hands over the nest of snakes. No one is more aware than I am of the impossibility of such utopian visions, which is why I prefer the tryptich to be opened only on special occasions. It represents the world as it could, but never can, be. Wherever the Jesuit priest happens to be, he opens the picture up on his table and looking at it apparently sustains him in his frequently gruelling work. Perhaps it can also sustain us as we seek to embody the vision of 'another Europe'.

Robert Kelly also told us about the Institute Catholique in Paris which is so liberal in its courses that Cardinal Ratzinger refuses to send students there. The basis of their teaching is to look to the human sciences to make sense of faith. We should also visit La Defence, a futuristic corner of Paris where a new church is being built to serve the people, the Cathedral at Evrey, and St Severin where they celebrate a liturgy similar to that at St James's Piccadilly, based on tradition but incorporating new ideas. Robert Kelly encouraged us to target young people on inter-university schemes which operate in affluent western countries. To balance this Donald wants to develop exchanges with people in central and eastern Europe, from Kiev, Warsaw, and Moscow.

We talked about the male domination of the Catholic Church where the congregations consist mostly of women. A number of the more active of these dedicate themselves to specific causes and could be interested in our project. He encouraged us to make contact with the Bayard Presse, a Catholic organisation which is influential and rich, being the fourth biggest publisher in France and dedicated to reaching people in their particular circumstances. They distribute informative and well produced magazines for children and adults, casting the net wide over all important issues and not specifically from a church point of view. If we identify an area of spending (like convening a conference of religious presses/publishers) then they might give funds for that.

Robert Kelly reminded us not to forget the Iona Community in Glasgow or Taizé where it would be best to contact Roger Schutz. I remembered a New Year's vigil at St James's when the church filled with a thousand teenagers who looked more as though they were at a quiet kind of rave than a service, nothing pious or self-righteous in their manner. They lit candles, sang, stayed for hours and hugged one another, eyes shining.

We discussed the principles behind the Soul of Europe, the kind of church communities we were looking for. A crucial factor to identify might be 'hospitality', at once ecclesial and personal. We would have to create new models, providing maximum structure of support but without defining in too much detail what should actually happen. Donald suggested the possibility of providing 'mentors', honorary curates, older people with vision and experience who could help younger priests in difficult urban areas.

The three of us continued our conversation over a simple lunch of steak, chips, salad, a bottle of wine and crusty French bread. We discussed the inter-denominational service at Chartres and I remembered the windows opposite the organ, the wildly staring warriors and bishops. Suddenly the size of our project frightened me, the impossible task of engaging with those in authority and persuading them to take our project seriously. Human imagination produces a great cathedral, but feels often powerless against the cynicism of those ambitious people who are convinced that only politics and money matter. We now planned to visit a few of these people in Brussels.

BRUSSELS

One of the first people of political influence to encourage Donald with our project was Lord Plumb of Coleshill. He agreed to meet Donald at the House of Lords, having received a copy of the letter we were sending to everybody explaining our objectives. Politicians like him received a version that diplomatically made a point of recognizing the importance of politics, business, and the market, but suggesting there were "other voices needing to be heard" in the debate over a united Europe. Lord Plumb sat down opposite Donald, looked him in the eye and said: "Why hasn't anyone thought of this before?" He used to be the President of the European Parliament and though about to retire from Brussels remained a popular and active figure there. He invited us to visit the European Parliament and offered to introduce us to those MEPs and Commissioners who might be helpful to the project. Without Lord Plumb there is no question that the Soul of Europe would not exist, not as it is now. He supported us firmly throughout our first year of hunting for funding and making friends, and found our first major sponsor. He did not toe the Tory line under Margaret Thatcher and made a point of telling her that he "was born an Englishman" and would "die a European". His position is clear and straightforward: we are now part of Europe and there is no going back on that issue. For that reason it is understandable why he supports the project so unreservedly. We are opening the debate about Europe far beyond the narrow confines of politics and the market and therefore will help educate future generations about the possibilities and nature of this new continental community. He also has links with Coventry Cathedral with its policies of reconciliation and peace-building, not only between

England and Germany after World War II, but all over the world where communities are still in conflict. Lord Plumb was sympathetic to Donald's Anglican constituency. He therefore arranged for us to meet MEPs with known religious affiliations, and this led to some bizarre encounters.

The European Parliament straddles Brussels like a monstrously oversized greenhouse. Apparently this glass castle will one day be empty because the Parliament will move to Strasbourg where they will have to build something twice as large to accommodate the new member states from central and eastern Europe. The effect on Brussels is oppressive: most of the city seemed to be under reconstruction and we exited the station stepping straight into a puddle on a stretch of wasteland where we eventually spied a taxi. Later, we walked up and down long streets where the names are written in tiny letters, though elegantly in an old-fashioned script, the city clearly not interested in helping foreigners find their way about. We then took several trams, buses and underground trains to the city centre. I sat for a few hours in a luxurious sauna, built on a lavish scale over several storeys, and allowed memories of the wedding and my anxieties about the next day's meetings to melt away. Sitting undisturbed in the jacuzzi I observed the young, attractive clientele following one another about, furtively and fearful of being rejected. I couldn't help wondering whether I might be looking at people we would meet the next day at the Parliament.

Despite the fact that the Cascade Hotel makes its business out of the Parliament's presence in their city, the staff were singularly unhelpful when we asked for directions. They misled us and gave us the most circuitous route, which involved trekking up and down long streets and eventually getting lost round the backside of the monster greenhouse. We arrived late, but the first MEP on our list had made an error with dates, and so we need not have panicked. However, it gave me the impression that work is not taken seriously here and that MEPs are relaxed about appointments.

Lord Plumb's assistants looked after us. Todd McClay had rather chilled me on the phone with his formality, implying we should mind our ps and qs, but he turned out to be amenable and friendly – because Lord Plumb had invited us, no doubt. He'd have given us short shrift under different circumstances. He behaved like a consultant, fair-haired, young, but looking prematurely middle-aged, with no trace of humour and a cautious demeanour that gave nothing away about what he was really thinking. Carlina Walton fetched us from reception and spent most of the time guiding us through the labyrinth that constitutes the interior of the greenhouse. Even she became confused about which lifts to take, which halls to cross to other lifts, and then which corridors to follow down and how to identify the different codes and letters to trace particular MEPs. Perhaps once MEPs have finally located their particular space in this version of Kafka's Castle, they remain isolated, too exhausted to know who might be next door, so in no danger of interfering or conspiring with anyone else. Carlina was a bright and attractive girl, still in the middle of her studies and supplementing her income by working as a sub-assistant to Lord Plumb. She knew everybody and had a word of helpful preparation before each meeting. On the first day she wore a trouser suit and platform heels which made her head bob as she trudged purposefully ahead of us. At first she seemed shy and cool, but we quickly relaxed together, exchanging opinions about the place, the absurdity and pretension of the building, and particularly the people there. An artist was setting up an installation and had begun to create a web of string leads all over the floor of the main lobby so that people would tread on them, look down and notice scraps of paper with meaningless scribbles on them, stuck to the floor. He looked the part of an artist in a black designer outfit and with a modishly shaved head. He reminded me of Tony Hancock's bitter satire of artistic pretentiousness in *The Rebel*, masquerading in cape and fedora at his opening night, style and appearance disguising emptiness of content and meaning. Several times we passed a monumental metal sculpture stretching up to the roof of the multi-storeyed building like powerful antlers. But the uniformity of the iron strips made it look like the twisted bars of a gigantic prison-cell window crushed into the space of the main lobby.

The first day began inauspiciously. The first MEP on our list, David Hallam, could not be found. Several minutes later we tracked down his assistant, a harassed young man, pasty and nervous, with eyes that looked in different directions. He had mixed up the dates and times of our visit which angered Carlina, as though the error were a personal affront. We wasted a few minutes talking to him and learned that Hallam was a 'very religious' man. Donald gave me one of those looks (the equivalent of raising eyes to the ceiling) and we knocked on the door of the next MEP, Veronica Hardstaff. No answer but her secretary's door opened and a timid, grey-haired woman in a mini-skirt and black stockings peered out, opening some post. This was in fact Veronica Hardstaff and she seemed about to burst into tears. Barely had we shaken hands than she announced that she had been demoted on the list of good candidates for the next election, in fact her name came so low that she had no chance of getting returned. "I will have to go back to supply teaching again," she groaned. Donald forgot about asking for help and switched into counselling mode. Veronica Hardstaff represented old-fashioned Labour, a stalwart of the hustings, somewhere to the left of Tony Benn, and because of the Labour landslide had surprisingly found herself in a position of power and influence. Before that she had been a professional heckler of Conservative foes who held the seats she never had the remotest chance of winning. Her life had been devoted to opposition and asking awkward questions. Now, unprepared, she had to deal with the responsibilities of a job in the European Parliament. Her interests were with eastern Europe but she had been given tasks with Agriculture and Fisheries and looked distinctly a fish out of water there. Now Tony Blair, ashamed of these Old-Labour warriors, had put a red line through their lists and Veronica Hardstaff became an early victim. Her office looked bare, the desk empty and nothing on the walls. Perhaps she had already packed, but it looked as though nothing had ever been there. We tried to cheer her up by promising to be in touch in September, when she might have recovered her fighting spirits, to ask for her help with eastern Europe – and then we left quickly. "So far it's been a waste of time," said Donald with the exhausted look of a man wondering why we had come here in the first place.

The warren of corridors became oppressive, empty and with all doors closed. Perhaps no one was there. The burrows disappeared round distant corners lined with offices. Metal containers stood in front of each door, stacked with papers for the MEPs and their secretaries, each of whom had an adjoining room. There was also an air of luxury about the place. "Good business for carpets," Donald observed as we strode along miles of expensive shagpile.

As we crossed over to the conservative MEPs' corridors the atmosphere changed markedly. We were greeted with old-fashioned courtesy by the crystal decanter tones of Sir Jack Stewart-Clarke's secretary, hair and twin-set in imitation of Margaret Thatcher, whom she alarmingly resembled. This part of the building felt more lived in, because the Conservatives were familiar with the place and felt at home here: this was their territory. It reminded me of a comment made about the film *The Ladykillers* in which a disorganized bunch of bumbling crooks squabble and the loot ends up in the pocket of an old lady. The comment described the crooks as representative of the post-War Labour Party, inexperienced in power, while the old lady personified the Conservatives, the natural born rulers who would simply take over when the Labour Party had made a mess of things. (Jeremy Paxman said to me shortly after the Labour victory, "It will end in tears, it always does!") Despite being the minority, the Conservatives here in Brussels have no intention of relinquishing their position and assume they will become the majority again. The Thatcher-clone secretary exchanged polite and witty pleasantries until the door opened from the chief's office and an arm appeared, ready to be shaken – or kissed maybe? Sir Jack was a throwback to the Macmillan years: a handsome, tall and gracious Tory nearing retirement, the kind depicted to perfection by Rex Harrison, ageless, always charming, sexy and therefore vote friendly to women (Donald's mother voted for Anthony Eden just for his looks), but with a cynical twinkle in the eye which implies that all this is a game, that life and certainly politics should not be taken in the least bit seriously. Sir Jack lounged back in his chair professing to know absolutely nothing about us or the Soul of Europe. It became rapidly clear that despite our careful preparation before coming to Brussels – and Todd McClay had certainly distributed all our leaflets – the sheer quantity of papers given to MEPs means that nothing gets read or remembered. Our leaflet was certainly there somewhere, buried under a stack of other papers, out of sight, out of mind. So Donald embarked on the first of a dozen presentations. Sir Jack did not seem to be listening, just smiling ironically as though finding Donald's enthusiasm rather touching and endearing. His eyes twinkling in a friendly manner, he announced that he was about to retire. Then there followed a long silence and I feared he would have nothing to say at all. He appeared to be thinking about how he could help. Without speaking he disappeared into his secretary's office where I heard her cut-glass voice say loudly in an irritated, querulous tone, "What is it exactly they are after?" At this her voice went into a sudden diminuendo as Sir Jack was clearly gesturing to her and she said still quite audibly, "Oh, are they still there?" Tories like the secretary are naturally patronizing. They like people to acknowledge their superiority. Donald felt at ease; he likes this kind of old-fashioned Tory with whom he converses as an equal. He respects their sense of duty, fundamental to their politics and often concealed under the disguise of indolence and seeming lack of concern. I had no idea these archaic characters still existed, assuming they were extinct. But I could not help being charmed by this handsome septuagenarian and imagined county women swooning into his arms. Sir Jack returned, but the information, as so much of what was to follow, turned out to be of no real use. Everyone we met talked about the 'Soul for Europe Fund', established by Jacques Delors, but Donald had already applied to this long before we decided to visit Brussels. There had been no need to come here just to hear this information. Why had we bothered to come? Donald had indicated it could be a PR exercise, and useful for us to meet MEPs and encourage their support. So far this didn't seem particularly productive. Then Sir Jack became expansive – after listening to us it was his turn to make us listen to him. He spoke with a slight edge of mockery about 'intergroups', organized to make presentations to MEPs in Strasbourg. Apparently they cover all kinds of subject matter. "We even touch the wilder shores of gays and lesbians," he announced with a barely suppressed chortle, as though the European Parliament had moved now beyond all rational bounds and he was clearly relieved to be leaving this mad bunch to enjoy a sensible retirement before matters got even worse. But he took a liking to us, probably because of Lord Plumb who had sent everybody we met a personal introduction. But Donald generally makes a good impression on these people. He shares their wit and air of authority, if not their superiority. They are impressed by him, even if they don't expect to be. Sir Jack gave us his personal address – a castle in Scotland – and said we should keep in touch and come and see him.

Lord Plumb had invited us to lunch in the main dining room. Carlina implied that this was a rare honour. "Only the bigwigs go there," she said in admiring tones. I could only keep thinking that as these MEPs are our servants, we vote them in and our money pays for them, such admiration might be misplaced, and I certainly intended to enjoy my slice of the pie on this gravy train. Lord Plumb presided at a large table with his family. His son, a timid man, appeared awestruck by his father, sitting like an eagle and clearly still lording it over the Parliament of which he had once been President. Two grandsons also sat at the table, both of them silent with respect for their grandfather. But the son's wife turned out to be a fearless and jolly Cotswold woman with her breasts so squeezed above her dress that I couldn't take my eyes off them, waiting for them to pop out altogether. Unintimidated by her surroundings she immediately started talking to me about horses, food and schools. Her first question to me went, "How many children do you have?" which caught me off guard and I choked on a piece of alfalfa garnishing the first course. This agony lasted several minutes and tears poured down my cheeks, but fortunately everybody was far too well behaved to pay attention. That is not only a direct first question, but it also elicits most of the information needed about a person. The first course consisted of raw fish, but marinaded in coconut, which at least gave it some flavour. The alfalfa remained lodged in my throat and eventually the mother began to sympathize with my discomfort. "Cough as much as you like!" she encouraged, knowing exactly how I felt. At the next table sat Glenys Kinnock with Joan Ruddock and some other less identifiable personalities. Mrs Kinnock seemed to think she knew me: she beamed and nodded as though acknowledging some important encounter earlier. I kept looking over my shoulder to ascertain whether she was communicating with someone behind me. Carlina had told us we would recognize famous faces here. She had earlier pointed out Nana Mouscouri in the corridors and told us how the singing star from a generation earlier, now turned politician, had stuck her own record sleeves all over her office door. Lord Plumb occasionally would get up during the meal and disappear, probably sighting someone he needed to collar. Several MEPs came up to the table to pay their respects, muttering sycophantically in his ear, and I gathered that Lord Plumb still has authority here, even though he is no longer President of the Parliament.

Carlina came to take us to our next appointment with another Conservative, Roy Perry, a younger Tory belonging to the breed of Portillo. Again the room looked as though he had been there for years, and he gave the impression of having been born for the job. Voting him in had nothing to do with it. His ruddy complexion indicated a life of pleasure, with plenty of drinks and parties. I began to take note of photographs on the desks, of wives and families, an oppressive statement of status and success to impress visitors rather than a reminder of distant dear ones. On Roy Perry's desk the family frame consisted of a complex photomontage of friends and relatives, women and men laughing and drinking together. His secretary, a willowy and exceedingly handsome young man, beavered away at a computer. I couldn't fathom what anyone actually did. The secretaries were evidently answering letters and typing something, but the MEPs didn't appear to have any task to fulfil, except to sit in their offices and wait for visitors. The meeting with Roy Perry turned out to be no more productive than any of the others. We were told to see a Stephen Biller who had his hands on most of the business we were interested in. Roy Perry then informed us of various schemes to do with European Youth Volunteers and cultural exchanges financed by Directorate Generals at the Commission. Clearly we should be talking to these important people with their hands on the pursestrings, and I began to wonder why we were wasting time with MEPs. We should be knocking on the door of Edith Cresson for instance and several other disgraced Commissioners who had been taking advantage of their position to employ cronies. We seemed to be in a double-bind. The MEPs couldn't help us – or rather, it turned out, the English ones were unwilling to because they felt insecure, anxious about losing their position and therefore not wanting to let on anything to anybody. And the Commissioners had all been sacked. Even though they were still carrying on their duties until the next elections, we couldn't rely on any permanent decisions or help from that quarter. Roy Perry claimed Edith Cresson to be a fine person, an excellent politician who had behaved inappropriately, but over nothing serious. Having successfully stalled us in our progress without showing anything but cordiality, Roy Perry took us next door to bask in the company of his handsome secretary, and smiled and chatted while sitting proprietorially on the desk, swinging his leg, and told us how he preferred to stay in hotels rather than go to the trouble of buying a flat in Brussels.

Feeling disillusioned and looking despairingly at each other, we followed Carlina down more furlongs of shagpile to see Leo Tindemans, the former Prime Minister of Belgium and an important contact. Our first non-British MEP provided a startling contrast to those we had just visited. First his son emerged from the office with an agitated expression, “Please wait, he’s in the middle of an important phone call!” It sounded like a death in the family or some cataclysmic political event. Then Leo Tindemans himself came out and welcomed us into his office with profuse expressions of politeness. Donald bowed subserviently before this eminent politician. “Thank you for seeing us!” “No! No!” cried Leo Tindemans, “Thank *you* for coming to see me!” For the first time we received respect from an MEP, and not a patronizing condescension which implied that we were wasting time. It now became clear that MEPs from mainland Europe are at ease in Brussels and know what the European Parliament is about. They also have some vision and awareness of why they are there. This would be confirmed next day when we saw Mme Haritos. At once we felt at home here. Leo Tindemans listened to us carefully and expressed an immediate and profound interest in the Soul of Europe. Yes we could and should use his name in all our applications. He would support this project strongly, and he emphasized that. He wrote out his home address and for the first time we felt a sense of achievement. Still no doors opened to funding, but at least we had the backing now of two major figures in the European Parliament, Lord Plumb and Leo Tindemans. He spoke about his involvement in trying to find a solution to the Yugoslavian crisis and recommended we get in touch with Geremek, a ‘good’ man and an important politician from Poland known to Donald. We should also see Mr Orega at the Commission and contact the Schuman Foundation for funds, but we might hear conflicting reports about this trust because of its political affiliations: Christian Democrat and therefore only interested in furthering the Conservative cause. Nevertheless Leo Tindemans offered us his help with any application. We thanked him again before leaving and again he insisted on reversing the situation and said it was he who should be thankful that we had thought to come to him for help. This is not empty humility, it is an awareness of his precise position as an MEP, a servant to the people who put him there.

So at last one door had opened and we felt that the day had

not been completely wasted. We sat in the Parliament debating chamber for a while, listening to a defensive South African politician being hauled over the coals because of corruption among his associates (the pot calling the kettle black, I thought) while he kept thanking the MEPs for agreeing to vote positively on an important trade agreement. As the agreement still needed to be signed they were asking him awkward questions and he shifted uncomfortably in his seat. Meanwhile waiters in bow-ties and black waistcoats served the MEPs coffee and cakes, moving stealthily from desk to desk where bottles of mineral water stood to attention next to cups and saucers. Most of the MEPs seemed quite uninterested in the debate. One young member entered halfway through, casting an arrogant glance at the visitors seated at the back behind the MEPs, lounged in his chair, loosened his tie and looked with boredom at the proceedings. But he indicated to the waiters with a flamboyant gesture that he needed attention. All round the debating room sat the instantaneous translators in their respective countries' booths. At least these people appeared to be working and they signalled to the waiters as well, requiring perpetual sustenance. Glenys Kinnock made a long speech and Lord Plumb added a few observations which elicited a respectful response from the South African. It had become excessively boring and just as we were planning to decamp, Todd McClay arrived to say he had fixed another meeting, this one with Ms Anita Pollack. She turned out to be a successful and high spirited Labour MEP, evidently enjoying the support of Blair which had been so ruthlessly taken from Veronica Hardstaff earlier. Anita Pollack would not be kicked out. Her office resembled a sitting room with sofas, rugs and pictures, with a large television set dominating. Her cheerful secretary produced some other names for us to chase up, acronyms like PHARE and TACIS which I couldn't make out exactly but had something to do with cultural exchanges with Eastern Europe. We should speak to Catherine Day, Directorate General 1A at the European Commission: yet another mysterious and powerful person with hands on the purse-strings. It was like trying to find the minotaur in the labyrinth: how could we access these influential people? Even if luck favoured us with an introduction – and none of the British MEPs were in the slightest prepared to help us directly – how could we rely on the Commissioner still being there? Most of them had been sacked for corruption. Money clearly existed, but only the Commissioners had access to it, and they were using it to finance their own interests. Donald and I were hitting our heads against the brick walls of this labyrinth, people supposed to be helping us simply deflecting us with information that was easy to give (and which we could have found for ourselves back home without needing to come all the way to Brussels to be fobbed off like this) and carefully insisting they could do nothing more practical to help us. Only Lord Plumb and Leo Tindemans were at least prepared to send notes of introduction and recommendation. Anita Pollack, like the other MEPs, said she knew nothing about the Soul of Europe, nothing had been received that we had distributed, and so Donald had to start from scratch again. However I felt that he always makes a good impression talking about the Soul of Europe and it probably makes no difference if they have read the leaflet or not. I stared at the tall piles of perpetually pending correspondence on their desks, while on the computer screens mesmerizing kaleidoscopic displays threatened to send me to sleep. However, Anita Pollack had an important engagement and needed to end the meeting urgently. The engagement that took precedence over our concerns with a more humane and peaceful Europe turned out to be a party downstairs to which we had also been invited on the offchance that we might bump into an important contact. The only contacts we needed were with Commissioners however, not with MEPs.

The party had been thrown as a farewell do for a retiring MEP. Champagne flowed among the crowds of MEPs gossiping and relieved to get out of their offices. Lord Plumb introduced Donald to a couple of MEPs whom it might be useful to meet the next day, including a bright-eyed woman from Denmark with good church connections there. Then another Danish MEP launched into an endless speech in such loud, hectoring Scandinavian English that we fled the junketings. On the way out we passed another party laid on for the artist and his installation in the main lobby. This group of cronies with shaved and semi-shaved heads, garishly dyed and wearing loose-fitting black designer clothes, larked about, quaffing champagne and behaving like naughty children being allowed in the holy of holies.

Outside the greenhouse, life in Brussels seemed subdued and to have no connection whatever with the Parliament in its midst. At a café we were served with a smile by a friendly waiter and his boss in leather trousers and ate some Belgian food, chicken stewed in a kind of soup with leeks. At a nearby table Donald observed a group of people whom we had seen being taken on a guided tour of the Parliament earlier that afternoon. An elderly woman had a silver perm specially for the occasion and sat with pursed lips not wanting to go home. They appeared to be in the middle of a lengthy process of dividing the bill and were still at it when we left.

We walked to the Parliament next day with heavy hearts. Even though Leo Tindemans had provided a slight opening of a door, it felt as though the MEPs on the other side were all leaning heavily against it to keep us out.

The first person pushing was Stephen Biller, a florid middle-aged man who wasted no time in giving us his religious credentials. He also had a sick wife to attend to, which made his halo glow even more noticeably. The walls were hung with photographs of orthodox icons. People who loudly claim their religiosity, which should be of no concern to anyone but themselves, generally use their 'goodness' as a cover for self-interest and being unhelpful to others. However we needed to cultivate Stephen Biller as it became clear that he had his fingers in every pie and spider-like kept an eye on a wide web of contacts. He tapped on his pocket computer and gave us name after name. But at the end of the day he could only recommend the 'Soul for Europe Fund' – yet again. (I could hear Donald's inaudible but deafening sigh.) And he indicated that the Schuman Trust would only support politically motivated ventures, i.e. those that furthered the interests of the Conservative Christian Democrats. As we left his office, situated at the end of a long corridor and tucked away round a corner, Stephen Biller laughed and commented; "You may be wondering why we are at the end of the passage. There's a very good reason for that! Ha! Ha!" Which made my flesh creep.

The morning had started depressingly and now took a plunge into the bizarre. For the next half hour, as soon as we had entered David Hallams's office, we were transported back a century and a half to some mid-western backwater in the States, scenes described vividly by Mark Twain in books like *Huckleberry Finn.* David Hallam sat behind his desk, eyes blazing, and immediately informed Donald that he wasn't going to help us in any way whatever, that the Church, or anything to do with the Church, should never ask for money or be given money, that we had to look after ourselves. "Every day people come and sit where you are sitting asking for money. Why should I give you money?" he shouted. Donald gave as good as he got but David Hallam remained impregnable and stoutly refused to help us.

Mr Kellett-Bowman, another MEP on the verge of retirement, waited for us with coffee at one of the bars. He enjoyed doing business there, noticing associates and friends in passing, beckoning to them and drawing them into conversation. He listened to us carefully, and slowly gave advice and several names. It turned out to be a maddeningly frustrating meeting because whenever he thought of someone who could help us financially he would hit his forehead and say, "Oh if only I'd known, so-and-so was sitting here only ten minutes ago." Collaring these people is apparently the only way to get attention. Otherwise the route to those with their hands on money is so complicated and fraught with difficulties that one might as well give up at the start. We could have met Jean-Louis Bourlanges who had access to the Budget for 2000, and had been sitting there having coffee only shortly before we arrived – as had a Terry Wyn whom everybody was recommending to us. Yet whenever we tried to fix a meeting with him, we were told he wasn't even in the Parliament. Mr Kellet-Bowman suggested we should apply to the Nuffield and

Rowntree Foundations in England. Donald almost groaned with despair; he'd applied months ago and had already been turned down. Had we really come all the way to Brussels to hear this advice? Then Mr Kellett-Bowman beckoned a white-haired man over and introduced us to a Jan Westenbrook who could give us some more information, a name or a trust, I can't remember now. But I do remember the way Mr Kellett-Bowman thanked the Dutchman profusely for his help, in a slightly ironic way – as though they were in on a game – and Jan Westenbrook smiled back cynically and remarked, "You don't have to thank me. I'm paid very good money to give you this information."

Todd McClay arranged two further meetings. The first was with Keith Jenkins, who had access to the 'Soul for Europe Fund'. Since Donald had made an application it was important to introduce ourselves and encourage its acceptance. Since the Church and Society Commission had religious connections and was therefore insignificant, the office did not merit a place in the plush smartness of the Parliament buildings, but had been relegated to an old house outside on a side street, a building looking as though it were about to be demolished. We knocked uncertainly on a door which in Soho would have had cards pinned to it telling us that Carol did whipping and cost £25 for a quarter of an hour. Behind us reared the monstrous chrome glasshouse, turning its back on us and Keith Jenkins. I imagined Stephen Biller sitting comfortably in his office decorated with icons, the other side of the non-reflecting glass, right there at the end of the corridor. Though we arrived early, Keith Jenkins answered the door, and having nothing else to do agreed to see us then and there. He took us into a big room full of large empty tables. Office plants with big leaves and straggling branches wilted in the dark corners. Evidently few people used this place. A striking feature was a fearsome bank of spotlights hanging from the ceiling which made me think we were in a chamber for questioning and torturing suspects. We sat on worn and frayed sofas while Keith Jenkins smiled at us amicably through his white beard. He gave us a potted history of his Methodist background and I could picture him spending hours engaged in gloomy conversations about the Church and the world in these dark rooms. He assured us that our application was being looked at but that the decision remained with the European Commission. Yet again we could not get to meet anyone with their hands on the actual money and no one we met was in the least prepared to go out of his or her way to either introduce us or work on our behalf with these mysterious powerful people, remote beings who had become god-like in their apparent influence and authority, and yet who were perpetually out of reach to us mere mortals. Keith Jenkins continued to smile and talk, evidently enjoying some company and comfortable in the knowledge that since he couldn't do anything practical to help us he didn't have to do anything at all. He dispensed advice such as telling us to find a Consortium of Foundations crossing national boundaries (i.e. Dutch and German, English and Danish etc) and contact the Charities Aid Foundation. We should note the minority Protestant Churches in Hungary and the Czech Republic. All of which Donald knew already.

We trudged disconsolately round the back of the greenhouse castle to our last meeting, with a Mme Haritos who had something to do with 'twinning'. We weren't expecting anything from her, 'twinning' being associated with brass bands and junketing. But she had an office in a Commissioner's building and therefore was closer to the pursestrings than anyone we had met so far. Having passed through security, leaving passports and then finding our own way in a smaller but nonetheless equally baffling labyrinth of corridors and offices, we reached Mme Haritos' office. From the moment this charming lady in her forties from Greece greeted us at the door the sun came out of the clouds. We sat there and did not even have to make a presentation. She knew already what we were about: Lord Plumb had written her an encouraging note. She clearly wanted to make 'twinning' more than brass bands and junketing and saw the Soul of Europe as being a visionary way of bringing cities together across Europe, opening doors to more important issues, in fact all the possibilities and aims that Donald had written about in the leaflet. She spoke quietly and to the point, alerting us to the problems of filling out the application to her, since we did not fit neatly into her remit. But she claimed adamantly she wanted to give us money for the project and immediately rang an associate in London, a Mrs Carol Maddison-Graham, whom she asked to help us with the application, guide us through the thorny issues, and do it in such a way that Mme Haritos could legitimately give us the funds. She gave more good advice, not a second wasted, such as how to make up the third of the budget we needed to find to match the two-thirds she could legitimately give us, suggesting we could find a free venue maybe for the conference the Soul of Europe was planning for next year, etc, etc. Donald for once had no talking to do, just listen. Then, while he spoke on the phone with Mrs Maddison-Graham, Mme Haritos came up to me and as though she understood all about the time we had been having these last two days, put her hand gently on my shoulder and repeated firmly that she would definitely help us, that we would get money from her. I suddenly found my eyes prickling with tears. Our very last meeting had suddenly proved productive, so unexpectedly, and from a source that was not British. Like Leo Tindemans, this European understood what the European Union stood for. It meant more than getting seats and holding on to a well-paid job, closing the door on everything else. It meant vision, doing something for people. They had been given access to power and funds and were there to release them for useful causes. We relaxed for a while and spoke about Mount Athos and a unique exhibition she had organized of icons from the monasteries there. She also spoke with a deep sadness about the chaos in Yugoslavia, noting that the Soul of Europe would be attending to these issues. Meanwhile my eyes became hypnotized for the last time in Brussels by a particularly complicated moving pattern on her desk-top computer. It depicted a labyrinth of pipe-like corridors growing into ever more complicated knots, like an infinite digestive tract, perpetually spreading and stretching into further knots and passages.

Postscript
Before leaving Brussels we had one last meeting, with a businessman recommended by a friend of Donald's in London. "He has plenty of money and will help you." So we arrived at another ancient office, even more dilapidated than the one housing the Church and Society Commission. The state of the front door should have alerted us to the fact that we would find no money here at all. But only after we sat down with a M. Merthes did we realise that we'd been sent on a wild goose chase. "I have absolutely no money," M. Merthes began straight away, "Not even to pay myself or my secretary! So if you are wanting money from me I'm sorry I can't help you." Then why had he offered to see us and why had he not warned us before we came to Brussels, when he knew precisely the reason for our visit? Despite being a businessman who worked with other businesses all over the world, particularly in underdeveloped countries, on improving business practices based on Christian values, none of these businesses had money. I doodled on my notepad and waited for the meeting to end quickly so that we could catch an earlier train to Amsterdam. Donald saw my thunder-look and politely told M. Merthes that we had to leave, at which point M. Merthes had a prick of conscience and offered to take us to the station. He saved us a taxi-ride, though his erratic driving through the Brussels rush-hour traffic made me wish we had ditched him back at his office. "Thank you!" I said with relief as we drove up to the building site outside the station, and he gave a loud laugh as he shook my hand, perfectly aware of having wasted our time.

A Further Postscript
A year after our visit to Brussels we learned that the Church and Society Commission no longer has access to the 'Soul for Europe Fund', no money forthcoming for any project at all. Our connection to this possible source of income came from the Lincoln Theological Institute and its associated charity, a small organisation calling itself Christianity and the Future of Europe (CAFE). We drove up to Sheffield where they are based in a Victorian

house in a leafy street outside the city centre. Two academics presided over the meeting with us and both seemed eager to welcome us on board. Canon Martyn Percy, young and ambitious, hoped that Donald's aims of developing concrete proposals, engaging in action as well as talk, would enrich the academic work of the Institute. Professor Ken Medhurst, a kindly older man, looking ill, tired and evidently hoping that we might inject new life and purpose into the charity, concurred and we assumed that we would eventually combine with CAFE. However, at the next Annual Meeting our application to merge with them was thrown out. The trustees, a group of elderly academics wearing anoraks and sitting dotted around a large room in the Methodist Central Hall in London, did not even speak to us or exchange eye contact, all of them staring grimly at piles of paper on their laps. It came as a shock to feel such hostility, and after we left they expressed their disapproval of Donald, whom they evidently disliked, and stipulated that all written evidence of our connection with them, on publicity material and covenant forms, should be expunged immediately. Our proposals to work in the Balkans horrified them and they did not want to be associated with such a dangerous project, one that they felt sure was bound to fail.

Ken Medhurst had encouraged us to apply for money from the Church and Society Commission, which is why we paid a visit to the derelict building round the backside of the European Parliament. We never heard from them afterwards because the Commissioners had withdrawn their support from an organisation they considered of no consequence. So even CAFE failed to get funds. Even though we could have helped fund as well as invigorate their moribund charity, these academics had taken such a dislike to Donald, personally as well as professionally, that they preferred to shut the door on us. The convenor at the Annual Meeting gave him a quarter of an hour to make a presentation, then tried to encourage questions. "Speak now, or for ever hold thy peace," she said, attempting to lighten the proceedings with a joke. But the grey academics looked even more grimly into their papers, stiffening and keeping their thin lips tight shut.

COVENTRY AND LONDON

January 2000

DIARY – PETER PELZ

Funds came through in the last few days of 1999. Chief among the donors was the Duke of Westminster, introduced to Donald by Lord Plumb. He asked one question, "What do you expect to happen?" Donald replied thoughtfully that he didn't know. The purpose of our journeys round Europe would be to establish what needed to happen. Out of these journeys we expected a number of projects to emerge. Donald puts it this way: "God has a way of sneaking up on you." So we couldn't guarantee concrete results yet. This impressed the Duke, who also begged Donald not to forget issues of the countryside. The project seemed to imply a concern only with urban communities. After visiting Bosnia we came to appreciate the importance of the Duke's particular concerns. He himself is a farmer and understands the problems of countryside neglect. The Duke then promised to match the funds we raised and gave us a deadline, 18 December, 1999. How we raised the money was no concern of his, but whatever we had in our account by that date, he would match. This promise elicited donations from various individual sources, people who have admired Donald in the past and were curious about the Soul of Europe and what might evolve.

Meanwhile we planned several journeys around Europe, starting in the Balkans. The aftermath of the recent NATO bombing of Serbia meant that a part of Europe had been ostracized. It seemed only right that we should pay our respects to a people who, for whatever political reasons, had suffered so much and still continue to suffer. This visit would inform all our other visits throughout Europe. The lessons we might learn there would give the Soul of Europe its impetus and purpose.

We therefore needed to pay a call on Canon Paul Oestreicher in Coventry, an expert on European Churches who had already been to Belgrade immediately after the NATO bombing campaign. To Donald he represents Cerberus guarding the gates, demanding the penny toll allowing access to beyond. We must sit at his feet, listen to his advice, and prepare ourselves for this our most important journey.

COVENTRY

The journey to Coventry from South Devon cuts through South West England and the Midlands. The road from Crediton to Tiverton is one of the most beautiful in England. This morning the dark farmsteads, tucked in the folds of meadows and hillocks, were waking to a faint winter dawn, mists and frost still lying in the dips. The road curves, winds, and climbs up steeply, following the back of a slope with views on either side. The pink sky illuminated fields, with indistinct shapes of sheep already grazing, and began to pick out the trees in copses clustered in hollows, along streams, and standing sentinel on the hilltops. On a clear day the panorama stretches for miles over the Devon countryside back towards Dartmoor.

Paul has appeared in my life ever since my father lectured with him for the Student Christian Movement over thirty years ago. Paul turns up everywhere. Like God he is so omnipresent that I long ago came to the conclusion that there are several Oestreicher clones doing the rounds. He never seems to change, even staying the same age, having been in his early forties ever since I can remember. His head looms at every gathering I have attended concerning church matters, easy to spot with the familiar reddish hair close cropped around the shining bald patch, eyes watchful and steady while he smiles through a bristly beard.

Paul used to be a colleague of my father's when they were involved in the 'Honest To God' movement in the Church of England, together with the then Bishop of Woolwich, John Robinson. The bishop died, my father became a lecturer in sociology in Australia, and Paul has continued a vital force in the Church, indispensable because of his experience and knowledge, the contacts he has with theologians, priests, and communities, not only in

England but also in the rest of Europe, particularly in Germany and the neighbouring countries. One of his most striking contributions to the Anglican Church consisted of strengthening links between Coventry and Dresden, two cities severely bombed by either side in the last war. This meant liaising with politicians as well as clergy and being involved in ceremonial and ritual. However, Paul prefers to align himself with marginal, alternative groups. He is an ally of gay and lesbian people and has been Chairman of Amnesty International. He once recommended a priest to Donald who had become an embarrassment to the German Church because of his association with the Baader Meinhof Red Army Faction which organized acts of urban terrorism in the 1970s, including assassinations of politicians, industrialists and bankers. The Germans were threatening to stop paying the all-important church tax while this priest continued to officiate in his Berlin parish. Kornelius Burckhardt constitutes a whole story on his own. Latterly Paul has forged links with churches in eastern Europe; I saw him at a gathering of Romanian Orthodox priests and students in Oxford, and his latest newsworthy activity was to visit Serbia directly after the NATO bombing in order to bring succour to the Anglican community in Belgrade. Being a New Zealander by birth, and having held on to that passport, he could enter the country at a time when the British were considered enemies. We now needed to pick his brains about contacts there, be warned of the pitfalls and dangers, and glean general information. His knowledge of the German churches would also be invaluable.

Paul is formidable. His bonhomie, ease, and authority barely conceal a determination which implies that he can never be satisfied with what he has achieved, that there is so much more work to be done. Perhaps he is conscious of not being English. My father felt that alienation acutely which eventually caused him to leave the Church and England. Paul's peers admire him but keep him at arm's length, letting him carry on his work, but they are reticent with their encouragement. Donald was nervous on the way to Coventry, as though afraid of getting a wigging from the man of experience, who might be contemptuous of our project. But Paul was gracious. He reminded Donald how he had supported him when he was running the lay training department in the Southwark Diocese many years ago. But when asking questions Donald looked like a naughty schoolboy, expecting punishment or a bad mark. Unintentionally, Paul did little to ease the tension, sitting with his back to the window so that the light fell on Donald and me, keeping himself in the shadow.

He had, however, generously prepared us lunch of vegetable soup, followed by fish in breadcrumbs and a chunky raw salad. (This obliterated memories of a disaster breakfast earlier at the Welcome Inn on the motorway, where a young chef cooked broken eggs in lashings of warm fat slowly till they were of a rubber texture and the limp bacon had cooled to a congealed mass of pale grease. These and the lukewarm coffee and leathery toast had provided a depressing start to the day. It is a hard act to balance a tray while carrying a case and having to pay the bill and search for knives and forks before being allowed to take a seat and occupy a table. The whole experience of eating in motorway cafés is an obstacle course.)

Paul gave us information. I jotted down names and recognized familiar ones, Dorothea Sölle, Marten Marquardt, Werner Pick, who still represent the lively, humane, and interesting side of the Lutheran Church, even after all these years. There were also a couple of women bishops to visit as well as the radical church movement called Kirchentag whose young and not-so-young crowds take over space in a number of city churches, setting up stalls and advertising the diversity of protest and alternatives on the edge of the comfortable and conservative traditional church.

As for Belgrade, Paul assured us we weren't likely to get murdered or tied to a radiator as hostages (an alarming prospect because I couldn't think of anyone who'd want to have us released and many who would probably pay the Serbs to keep us there!). We might get kicked in the streets for being British, but apart from that we only had to fear the loquaciousness of the Serb people who would probably lecture us incessantly while being most hospitable. I have already gathered that from our contact in Belgrade, who can't wait to bombard us with information, and probably tell us off as well, while pointing out the broken bridges and NATO bomb damage. Paul gave us a description of the Anglican community there. It consists of English wives of Serbs, Commonwealth people working in Belgrade (a Ghanaian and an Indian are the churchwardens), young Serbs disaffected with the extreme nationalist and traditionalist Orthodox Church – these perhaps the most interesting people to meet – and the treasurer, an English woman who happens to be fervently Serbian nationalist, pro-Milosevic and aggressively anti-British. The Anglican community is small and meets in a Catholic space, a building belonging to Caritas, one of the main Catholic charities. The Catholics are held in deepest suspicion by the Orthodox. Clearly, given recent events, we have to be diplomatic and try and keep to the right side of the Serbs. After all we are not there for any political reasons. We want to learn about the situation, find what the real needs are, and take away an agenda to share with communities in the other parts of Europe we intend visiting later. So we should be discreet when visiting the Women in Black and other dissident people – rather like being in old-style Communism.

Paul kept looking at us out of the darkness sharply, trying to fathom the reason for this journey to such a remote and troubled part of Europe. It is difficult to answer that except that if Europe wants to consider itself as an entity, then regions like Serbia need eventually to be incorporated. The Balkans are a running sore in the body of Europe, and so it has to be the first place on our list of visits, however uncomfortable or even perilous.

Paul's house made an impression on me which I mulled over throughout the return journey. He appreciates art. Pictures decorate every wall. The kitchen is lined with postcards. Prints of Dürer's *Crouching Hare* and *Praying Hands* have pride of place as they do in every cultured Lutheran household. Even the lavatories are decorated with humorous posters, depicting traditional images of Adam and Eve covering their genitals with shopping bags sporting famous names from the world of fashion. Most of the original pictures depicted peaceful landscapes and figure line drawings. He told me how famous most of the artists had become after he had bought the pictures. I was reminded sharply of my failure in this department. Though he had once bought a drawing of mine, many years earlier, and which I did not see hanging anywhere, I had not become famous. Before we left, Paul showed us what he called the 'best pictures' in the downstairs living room.

A portrait of his grandfather from the German, as opposed to Jewish, side of the family, hung in pride of place over the fireplace. He had been a prison warden in Thuringia during the early decades of the twentieth century, at the time of the rise of Hitler and fascism. He had apparently been a kindly warden refusing to take political prisoners, which must have put his position and life in danger, a principled dissident like his grandson. The colours were muted and the style almost primitive. A hunting hat planted firmly on his head emphasized the typically Germanic features with a sharply aquiline nose, cool blue eyes and prominent cheekbones. A spindly fir tree stood solitary in the indistinct, sketchy background, an apology, a lonely echo of the German forests that fill the region there. Paul judged correctly; this painting stood out from the rest. It spoke of a period of history, of a determined but gentle ancestor, alone in the German political landscape of his time. The undefined background accentuated this sense of isolation, as though all support had been taken away from him. The painting left me with a melancholy impression of the soul being drained away, the warmth and security of the natural world being denied, leaving uncertainty for the future, loss and even fear. Somehow the painting spoke of the end of a culture and looked to a bleak future which still has not regained its foothold in the old certainties of faith and nature. The wizened fir tree, missing so many branches and with barely any needles, seemed like a bleak discord, an empty dissonance from which even the suggestion and promise of harmony and therefore hope had been removed.

Two smaller portraits, in black and white, of ancestors from further back in time, at the turn of the nineteenth century, hung to the right of the fireplace. These belonged to the Jewish part of Paul's family. The strikingly sensual Semitic features were encased in tightfitting sober Lutheran clothing, the generous bosom of the mother squeezed into a lacy Victorian bodice. They must have been contemporaries of Felix Mendelsohn and their evident prosperity and success indicated a period of German history when culture, in particular music and literature, overruled the bigotry and racism which would one day wreak mayhem. The portraits reminded me of the Jewish German poet Heine, possibly their contemporary, who actually prophesied the events that disfigured the twentieth century. "Beware of those buried ancient German gods," he wrote, and went on to describe how they would one day soon be heard rumbling back to life, and their juggernaut tread would destroy everything in their path. Heine, a witty intellectual who also possessed a painfully sensitive poetic sensibility, expressed an acute understanding of the undercurrents of history.

The faces of these ancestors dominated the room. People would want to sit elsewhere. There were too many reminders of history. The room where they hang remains empty and cold. The faces stare and keep watch in the perpetual silence. Even Paul preferred to take us upstairs to another sitting room.

LONDON

We had already arranged to visit Serbia in the autumn of 1999, but NATO bombing there had put an end to those plans. We were still waiting for funds but had promised our contact there, Lazar Markovic, that immediately we had the money we would come. He knew that we wanted to see the religious leaders and had an itinerary where we would learn about the Balkans and their present plight. Gaining a visa to enter Serbia is still not assured and those with invitations from the Orthodox Church which persistently attacks Milosevic and asks him to stand down are not recognized. Even the Bishop of London, Richard Chartres, suffered the indignity of being turned back at the border. We left it to Lazar to decide what kind of invitation would permit our entry. He asked us to write and publish an article in the main newspapers attacking NATO and expressing our sympathy for the suffering Serbs. After the recent horrors of Kosovo anti-Serb feeling in Europe ran at an all time high. Only now that reports of Muslim atrocities in Kosovo are beginning to appear do the papers write more sympathetically about Serbs. But then we had to rely on a personal invitation from Lazar. We were tourists coming to visit a friend. Nothing more. We should not mention the Soul of Europe or our intentions to meet with religious leaders. Even so, we could not guarantee that such an innocuous invitation would make a visa forthcoming. We might have to accept failure.

Today it feels like D-Day, storming the Serbian Embassy, which has the power to block the plans for our first important and symbolic journey.

There is also the meeting of the Advisory Council: we are to put our proposals to a group of busy people and seek their approval. Donald fears that no one will turn up, like those Sundays in church, peering round the vestry door, checking the numbers in the congregation. We now have the funds and so this particular meeting should constitute a formal launch of the project.

We breakfasted in the RAC Club, with only a couple of other guests at distant ends of the room, while several eager early birds swam their lengths fiercely and intently in the swimming pool on the floor below. I observed them warding off age by keeping their bodies in lithe shape, breaststroking like supple athletic fish. I stared at the large sylvan landscape paintings fitted like murals across the expanse of wall in the dining room. The air of urgency in the other guests, hastily swallowing healthy juice and a light breakfast, in order to pursue important business, against the clamorous crescendo of heavy traffic along Pall Mall outside the window, contrasted with the calm of these paintings. The landscapes are devoid of human presence. Large trees spread luxurious foliage over distant horizons, rocks, waterfalls and limitless countryside where there is not a single sign of habitation or even of any living creature.

The Yugoslav Consulate could not have provided a greater contrast to the splendour of the RAC Club. The consulate fits apologetically inside the Cyprus Embassy. The building looks neglected and a notice written in felt tip on card points the way to the visa application door. The room could have been a derelict post office. Two mournful officials waited behind the glass partitions. No crowds were applying for permits, there clearly being no desire to visit Serbia. Only one other person stood before us at the visa window, a short man in scruffy clothes. While we waited just three other people joined the queue. Among them was a girl who spoke through a mobile, unconcerned about being overheard – evidently a journalist preparing to go to the least comfortable spots in the world. "It's Bangladesh after…" she announced over the phone. Two young male backpackers examined the xeroxed information sheets scattered over the tables and shelves. A map of Serbia, printed on glossy paper, gave the impression of a pleasant holiday destination, marked with numerous monasteries and historic sites, even in Kosovo, as though no wars had taken place there at all. Another even more lavish brochure extolled the beauties of Montenegro's beaches, still seen as part of Serbia though the regular military exercises of Serbian troops along the border warn the people to remain within Milosevic's bear-like embrace and not to become another Kosovo.

The official dealing with our visas treated us politely, but looked beaten and melancholy as though aware of Serbia's pariah status; he was carrying out his duties with an air of atonement. He wanted to make the procedure as easy as possible for us. Lazar's letter did not even seem important, although the invitation and address were deemed necessary. I could not believe how easily and quickly matters proceeded. I paid cash. We were careful not to say anything, and avoided drawing attention to ourselves, just wanting to get the visas into our passports and be out of the door. The man in front of us had told the official how he planned to take a video camera to "film schools and such like…". We kept quiet about our plans. But the official seemed simply relieved that we wanted to go to Serbia at all.

As we left I noted the dinginess of the office and the picture of Milosevic hanging slightly askew like an afterthought, small and perfunctory on the otherwise empty wall. It reminded me of the old days of Communism, as though Yugoslavia hadn't left that part of its history behind yet, but nonetheless rapid and even catastrophic changes had been making it all irrelevant.

We lunched in an Italian restaurant. The friendly waiters might have been from Serbia: they spoke little English and seemed relieved to be working at all. Occasionally they looked alarmed, eyes turning from friendly helpfulness to pinpricks of fearful concern, as though aware of their perilous insecurity: one false move, one mistake and they might be out of a job. The boss hovered behind, grim-faced and watchful, but unctuously servile with us customers.

The Council meeting turned out unexpectedly eventful. I had underestimated the intellectual calibre of its members who plied us with searching questions about our plans. We needed all our wits to create an impression of knowing what we were doing, when in fact we had as many doubts and questions as the Council members.

Lord Plumb arrived in hearty spirits, looking bright-eyed, lively and at least ten years younger than when I last saw him weighed down by European responsibilities in Brussels. He no longer looked remote, irritated, and dyspeptic, constantly being approached by members and colleagues with Uriah Heep expressions whispering requests in his ear. Now he had a mischievous smile and twinkle in the eye. Lord Plumb is a seasoned raconteur, used to entertaining a packed dinner table, stringing jokes with expertly delivered punch lines. At a crucial stage of the meeting he also proved himself to be a skilful chairman and handled a crisis with exemplary finesse.

He arrived attended as usual by Dr Puck Wertwyn. With grey hair lacquered to a stiff helmet, she made me feel uneasy. She evidently knows that I am unqualified for my task but admires Donald. She smiled at him approvingly, then fixed me with a glacial stare that questioned my competence. Later in the meeting she admitted to being a crime researcher; which explains her misgivings about me. She probably knows of crimes I don't even realise I've committed.

I missed the presence of our first supporter, John Banks. He runs a busy advertising agency and encouraged Donald to establish a network of European churches along the lines of St James's in Piccadilly. He took the trouble to attend Donald's leaving party and listened carefully to Donald's proposals. At several meetings in his Baker Street office he helped us to clarify our objectives, and then printed our first publicity material which succeeded in raising our first funds. It would have been only right to celebrate our first success with him, and to be able to show him that his faith in us was vindicated. He always gives astute down-to-earth advice, a cigar clamped in the middle of his mouth.

In his place sat Redmond Mullin, a successful fund raiser, who used to be a Jesuit novice. Now married, he has a large number of children. One of his staff used to speak of him in hushed tones, as of someone at the top of his profession, which he quite readily admits to being. "I only deal in millions." On our first visit to his house on Dartmoor to discuss the project we discovered a shared enthusiasm for *Tokyo Story* by the Japanese film director, Ozu. The film examines the generation gap between an elderly couple and their children after the Second World War. The hard-working children have no time for their parents and finally the mother dies, leaving the father on his own, far from the rest of the family. It is an everyday story, but Ozu manages to express depths of feeling and an understanding of the wider political and social implications, the tragedy of life in the twentieth century after a scarring war and the need to recognize new affiliations. The most significant relationship turns out unexpectedly to be between the widow of the one son killed in the war and the parents. They at first reject the girl because of their inability to come to terms with his death. Yet this daughter-in-law, who perpetually reminds them of their loss, relates to them and looks after them better than their own children. This film manages to say so much about war and loss, about human beings trying to make sense of a new world where traditional values no longer exist, about life's disappointments and about time passing regardless of our griefs and pains, that its impact is overwhelming. The film shows how art can directly influence our response to the world. It is not a matter of changing people, but encouraging an empathy which will make the hardships of life perhaps a little easier to bear. Donald and Redmond involve themselves in the Soul of Europe from a deep sense of commitment which has its roots in religion. Works of the imagination, like *Tokyo Story*, are the source of my commitment. It no longer becomes a matter of choice. Given the opportunity to do this kind of work in Europe, the decision is straightforward. It is a privilege.

Another formidably qualified entrepreneur sat next to Redmond Mullin. Stephen Wenman is polite, kind, and friendly, with that ease of manner which is part and parcel of an apparently effortless business acumen. He contributed encouragingly and thoughtfully at all stages of the meeting, looking at everybody attentively. He never stops working. Wherever he is in the world he rings me up in the evening and gets me to work on complicated fundraising letters. He enjoys long conversations with Donald about religion. At their first meeting he described how he worked hard throughout his life because of his ambition and also because he was successful at it, but realised the pointlessness of work just for its own sake. Since then his life has changed. Devoted to supporting the work of the NSPCC he also responds immediately to all our memoranda. We are a rival for his attentions and he calls us his 'mistress', which we take as a compliment. The energy he devoted to work he now channels into voracious reading and learning, and generous commitment of time to the charity and also to us.

The Bishop of Aston, John Austin, arrived from Birmingham, a friend and colleague of Donald's going back thirty years. In those early days, while in Southwark, John Austin commissioned me to paint a mural depicting the Ascension: a massive nude Christ figure leaping across an outside brick wall. It caused a rumpus, was included in the Phaidon Book of Murals, and is one of my favourite works. I can only guess at the flak John had to suffer over that commission, but he never let on. I remember someone threw well-aimed mud to cover the swinging genitals. He speaks quite slowly, as though about to stutter, but clearly and without hesitation, which is a boon to secretaries and to me, writing everything down in longhand. His advice always follows deep thought on the matter, and he does not speak until he is sure of his counsel. This he gave at the meeting, encouraging us with the journeys but suggesting we keep clear objectives and don't waste energy by spreading ourselves thinly. He spelled out what Donald and I already knew, but it was helpful to hear all the same. We have no intention of coming back empty-handed and are both clear about preparing the ground before we even arrive at various destinations. The visits should basically strengthen bonds and encourage the contacts we make to create 'embryonic networks' wherever we go.

Opposite the bishop sat another formidable figure, Eileen Barker, Professor of Religious Studies at the London School of Economics. Her shock of white hair frames a warm friendly face that encases a mind in perpetual motion. She never stops working and even at the table pounded away at her laptop. "I'm off to Copenhagen to give a lecture, at six o'clock tomorrow morning," she announced to Donald in passing. When she speaks, which isn't often, every word is weighed and you write it down. She warned about the ethnic groups in Eastern Europe where we have to tread carefully. "It's easy to love your neighbour," she said, "when he lives two thousand miles away and needs a passport."

Anthony Airey, a gentleman's tailor in Saville Row and now our treasurer, arrived like myself, breathless. His is the most thankless task and to my amazement he appears to enjoy it. He embarked on his financial report. It was an uneasy moment for Donald and me. Having worked so hard to raise the funds we now feared the Council members would decide not to let us have any of them. "I had a discussion with myself," announced Donald, "no one else being around, and decided I was going to pay myself this amount..." Fortunately everyone agreed.

At this point a bizarre turn of events livened up the treasurer's report and created a diversion. The door opened and a white-haired man with peaky features and wearing a grey suit entered and stood his ground. At first we thought he'd come to the wrong meeting, but he insisted on seeing Lord Plumb. Not even Donald recognised him as Sidney Shipton, the right-hand man of Sir Sigmund Sternberg, a veteran of Jewish–Christian relations and now the founder of the Three Faiths Forum, which organizes conferences and seminars encouraging the association of Jews, Christians and Muslims. I heard the chains of Marley's ghost rattle across the floor as this unwelcome visitor showed no intention of leaving but crossed the room to join the meeting he had been sent to gatecrash.

Lord Plumb gave a brilliant display of chairmanship. Pretending to be interested in what Sidney Shipton had to say, Lord Plumb placed his elbow on the table, pressed his hand under his chin, turned sideways to attend to every word, fixed Sidney Shipton with a steady gaze and allowed him to say his piece, carefully avoiding telling him anything. My heart missed a beat as I realized that in front of everyone at the table, including Sidney Shipton, lay my agenda for the meeting with an item concerning the Three Faiths Forum. Sidney Shipton had evidently been sent to get his feet under the table and not to leave until he'd learnt of our plans. But Lord Plumb got him to divulge his own. First he complained about having given Donald a valuable list of names and contacts, and hoped we would not be poaching on their territory. Donald gave his assurances. Sidney Shipton then told everybody that there already was a Soul of Europe organisation in Europe, a far right evangelical group in Strasbourg. "So sorry to be negative," he said. Donald said he knew of this particular Soul of Europe venture and it was of no importance. No one could possibly confuse us and besides, this evangelical group had only a small following. Having set up a web site under the address of SoulofEurope.com, and not been blocked by prior claim to the title, I knew that there could be no other significant organisation with our name on it. Then Lord Plumb asked: "Now before you leave, would any of the Council members like to ask a question of you?" Of course no one wanted to ask anything, lowering their eyes in embarrassment and wanting just to get rid of the man who had interrupted a private meeting. "Thank you so much for coming," Lord Plumb then said, with a tone of finality, moving to face away from Sidney Shipton who had no choice but to leave, which he did.

This lively diversion had Redmond Mullin turning crimson and shaking with mirth. No one had sent the Three Faiths Forum any information about this meeting, not even the date, time or place, which made the appearance of Sidney Shipton so unexpected.

The treasurer's report then continued, but the interruption had livened this usually tiresome part of the meeting. After talk of investments, trustees, and charity status, we proceeded with more agreeable issues concerning the travels and purpose of the project. It is exhausting to be in the wakeful and intensely supportive presence of formidable minds. They each had something to comment on. Donald at first felt cornered. This was his project after all. They had been invited just to agree with him, and so why did they all persist in making authoritative observations and giving such astute counsel? They performed their duty as Council members seriously. In retrospect when we had picked ourselves up from the floor after they had all swept out over us in grand procession, we realized we had been firmly supported and encouraged, and indeed had been given permission to carry out what we always planned.

With the funds in place, the visit to Serbia assured, and the Council having given us their blessing, we needed to look beyond the first journey and prepare ourselves for meetings with influential people elsewhere in Europe. Charles Hill at Church House, Westminster, promised to give us names and addresses in Scandinavia where the churches are known to support imaginative ventures.

All places of administration are intimidating. Vicars and priests deal with buildings, services, communities, and the problems of parishioners. Administrators possess higher qualifications and make decisions while keeping a distance from these everyday problems. Our project focuses on those who work on the ground, who will welcome our support and concern, yet from now on we came into conflict with administrators who viewed our activities with suspicion and our demands for help with dismay. The division of the world between those who deal constantly with human issues and those who administer reflects the divisions in Europe, between poor and rich, between the advantaged and disadvantaged, between those less and more qualified. Discovering how these divisions are so often unbridgeable chasms became one of the bitterest experiences on our travels.

A Catholic priest in Bihac is at the end of his tether attempting to care for his people, just finding them homes and food. He listened to our proposals barely able to contain his frustration. Then he said; "You come with great ideas, then go away to discuss them. Perhaps you will not be able to help us and will forget about us. I cannot wait. I have no time. I cannot even feed, clothe and house my people." In affluent cities in western and northern Europe administrators, people with influence, and the power and the money to help, deflected our requests with all the skills for which they are qualified. They sat in expensively furnished rooms. No, they couldn't help. No funds. They had already done so much, implying that the poor are a nuisance, always demanding attention. The best part of being an administrator is that work can be left at the end of the day. The offices lock the issues into filing cabinets and evenings, leisure time, and holidays can be spent in the comfort of prosperous homes in pleasant domestic pursuits, being entertained. "Come back later," they told us, offering a faint glimmer of hope. We should return with more and better proposals. But Bihac cannot wait. The chasm waits in vain for a bridge. Distance, both physical and psychological, keeps the divisions deep and emphatic. We can put the issues out of mind: they belong far away, somewhere else. Not thinking about them creates apathy. Besides, don't we all have enough problems of our own?

Having the money to carry on the project makes it feel almost indecent to continue on our visits around London and the country. We should be on our way round Europe. We were so used to begging that when we arrived at the desk of yet another man of influence without needing to ask for money, I felt as though we had gorged on a meal at someone else's expense. It didn't seem quite right, the boot on the other foot, now in a position to call the shots, no longer penny pinching nor wondering fearfully what the response might be to our requests. The typical scenario was: "Do you know of anyone who would be prepared to help us? Or can you tell us of someone who might be able to open doors to others who might be prepared to?" This implied: "You yourself don't have to worry about having to refuse to help us, even though we know that you're in an excellent position to do so and could finance the project on your own without missing a penny. We're making it easy for you and you can forget about us the moment we've left the room!"

Donald displays once again all his usual confidence and sharpness, not petering out in mid-flow when he notices the face opposite turning blank. He then instinctively realized that the words were a waste of time and his mind already became distracted by some other more pleasant alternative to being there. There is a spring in our step now and we are thinking positively again.

We needed to be cheerful as we entered Church House with its large and empty corridors, and the sense of being excluded from yet another club as the doorman eyed us suspiciously. For a moment I believed I'd brought a bomb into the building.

The Revd Dr Charles Hill is the specialist on inter-church matters between the Scandinavian churches and the Church of England. He knows personally the administrators and people of influence we need to contact. We squeezed through a party crowding one of the corridors, the staff drinking wine and socializing cheerfully, evidently glad to get out of their prison offices. Donald recognized Mary Tanner, a distinguished, lively-looking woman who expressed serious interest in our project. While Donald talked to her, other people pushed forwards to share in the dialogue. The women in Church House were friendly and sympathetic. The men reminded me of ecclesiastical officials who used to visit my father when he was still a priest in Lancashire. Their faces expressed the sigh of resigned exasperation because they had the unenviable task of dealing with a difficult and noisy vicar, someone who, their heads shaking with irritation, didn't apparently even believe in God. These men are intense people, absolutely convinced of their own rightness and intelligence. They engage in serious conversations eyeball to eyeball; they could not be mistaken for bus drivers or coal miners.

Apart from giving us an exhaustive list of addresses and contacts Charles Hill had very little more to say. When a harassed-looking woman burst hysterically into the office telling him to attend to some matter urgently and immediately, we left.

SERBIA

24 February – 2 March 2000

DONALD REEVES

REPORT TO ADVISORY COUNCIL

Introduction

We were invited to Serbia by Lazar Predrag Markovic. Lazar, thirty-six years old, is Serbian, and he lives in Belgrade. He was baptized into the Orthodox Church ten years ago. He is a journalist and art historian. He speaks good English. He has travelled extensively in Europe, mostly as a speaker at conferences arranged by the World Student Christian Federation. He is the editor of *Iskon*, a magazine exploring the interface between Orthodoxy and the Arts. He is also Vice-President of the Balkan Orthodox Youth Association which operates in all the Balkan countries.

Shortly before we left, at our Advisory Council meeting, the point was made that we should proceed in an informed yet open manner, but that we should also return having left something for Serbia. We should also have acted as a catalyst for future work. We have achieved successful outcomes and have certainly been catalysts.

The Visit

Visits were arranged to the Serbian Orthodox Church. We went to the patriarchate where we had three meetings with the patriarch, His Holiness Pavle. We also met the bishop of Branichevo, Bishop Ignatije, and visited three monasteries. We visited the office of the chief rabbi of Yugoslavia, Rabbi Isak Asiel, and had long meetings with the mufti of the Belgrade Islamic Community, Mufti Hamdija Jusufspahic, and with the Roman Catholic archbishop of Belgrade, Archbishop Perko.

Alongside visits to the religious institutions (and to two refugee camps for Serbian refugees from Kosovo, run by the patriarchate outside Belgrade) we visited several non-governmental organizations, the Women in Black, the Centre for Democracy Foundation, the Anti-War Coalition, the 'Most' ('Bridge') Association for Cooperation and Mediation, and the Centre for Cultural Decontamination, all thriving and active despite the political uncertainties in Serbia.

We had several social gatherings with theologians, professors, artists and journalists.

The visits took the same form: Lazar Markovic introduced us, I gave a brief presentation of the aims of the Soul of Europe, then an exchange of views followed.

Four Successes

1. Cooperation Between the Religious Leaders

We provided new impetus for cooperation between the patriarch of the Serbian Orthodox Church, the mufti, the chief rabbi, and the Roman Catholic archbishop.

The Jewish and Catholic communities are small compared to the Islamic community which numbers about 200,000. All three communities are dwarfed by the Serbian Orthodox Church. Nevertheless, at the level of leadership there have been cordial relationships endorsing a style of coexistence which is peaceful, although they meet only rarely.

Given the demonization of Serbia by the Western media, I thought it would be right to show that there is hope from Belgrade.

I asked the patriarch if he would call a special meeting to which the main religious leaders would be invited. He agreed to this proposal and they all came together on 1st March. Sky News filmed the gathering and interviewed me afterwards. The meeting was widely reported in Serbia, on television and radio, and also internationally. I believe the leaders will now begin to work together on substantial matters on a regular basis, thus being an example to the communities they serve. For example, they will jointly put pressure on the government to provide a separate cemetery for Muslims.

2. Links Between Serbian Orthodox Monasteries and Western Europe

As a result of our visit, several monasteries of the Serbian Orthodox Church will prepare to receive guests from western Europe. Serbian monasteries are often set in attractive and remote rural areas. Then we hope groups from western Europe, particularly younger people from all denominations, will be welcome to experience the Orthodox liturgy, meet local people and contribute to the life and work of the monasteries, participating in restoration programmes. The details are now being worked out, but there is already goodwill for this project.

3. Travelling Exhibitions

There will be an exchange of exhibitions by Serbian artists and iconographers and western European artists. There was of course much enthusiasm for such a project given that Serbian artists are isolated from the European art world.

Important as they all are in opening up Serbia to the rest of Europe, they are gestures compared to the major outcome of our visit.

This is the Bosnian Project.

4. The Bosnian Project

At the meeting of the religious leaders on 1st March, I shared a proposal which had emerged and taken shape throughout a number of conversations with a wide range of people.

This is that the Soul of Europe should establish a project in Bosnia. In a chosen town, a war-damaged mosque, a war-damaged Catholic church, and a war-damaged Orthodox church should be restored brick by brick and become living places of worship. The European aspect of this initiative is crucial: young people of every denomination from all over Europe will be invited to contribute their labour, working closely with local people.

The project will be a tangible attempt at reconciliation. The rebuilding will provide a unique opportunity for Muslims, Orthodox, and Catholics to work and live together.

As the buildings are restored, so a centre for reconciliation, mutual understanding and respect, for justice and peace between all faiths and all people, will be established.

Alongside this aspect of the project will be another: an attempt to provide economic regeneration for the area in which the re-building takes place.

I have asked Lazar Markovic to undertake a preliminary in-vestigation. Within two months he will have produced his report, indicating possible areas where the project could be based. He will proceed by meeting religious leaders in the churches and mosques in Bosnia. Once a local community has agreed in prin-ciple to explore this idea, I will meet with them as well as with government officials and with United Nations officials. After as much consultation as is necessary, the project will be launched.

There will of course be many difficulties: funding, establishing the right international organization, raising the interest of young people, finding the best agencies for economic regeneration and, above all, working with the local communities.

But such a project embodies the vision of the Soul of Europe. As an old style former communist atheist in Belgrade said to me: "This is just what religions at their very best should do together."

DIARY

PETER PELZ

Something needs to be said about Western perceptions of Serbia. Recent history and the catastrophe in Kosovo, the ambiguous relationship between the Western powers and Milosevic, on the one hand accused of war crimes and on the other his position made seemingly secure by our policies, the general demonization of Serbs in the Western media – all these factors contribute to a fear and mistrust of the country as a whole. As we entered the country we felt afraid and before we left, two Serb journalists as-sured us that we had every reason to be so. While no Serbs we met excused themselves from the criminal atrocities committed in their name, they are nonetheless deeply bitter about the one-sided reporting of the Balkan crisis in the Western press. The crowds of Kosovan refugees regularly depicted on television, accompanied by stories of rapes, murders and burnings, turned the Albanian Muslims into pitiful victims, so that any balanced judgement of the situation became impossible. Gradually, carefully considered documentaries and reporting from independent minded journalists began to shift this one-sided perspective. Now Serbs are also victims, this time of Albanian backed KLA atrocities, and the majority of people in Serbia, those who always opposed the actions of their president, have to witness the violation of their culture. Already eighty churches, which had been built and worshipped in long before the Albanians began to occupy Kosovo, a heartland culture which not even several centuries of Ottoman Muslim domination ever touched, have been destroyed under the watchful eye of KFOR troops.

Many Serbs believed that reporting of their atrocities was exaggerated and they want to be treated with fairness. There was bitterness about the support given to Milosevic by NATO and the West in general: they noted that the only town in Serbia not bombed by NATO planes was Milosevic's hometown. The sanctions and the bombing appeared to strengthen his position. Serbs also questioned the motives of NATO in waging the bombing campaign at all. Many believe NATO wants to establish a military base in Kosovo for political and economic reasons of its own, probably to do with Russia and Asia, which have no connection with protecting victims of atrocities in the Balkans. Serbs have come to the conclusion that it is in the interests of the West to keep the Balkans, in particular Serbia, weak and ineffectual.

Nonetheless, intelligent Serbs, thoughtful about recent history, though preserving their characteristic sense of pride and dignity and therefore seeming arrogantly defensive and maybe even unapologetic, were grieving over the criminal depths to which their country had sunk. As Lazar himself put it: "We were once the victims, persecuted, misunderstood and hated by Turks, Albanians and Croats for centuries; now we have become as bad as all the rest, criminals and murderers."

The wars, embargos and sanctions have turned Serbia into a dangerous country. Milosevic remained impregnable in his bunker.

The Mafia were visibly active on the streets. It was difficult for law-abiding citizens to survive without recourse to criminal activity. Though we carefully avoided contact with politicians and gangsters, their presence and influence were a dominant feature of the whole visit. No conversation passed without mention of Milosevic and we could not fail to observe the blatant activities of the Mafia. Continued isolation of Serbia looked likely to prolong this state of affairs. Criminals would thrive and people would suffer.

Looking Back

Culture shock hit us unexpectedly when we returned to Budapest at the end of our visit. It was supposed to happen arriving in Belgrade. Coming back to Vienna after travelling through Slovakia and Poland some years ago it hit me in a similar way. In contrast to the sociability and traditional hospitality of even the poorest, life in western Europe seemed cold and inhuman, a market place in which people are reduced to products buying products. People in eastern Europe are responsive, even if it was being spat at by girls outside a restaurant in Belgrade who overheard us speaking in English. They turned round and shouted, "Fuck off!" Usually the people we encountered were warm and kind, always making a special ritual over a welcome drink and preparing generous meals. Doors opened. In Budapest it felt like a steel door being slammed in our faces and concrete walls rising all round. Serbia was another world. In the Budapest hotel guests were cocooned in luxury, but not intimidated by the plush furnishings, because this was what they had paid for, they had earned it, it was no less than they expected. The massive elegance of Belgrade's Hyatt Regency dwarfed the guests. There were fewer of them anyway. Figures disappeared in the vastness of polished marble, monumental staircases, cavernous corridors and hallways, sunken gardens, balustrades and echoing spaces. Even the staff tiptoed furtively, vanishing from view after pouring coffee or clearing tables. People seemed to want to remain invisible, perhaps because this was not a safe place. Killings did take place here. One room where a gangster was shot has a price supplement attached.

The Hyatt Regency bore no relationship to the rest of Belgrade and Serbia. It was an oasis of luxury in a desert of untended, derelict, or unfinished buildings. It looked like a brightly coloured bauble in a wasteland. On the other hand, the view from the Radisson Beke in Budapest was of elegant buildings in the Austro-Hungarian imperial style, covered with caryatids and ornamental balconies. On the ground floor of these houses people wandered in and out of sophisticated shops selling designer spectacles, bags, and artefacts. Hungarians passed by, still shabbily dressed, mostly too poor to afford such quality goods.

The view from the Hyatt Regency in Belgrade was of rubble, as though NATO bombs had demolished the neighbourhood, which happened to be just a neglected building site. The shell of one huge building opposite had been a grandiose project that ran out of money when the boom years of late Communism collapsed. The windows without panes stared blankly, wind whistling through the empty spaces. Beyond stood range after range of twentieth-century communist tower blocks, concrete and indestructible: it was brutal architecture. In between lay a wasteland crossed by roads and traffic. Romanian traders gathered along the edges of the rubble standing next to plastic carrier bags with small piles of odds and ends, a few bunches of mud-clogged carrots, bottles of juice and cheap clothes. Occasionally a car parked surreptitiously in a corner of the wasteland and advertised black market petrol on a hastily scrawled piece of cardboard.

The Hyatt Regency stood on a street with other large, expensive modern buildings including the Foreign Media offices, the Intercontinental Hotel (where the head gangster Arkan recently died, shot by an assassin), and some other nameless places looking smart and forbidding with their dark reflecting glass. In the car parks outside, scruffy gypsy children roamed, waiting to harass car owners. These urchins resembled those undernourished children in documentaries about the Great Depression between the First and Second World Wars. They mobbed us, and when we gave them a two hundred dinar note (roughly three pounds) they rushed off in triumph waving the crumpled note in the air like a trophy. "They can buy some food," I said. Lazar commented drily that it might be better if they bought some soap. "But what would these kids want with soap?" he added wistfully.

Three Ms dominated our time in Serbia – though we barely touched any of them. But on the last day each made a potent impression.

The Mafia first. They were ever visible in their shiny new western cars. Who else can afford these Mercedes and BMWs here in Serbia? Though I had glimpsed behind the steering wheels either young hoodlums with their mobiles or fat entrepreneurs, cigars clenched between puffy lips, exuding a quiet menace from the security of their hi-tech cocoons, only on the last day did I come face to face with one of them.

Lazar had to pick up his passport from the landlord of the flat where we stayed in central Belgrade. The passport had served as a form of insurance. We drove past the wasteland around the Hyatt Regency and eventually arrived at one of the many concrete tower blocks visible on the Belgrade skyline. A flashy car drove alongside us and disgorged two passengers. I was photographing the view from the back seat, when Lazar suddenly turned round, eyes blazing and gestured me violently to hide the camera. "If they see you filming them they will kill you, immediately." The hoodlums were straightening their jackets and orientating themselves. Just for a fraction of a moment my eyes locked with those of one of the men. I looked into two bottomless pools of blackness. The man looked in his mid forties, an experienced henchman, a startling contrast to the familiar sleek fat bosses with cigars, dark glasses, and half-naked adolescent girls attached like trophies. These always reminded me of the thieves who held a knife to my throat on the train back from Kiev six years earlier, incongruously Armani-suited with tiny embroidered Gucci shoes, puffy faced and already going to seed with all the spending and high living. Nor was this Serb a young beginner, an adolescent bored with his lack of future, bursting with energy and therefore only too keen to enjoy the fast, furious, and risky business of being a gangster. Live like a king for a week rather than suffer a lifetime of poverty. This man looked steeped in violent crime, not primarily interested in wealth, power, or even women accessories, but simply used to this way of life, knowing no other. Black dominated from his long greasy hair, bristly unshaved face, shabby leather jacket, and trousers down to his shoes. The eyes reminded me of William Blake's lines describing those "born to endless night". The look he gave me, for all of a fraction of a second, sized me up. It even welcomed me into the pit as it might any of his colleagues in crime and particularly his victims before killing them, embracing them into death, as Lightborn does the frightened king at the end of Marlowe's *Edward II.* The Serb then dismissed me from his gaze, hunched his shoulders, and slouched off into the concrete with his mate. History evidenced itself in this figure who for centuries might have ridden a horse across Serbia, fighting Turks, joining in the massacre of communities with cool indifference, a way of life as natural to him as eating and sleeping. Now his skill is of use to the Mafia and he fits easily into the subversive cycle of wheeling, dealing, and killing. For a fraction of a second I became another victim.

The second M represented Milosevic: an ever-present, invisible menace – a power that somehow had everyone in its thrall, though never to be met with; he was always at a distance, but hovered over every conversation, every encounter. He reminded me of the sinister Dr Mabuse in Fritz Lang's subversive early German films that warn of the rise of Fascism. Dr Mabuse manipulated people through terror, and managed this all the more effectively by keeping himself invisible. The source of power unknown, he remained untouchable.

During the drive to Hungary through the flat Serbian countryside, stretching fertile for miles in every direction, Lazar informed us that Milosevic had no power base. Belgrade and the big cities were lost to him anyway. In free elections he would lose, as was proved later in the year. But even in the countryside, where he might have manipulated the loyalties of simple peasants with warnings about devious Western imperialists, ordinary folk did not care, so long as they could survive. Politics were irrelevant to them, a game played by invisible power mongers.

My impression was that even ordinary, less thoughtful Serbs were aware of Milosevic's desperate measures to hold on to power. Elections were approaching and the sheer crudity of the defacing of the opposition leader's posters must have made even the dumbest voter know that Milosevic ordered it. Somebody had been paid to take an aerosol can to every poster, spraying slogans along the lines of 'NATO slave', 'Janissary', etc. Janissaries were people who were taken from all over the Ottoman Empire to Turkey and trained as an elite fighting force. There was something absurdly pedantic about these slogans; no attempt had been made to make the daubs look like a genuine protest.

Milosevic had no fear of non-governmental organisations that thrive in Serbia. We visited five – more about them later. Unless they took up arms, Milosevic would not waste any effort in eliminating them. They also bolstered his reputation for being liberal, tolerant, and democratic. He reckoned on the unfortunate characteristic among all Serbs of blaming others for their misfortunes, a character trait no different from that of any other nationality including the British. It was always somebody else who was responsible for the catastrophe in Serbia. NATO seemed to play into Milosevic's hands, and the bombing of Belgrade helped him survive. Lazar said, "Milosevic and the western Mafia destroyed my life." Lazar was determined to change his life for the better, seizing the opportunity we were giving him. He had always resisted the temptation to resort to subterfuge and crime, like stealing from humanitarian aid, which happened frequently in Serbia. Instead he kept faith with Orthodoxy, his religion, and he preserved his natural sympathy and compassion for others, those even less able than himself to make a living. An intelligent, thoughtful, well-read young man, his analysis of the political, social, and economic situation of his country was acute. It was expressed in bitterly ironic asides. As we drove northwards to the Hungarian border we passed heavily armed police, imposing in their blue uniforms which made them look fat, slow, and intractable, interrogating drivers on the roadside, investigating the contents of cars and clearly expecting bribes and pay-offs. Lazar muttered a stream of irony: "Our fine police…how kind they are…they love us so tenderly…they protect us from criminals and evil people, from NATO bombs, from wicked foreigners …they watch over us…"

The third M was for mongrels.

There was the constant presence of abandoned dogs. They lurked near rubbish bins, outside restaurants, anywhere they might find a morsel. It was not so much their starved, shivering, dirty appearance that was upsetting, but the look in their eyes. They did not understand what had happened to them. They were dumb beasts who looked desperately for a human being to take care of them, whom they could serve and be attached to. Like the peasant boy abandoned by his uncle in the market place somewhere in Mexico City at the start of Luis Bunuel's *Los Olvidados*, these creatures waited forlornly and patiently for their master and protector. The sight of refugees was not as disturbing as these abandoned dogs. The men and women huddling together in crowds outside the patriarchate waiting for food and aid expressed defiance along with their desperation. These Serbian refugees from Kosovo had lost by the flick of a coin and knew it. Given a different political outcome they would have inflicted their present suffering on others, and it might be their neighbours who were having to scrape a living on the streets of some city, waiting for a toilet to be installed in their camp or for help to come from some foreign agency. Guilt exacerbates defiance. The refugees in the camps followed us around eagerly, expecting some immediate improvement in their condition: they too were cynical in their opinions. It was well known that barely ten per cent of all aid actually reached the people who needed it. So this defiance and cynicism gave them pride and resilience as they stuck close together for support and survival. As for the dogs, they suddenly found themselves thrown out of home and security. Occasionally they joined in packs. Just such a rabble of mongrels once chased us viciously down the road, venting their fury on our car, yelping, squealing, howling, barking, baring their teeth. I felt no fear, just relief that they had found one another and could together express their outrage at human beings who had betrayed them.

On the road to the Hungarian border I saw a dog standing in the middle of a vast ploughed field, part of a landscape empty of human habitation that stretched to the horizon. It had clearly been chucked from a passing vehicle. It looked in every direction for mile on mile and could see no help or company. Its tail hung between its hind legs and, though far away, I detected that moist glint of hopeless bereavement in the eye. What would happen when night fell, as it would shortly? Where would it go? How could it survive? There it stood, black and lonely, waiting, wondering, grieving, while cars whistled past.

A fourth M might have been monasteries. Considering the nature of our visit, religion naturally dominated our time in Serbia. So the prospect of visiting another monastery on the return journey was depressing, particularly as we were already late and hoping to reach Budapest before midnight: yet more imitation fake icons, the figures and faces ironed out to bland uniformity, the colours garish; yet more monks looking pious and withdrawn.

We crossed the Danube on the road to Novi Sad (which means 'New Garden' and looks like an industrial wasteland) and watched out for NATO bomb damage to bridges and infrastructure. We noted the neat rows of idyllic summer houses lining the sloping southern shores of the wide meandering river. They were the dachas built by officials in the heady economic boom years before the collapse of Communism. Flood waters along the northern shores of the Danube make it inadvisable to build there, and the muddy flats must provide a melancholy view from the weekend homes.

The monastery lay beyond the town of Kovilije. We bumped along the narrow cobbled street past dozens of traditional neat Serbian houses, which, although functional, were beautiful in their simplicity, with even the occasional attractive gable. We observed people sitting outside, chatting, smiling at us, carts laden with manure and logs, chickens scratching, old women in kerchiefs leaning on fences, and gardens with carefully pruned fruit trees. Here was a place time had forgotten. The cobbled road continued for several miles as friendly people pointed us in the direction of the distant monastery.

The place seemed quite deserted. Sun shone on the white walls of the old chapel, cold inside with its peeling frescoes. A tower stood at the entrance with bells of different sizes attached to a wooden framework. Several empty wine casks cluttered the entrance to the main lodging area. There was not a person in sight. A stillness lay over the flat fields stretching back to the town in the distance, and the sky flung its vast dome over the horizon, tiny white clouds slowly making their way across.

We knocked but no one answered. We nosed our way down long chilly corridors peering at reproductions of famous Serbian paintings. They included a reproduction of a nineteenth-century commission: Patriarch Arsenije leading the Serbs out of Kosovo in the Middle Ages, wounded warriors accompanying women, children and flocks of sheep in a cloud of dust. This portrayal of an historical event so offended the patriarch who commissioned the picture – "you have depicted a rabble!" – that the artist had to repaint it, omitting the sheep. The original version doesn't look like a rabble at all, rather a defiant group of people determined to carry on their life somewhere else. It is the old Serb story of being ousted from their homeland, perpetually persecuted. Old photographs of the Yugoslav Royal Family were interspersed with paintings and photographs of patriarchs and faded paintings of St Michael triumphing over a particularly sexy looking devil, lithe and muscular. There were also some landscapes and folk paintings of the chapel. Old manuscripts lay open under glass, and the sun shone through dusty windows which looked out on to extensive gardens and orchards. We climbed to the top storey, with still no sign of anyone. Then a door opened further down the corridor and an alarmed face peered out only to disappear again. Eventually we caught one of these furtive figures who fetched a tall young monk. He welcomed us with a beaming smile.

We were too late for lunch, which Lazar had hoped for, but the monk gave us a traditional warm welcome, taking us to the reception room, the best room in the house, one with heat, a table, and several comfortable chairs. This room had once been beautifully decorated with gold-tinted wallpaper and an antique tiled stove in the corner. The paper had faded and peeled at the edges with large damp patches, but the place felt as though it were about to be renovated. Already some new chunky pine furniture, polished and carved in a straightforward, simple country fashion, had been installed: two large wardrobes, a wide coffee table, and the armchairs we were sitting in. The portraits on the fading wallpaper of the king and several grim-looking patriarchs seemed remnants of an old order, the smiling young monk representing the change. Tall and gangling, he even resembled a new broom ready to sweep away the fusty old traditions and cobwebs. He offered us homemade quince brandy and Turkish coffee: they were served to us by a babushka in kerchief, crumpled grey stockings, and comfortable slippers. She carried the delicate china and glasses on a metal tray, which resembled a pyramid with a large handle for carrying. Wherever we went we had been greeted with the same Serb hospitality. However poor the place we visited, we would always be served brandy and coffee in the best china, ritually with style, reminiscent of the Japanese tea ceremony. However poor the people, the elegance and quality of service remained constant.

The babushka turned out to be the mother of Bishop Porphirije who headed the community in this monastery. It was a unique place in Serbia because the monks were all young. The community was only just establishing itself, which accounted for the place seeming to be in the process of change from old to new. The bishop represented a new breed of Orthodox monasticism, opening up the old traditions and welcoming new ideas, new generations.

The smiling monk began with a long and tedious ancient history of the monastery, a familiar litany of violence, destruction, and massacres. The place was for ever being sacked and burnt, then being rebuilt. Now a group of young monks had been gathered together by the bishop to renovate the place, turn it into a kind of family or commune rather than the way it used to be with strict monastic rules. The monk rather emphasized this point, looking at us intently. I could only guess at what that implied, but perhaps the more liberal rules accounted for his pleasant demeanour, a striking contrast to the grim asceticism of other monks we had met recently.

We could hear a soprano being taught the art of Byzantine chant in the next room: evidently women were welcome here. While we talked, a young couple sat in a corner of the room waiting to meet the bishop, two fresh and eager faces. They bore out the monk's statement that mostly young people wanted to join the community. However, far too many apply and there was only limited space. Given the situation in Serbia, that came as no surprise. However, young people would be trying to join this community whatever the political situation. They came from all over the world, monks from as far away as America and Australia.

The sun shone through all the windows, and as we were shown round the place it felt as if a fresh breeze was blowing through a fusty tradition. The new chapel on the top floor had a light and airy feel to it, perhaps because the icon painters hadn't started on the walls or iconostasis yet. A couple of small ancient icons lay on the altar, and the rays of the sun shafting through the narrow windows on to the honey coloured stone warmed the space, making it ideal for quiet worship and meditation. Along the corridor we visited the painting studio where a monk continued to work on a new icon, paying no attention to us, totally absorbed in his craft. The windows around him looked onto the large orchards and vegetable gardens, beehives and cattle sheds, poultry scratching and two cats prowling. Beyond a thicket a backwater of the Danube flowed lazily past. This monk looked severe in his concentration, irritated by the intrusion of a noisy group of tourists. Lazar kept urging me to film and take photographs. It was one of the few moments I could have hurled the equipment at him. The light-filled studio, the tubes of paints, the palette streaked with colours, the jar of water, and the repose of the hand of the young painter as it rested on the easel made time stand still, opening into eternity. The icon was, however, yet another imitation, a bland copy, like several lying around the studio. This is a discovery for the new generation in post-communist times. An ancient tradition is being resurrected, understood, and appreciated as though for the first time. The iconography and the special skills need to be learned. However, despite the blandness of the new icons the colours burned with garish intensity. The new artists have fallen in love with their tradition and can't help themselves in slavishly imitating and ironing out what they might think of as clumsy errors by the ancient painters. One day they will see that these very imperfections, the elongations and distortions, are in fact what make the old icons so astounding and beautiful. They are a catalogue of psychological insights, pious fervour, and human striving after the divine in a brutal society which, by its nature, mocks, discourages, and contradicts the life of the spirit. The next generations will not only understand this, they will dismiss the facile imitations and create the next masterpieces of iconography which will reflect the realities and aspirations of their own lives and times.

By now sunlight flooded every corner of the monastery, the staircases, the corridors, and each room. As we left, Bishop Porphirije arrived. He was a charismatic priest, film-star handsome and still in his thirties. He had a rare manner of greeting: attending to each person separately, locking eyes, pausing before giving a long handshake, and gazing with quiet intensity as though memorizing every feature. So he looked at me with his large friendly eyes set in an ivory smooth face, framed in the traditional beard, and invited us all to come and stay again, though next time for much longer. He then insisted on waving us goodbye as we drove out of the monastery grounds, fixing us with a loving soulful gaze as we returned along the narrow cobbled road past the old houses and carts with manure, the gossipping women, the men smiling, and the poultry scratching beneath the winter-trimmed fruit trees.

Trying to reach the road to Budapest, we made a wrong

turning, there being no signs in any direction, and followed the cobbled road to its end. It crossed a bridge and without leading to a slip road eventually vanished into a muddy field. We barely managed to turn the car round. It seemed somehow appropriate at that moment to have ended up wedged in the rich and viscous Serbian soil, the distant churches of Kovilije pointing slender fingers into the blue canopy of the sky flecked with white clouds, and the countryside enveloping us in a silence broken only by the suddenly soaring song of a lark.

Setting off for Belgrade

Till recently I had held the opinion that the whole of Yugoslavia, from the borders with Austria and Hungary to Greece, should be left to its own devices, with a barbed wire fence placed all round so the different ethnic groups could fight undisturbed. It would not be until our visit to Bosnia that I grasped the extent of my ignorance. This had been no civil war. The ethnic cleansing had been a holocaust against the Muslim population. In my unawareness the history of the region appeared to consist of one group after another persecuting the others. All groups were reckoned to be equally guilty. Serbs seemed to be the latest scourge of the region, but hadn't the Croats and Muslims also committed atrocities in the past? Each group became a victim of the others. Generation after generation continued the cycle of violence. History endlessly repeated itself. What could we possibly contribute to changing the relentless vicious circle? The scale and horror of the atrocities seemed designed to terrify and warn off visitors. "This is what we are capable of; come at your peril."

We were now on our way to the dark heart of this country, with an impossible objective: to bring the leaders of the main faiths together into one room, Orthodox, Muslim, Jewish, and Catholic. If we succeeded in this then the Soul of Europe would gain credibility. We would have taken a modest new step and provided a basis for the possibility of change.

The urgency and importance of this visit took time to register. We had originally thought along the lines of exploring the more familiar regions of western Europe where there are enough problems, especially between the different faiths and ethnic groups. The Germans, French, and English should learn to talk to one another and share their experiences. We are after all part of Europe and we should spend more time discussing issues of people rather than perpetually arguing about economics, farm produce, and currency. The poorer eastern European countries ought to be included in the conversation, now that they are queuing up to join the European Union. The Balkans seemed a different part of the world altogether: I could not even perceive them as being European. They are, however, an important part of Europe, a bridge between East and West, where the three major Abrahamic faiths have coexisted for a thousand years. So despite our reservations about this region, locked in a medieval mind-set of warfare, revenge, ethnic hatreds, and lethal grudges, we knew we had to go there first. Balkan history is hard to digest. The killings and grudges are not simply between different ethnic groups. The fiercest often occur within each ethnic group. Reading Tim Judah's *The Serbs,* a gruelling and detailed account of endlessly repeating massacres, can inspire an hallucination in which a Serb suddenly feels such a grudge against himself that he commits self-slaughter in a fit of righteous hysteria. A bizarre incident is recounted in the *Guinness Book of Records*, reckoned to be the craziest act of violence ever, when three drunken chainsaw-wielding Yugoslav peasants tried to outdo one another on New Year's Eve. One cut off his own arm, then another cut off his own leg. The third trumped them all by swinging a chainsaw and chopping off his own head.

We left with fears that the Serbs might kill us, or that we might fall victim to crossfire. While they shoot one another, and one government official or gangster after the other, we might get caught in a hail of bullets. We cracked jokes with friends before leaving, picturing ourselves spending the next few years tied to a radiator in Belgrade. Our laughter had a hollow ring to it.

It was more likely that we would enjoy legendary Serbian hospitality and we were looking forward to meeting people. We have already been scheduled to meet each church leader separately. But would Donald manage to persuade them to meet one another and be photographed together? Our ignorance about this country shamed us. For instance we had no idea that there was a Muslim mufti in Belgrade, let alone a mosque. We also looked forward to meeting our contact there, Lazar Markovic.

A year ago, Donald accompanied Robert Runcie, the former Archbishop of Canterbury, to Mount Athos. Donald wrote a vivid account of this journey for *The Tablet.* They travelled by boat and truck from one monastery to the other, middle-aged gentlemen with clerical robes billowing in the wind, coping with rough roads and varying hospitality. They were even thrown out of one monastery by an irascible Serbian priest who objected to people from a different denomination desecrating his church. This incident reminded me of the chapter in Dostoevsky's *The Brothers Karamazov* when several priests at a holy place in Russia engage in a public quarrel, wagging fingers, shouting and denouncing one another.

Donald and Robert Runcie had just arrived at one of these monasteries on Mount Athos and were discussing ways of avoiding yet another lengthy service, when they heard voices in the courtyard below Robert's bedroom. They leaned out of the window and two young men sitting on a bench looked up. Robert's purple cassock intrigued them. They waved and started up a conversation. Donald joined them in the courtyard, and so began our association with Lazar. He had come to Mount Athos on a pilgrimage with his friend, an icon painter.

E-mails are Lazar's chief mode of communication with the world outside Belgrade. They regularly furnished the West with information and propaganda about the Balkan war, during and after NATO's bombing campaign. Lazar e-mailed Donald regularly. The Soul of Europe, then in its infancy, was in the process of developing its aims. The Balkans were not yet necessarily a part of them, given the conservatism of the Orthodox Church and its suspicion of foreigners and other denominations in particular. The Balkans seemed the last place to be involved with the Soul of Europe. Then the political situation in the region deteriorated as the year 1999 proceeded, and a sense of desperation crept into Lazar's messages. For ten years he had put his life on hold. His problems multiplied: he had no prospect of work, no money. An invitation from Scandinavia to give a lecture on Serbian iconography helped, temporarily. We began to make arrangements for a visit to Serbia in the autumn of 1999, a fact-finding tour to see how the Orthodox Church might react to the Soul of Europe. Lazar could act as our guide and interpreter. Then NATO intervened with its bombing campaign on Serbia. The visit had to be postponed till now.

Lazar had prepared a varied, packed, and interesting itinerary. Tomorrow we would meet him for the first time. He told us to look out for him outside Budapest airport. He had hired a white VW Golf next to which he would wait for us (because it might be stolen if he left it even for an instant), and in this his final e-mail before we left home he added, in a rare lapse of spelling, that he would probably see us first and be "weaving"!

Budapest

We saw no sign of Lazar when we arrived.

Having passed through the customs and passport control and walked along the smart, polished marble hallways of the new airport into the reception area where several shabbily dressed men held placards saying BELGRADE (taxis replacing the lack of direct air transport from Great Britain to Serbia), we stood outside in the bitter cold and nobody was either weaving or waving. There was no white VW Golf either, not even in the car park below. We felt uncomfortable being observed and photographed by three suspicious looking young men on the parapet above. After a quarter of an hour pacing up and down, searching in every direction, we began to face up to the fact that we might have been stood up. We waited another quarter of an hour. Several planes disgorged passengers and while a crowd from the latest flight filed into a waiting bus, the long-awaited white VW Golf screeched at top speed round the corner and dived straight into the one and only parking space in front of us.

The day proceeded in chaotic fashion. Lazar had arranged for us to meet two young Hungarians in Budapest. It was three o'clock in the afternoon and we still had to drive to Belgrade, over three hundred miles away, which alarmed us. "We are late already," said Lazar, in what became his signature tune. Having explained unconvincingly that he had been waiting for us at the wrong airport, he devoured a large cream cake with his coffee before rushing into the city centre. It is difficult to navigate in Budapest simply because there are scarcely any road signs. We asked one person after the other, but no one spoke a common language. Eventually, after driving up several one way streets in the wrong direction, much to the consternation of oncoming cars, and performing rapid illegal U turns on the main boulevards in the face of oncoming trams and buses, then hurtling down side streets in vaguely the right direction, we found the street where two shivering youngsters, a boy and a girl, were patiently waiting for us outside an Internet café. While we got to know them, Lazar disappeared for half an hour, trying to contact someone on the Internet. Donald launched into presentation mode, beginning the spiel about the Soul of Europe and its aims while I observed the numbers of young people of Budapest, shy and diffident, enjoying the spacious elegance of this old fashioned coffee house, computers standing on tables in what would have once been a minstrel's gallery.

Lazar is a robustly built, tall man who looks intently at everybody he addresses. He gives the impression of a strong personality capable of organizing anything. He cuts a dash, dressing casually and stylishly in loose fitting clothes. He walks with determination, always needing to get somewhere, probably 'late already', whistling or humming a rock tune. His high forehead is topped by a healthy mass of black hair which juts out at the front in a characteristic tousled quiff, as though he had passed his hands through it instead of a brush. This quiff emphasizes his watchfulness and attentiveness.

It was now half past five in the afternoon. We arranged to meet the young couple on our return from Serbia, and Lazar, having insisted on our buying leg wallets in the event of being mugged, put us into the VW and drove off blindly, hoping he was in the right direction for Belgrade. "It is a big city," said Lazar, "there will be signs everywhere." Not a single sign. We ploughed down lengthy boulevards, crossed lights and roundabouts, but failed to see a direction to any place whatever. We passed miles of dark flats and a few shopping precincts until we reached the outskirts of the city, at which point the road became rougher, pitted with holes. Night began to fall. Eventually we passed through the outer suburbs and reached the countryside. Only then did a minuscule sign indicate that we were on the road to the Ukraine. Lazar made a violently rapid U turn on the main road, but refused to go all the way back into Budapest centre where our troubles had started. Instead we proceeded in a southerly direction down a back street, narrow, bumpy, and potholed. Budapest commuters lived here evidently, but when we stopped a woman getting out of her car and asked which way to Belgrade, she shook her head unhelpfully. So in pitch blackness we continued back to the city centre, tired, stressed, and aware that we had not even started the long journey.

In the middle of the gloom, grime, and urban blankness, with roads, railway lines, tramlines, and traffic crisscrossing from unexpected directions, and Lazar driving at full speed wherever he thought there might be a road sign, we came across a brightly lit petrol station which would be considered smart in England, spotlessly clean and well stocked with drinks and sweets, looking as incongruous as Las Vegas in the desert. A man gave incomprehensible directions in Hungarian, and we plunged back into the urban darkness, as lost as ever. Eventually a German-speaking mechanic at the next filling station gave us clearer instructions, and all of a sudden, at a major road intersection with traffic coming from seven directions, together with trams and trains, we luckily glimpsed a tiny sign to Szeged. Szeged is on the way to Belgrade.

Lazar had already driven four hundred miles to meet us, so the journey became steadily more difficult. It would be impossible to reach Belgrade before the next morning. We also worried about the border, possible complications awaiting us there, and the menace beyond the border, Serbia. Lazar spoke animatedly and without stopping as we hurtled through the night across the flat Hungarian plain, the road getting emptier, Serbia coming ever closer. The fact that Hungary resolutely refused to mention its neighbouring country on the few signposts we came across made us even more uneasy, as though it were a place we should not be visiting.

Lazar gave us a history lesson about the depressing massacres, and we expressed astonishment that there were any Serbs left alive. I remembered *The Serbs* by Tim Judah and how I could hardly read more than two pages at a time, with so many atrocities over the centuries (heads on stakes, women and children torn to pieces). Lazar's family came from Montenegro. The Montenegrins were traditionally bandits, and that relatively small corner of the Balkans was always dangerous even to the invading Turks who never managed to conquer and colonize it. A little of that banditry could be sensed in Lazar's driving, aggressive as though other drivers were enemies to be vanquished. Yet he can also be gentle and affectionate, thoughtful and compassionate. He spoke about the contrasting characteristics typical of the people and the history of this region, the paradoxical contrasts in personality, the country unreconciled and therefore prone to excessively barbaric eruptions, but also capable of peaceful coexistence. There is talk of 'love' between the religions and even between the ethnic groups. Yet the reality, as so painfully experienced in recent times, is full of bitter vengeance and destruction. Lazar is a free thinker, open-minded, intelligent, well educated and with a sharp mind. Communism collapsed shortly after he left University, but he had already questioned the old dogmas and registered his rebellion by becoming a drummer in a rock band. Then, through a girlfriend, he discovered the Bible and was baptized into the Orthodox Church, a change of direction even more remarkable considering his atheistic hardline communist upbringing and environment. The importance to Lazar of Orthodox Christianity lies in its teaching about 'loving' one another. The word 'love' in western Christian usage can often be meaningless, implying at best tolerance and mutual respect, but basically allowing the faithful to preserve privacy and individuality at the expense of others ("we can do as we please so long as we go to church"). For Lazar 'love' means a strong emotion of empathy with other people and a desire to strive for perfection in human relationships. He regularly interrupted his autobiography by furiously berating oncoming drivers for overtaking or for not dipping their headlights. He earns little, but he always shares what he has with his aged and sick father, and occasionally gives even that to his family in Montenegro who are paupers, just to keep them from starving. Lazar spoke to us about every part of his life, but when he spoke of his mother a curtain fell over the conversation. It is another paradox in his personality, that although he is brimful of self-confidence and self-esteem, he fears to deal with his emotions. He still cannot speak about the death from cancer of his mother.

We discussed our strategy for the next few days, the methods whereby we could persuade the religious leaders to meet under the same roof, be photographed by the world press, and so prove that the Soul of Europe means business and can bring about such seemingly impossible outcomes.

Suddenly a sign to Belgrade appeared out of the blackness, small and insignificant, but it warned of the approaching border. Almost immediately we ran into the back of a long queue of waiting vehicles. The man smoking patiently in the car in front told us that the wait would be about two hours. This is usual in the evenings when Serbs are returning from Hungary with cars loaded with goods, otherwise unavailable because of western European sanctions. The border guards search for drugs: hence the delay. The drivers looked down at heel and nervous, chain-smoking and stretching their legs. They would have to unload boxes packed with bottles and cans. But the queue moved quicker than expected. After an hour the Hungarian guards joked testily with us, provoking Lazar with facetious comments about Milosevic. We laughed and agreed with him, only guessing the jokes. So he allowed us through to where a severe-looking Serb guard, a fair-haired woman, middle-aged, thin and straight-backed, cast an eye rapidly over our passports and let us through immediately, but only on condition that we registered with the police in Belgrade. This would interrupt our busy schedule, much to the irritation of Lazar, but at least we were through to Serbia. And we needed to remember we were guests, not on business. Beyond the border the road lay lightless and desolate.

Arriving in Belgrade

Midnight approached as we crossed the border into Serbia and we needed sustenance. Lazar told us of a restaurant on a lake. "Our football team comes here. It is good and very popular!" We drove through a village and parked in the forecourt of a travel lodge. Several parties were reaching a climax inside. Pillars and hedges of pot plants divided the spacious room so groups could dine in privacy. Folk musicians played on fiddles, bass, and accordion, moving behind a row of guests seated at a long banquet table where a lavish meal had just been consumed and many bottles of wine waited to be drunk. A recent television documentary had filmed a young Serbian soldier being serenaded and feted before leaving to fight on the front line in Kosovo. Here it was a birthday party and the people were mostly elderly. The other parties and groups consisted entirely of men. They looked like businessmen taking their socializing seriously, tucking into a large quantity of dishes washed down with copious amounts of beer and spirits. They talked animatedly, laughing and occasionally tearful as they listened to the non-stop stream of folk dances and songs being played by a band of evidently classically trained professionals. Sometimes the guests would join in the singing. The musicians concentrated on the birthday party where the only women in the restaurant were sitting, smiling and blushing at the attention, the violinist inclining his head towards them.

The all-male groups might have been Mafia and we prepared to duck when the shooting started. Meanwhile courteous waiters attended to everyone's needs, each table glistening with heavy polished cutlery on starched linen cloths.

They offered us local rakija, a dry and potent pear-flavoured aperitif. Lazar, being a vegetarian, satisfied himself with an omelette and baked mushrooms, each one swimming in a lake of oil. After a thick meat and vegetable soup, the evening speciality turned out to be lightly grilled goose liver on a bed of rice, delicately prepared with the meat still pink inside but crisp on the surface. Lazar made the mistake of drinking a glass of wine. This made him sleepy later in the journey and Donald had to keep pinching him, talking and finding ways of engaging his interest just to keep his mind on the road.

As we left the restaurant and drove out of the car park, Lazar began a lengthy conversation with the attendant, a young man living in a shed and paid to keep an eye on the cars. The man became quite animated and bent down to look at us through the windows with large soft brown eyes. Barely twenty years old, he spoke softly but in a torrent that meant our journey would be delayed. Lazar took no heed of the late hour and persisted in questioning him. This young man had fought in Arkan's army. Apparently oblivious of his master's assassination, he spoke of his gratitude to Arkan who had rescued him from a life of village poverty in a remote area of Serbia, given him clothes, paid him enough to look after his family and, when the army disbanded, found him this job. Looking closely at his smooth-skinned, fresh young face, it was hard to envisage him as a soldier massacring Kosovan Muslims, and impossible to imagine him armed, though he specifically told us that Arkan had given him a rifle. Just this kind of young man joined the Serb army in Kosovo, and when KFOR troops moved in he would have been seen on television newsreels reluctantly retreating back to Belgrade defiantly sticking fingers in the air.

Lazar looked at us pointedly as though to warn us now to pay attention to every encounter.

We filled the petrol tank at a brightly lit garage on the road to Belgrade. Sanctions impede the supply of petrol, but somehow the government and gangsters owning this gas station have no diffculty with supplies. We had to pay in deutschmarks so that the pump owners need not declare their earnings. The place buzzed with life even at two o'clock in the morning. A party celebrated noisily inside. Lazar talked to the young doe-eyed attendant here and discovered yet another young soldier disbanded from Arkan's army.

The last hundred miles seemed to last for ever. Lazar kept leaning on the wheel and nodding off. Donald next to him tried to find topics of interest to engage Lazar's mind. Fright kept us awake.

At one point Lazar straightened up and announced with solemnity that we had reached an important place. "Here, on this bridge over the Danube, we cross the line between Europe and Asia." Historically and geographically the Danube to the south of Novi Sad marked the point beyond which the Turks failed to colonize Europe. No difference is discernible, but on crossing the border earlier it had felt we had entered an alien world.

We arrived in Belgrade at four o'clock in the morning. Lazar informed us earlier in Hungary that we were scheduled to meet the patriarch at nine o'clock. Most of the journey had been taken up with discussing this crucial encounter on which the main objectives of the Soul of Europe depended. So our most important meeting would take place in just a few hours time and we had yet to sleep. The dark outskirts of Belgrade soon merged with the lights of the city centre, and having crossed the River Sava we turned right into a derelict car park, the ground pitted with rubble and dislodged stones. We staggered, half asleep and freezing cold, into an old-fashioned block of flats, the entrance bleak and functional, a twisted lattice of iron bars blocking off the basement. We stepped into the lift and the lino flooring sank an inch under our feet, so, for a moment we felt the sensation of falling. Lazar had been enthusiastic about this apartment telling us that the owner was related to a rich government official. He went on to say that the flat might be turned into a brothel or used for making sex videos. The sitting room was spacious, with several armchairs and a dresser containing a large collection of cut glass. Grey, unwashed net curtains draped over the windows leading onto a narrow metal balcony. The kitchen smelled of stale cabbage. The main bedroom looked straight out on to the main road between Budapest and Istanbul, the traffic roar perpetual. Here the grimy net curtains were torn and ragged. In the smaller bedroom what looked like two pieces of conceptual art on the wall turned out on closer inspection to be a cluster of naked wires missing their light fittings. We were so tired that we could have slept on a traffic island. We lay down fully clothed, Donald in the main bedroom but perpetually wakened by the heavy lorries outside, myself on a smaller bed in the small room, and Lazar on two armchairs pushed together in the sitting room.

In four hours we needed to be on best form to meet the patriarch himself, on whose goodwill the fate of our trip to Serbia depended.

Meeting Patriarch Pavle

The patriarchate is a nondescript, functional civic building, the corridors dark and cavernous. A babushka in a kerchief was mopping the stone staircase that led to several floors above. We waited for a while in an anteroom to an office where the patriarch's secretary appeared to be administering the work of the diocese singlehandedly, constantly dashing in and out. Another priest arrived who spoke animatedly about two refugee camps in his charge outside Belgrade. He wanted to take us there after the meeting. The atmosphere was cool and chilled even further as we were eventually shown up to the first floor where the patriarch was waiting for us. A tall young man in a grey suit accompanied us. His eyes expressed perpetual alarm. We passed the babushka and her bucket before being ushered into a large room with a large nineteenth-century painting depicting the conversion of St Lazar on the wall. The patriarch stood at the entrance to his reception room, a tiny elderly man with a long white beard, wearing a simple black fez and a black cassock. He looked nervous and defensive. Perhaps as English people we might still be perceived as enemies. Not so long ago we had been dropping bombs on Belgrade. Perhaps we were coming to criticize and dictate. At any rate, though he gave us a polite welcome and sat us down, we felt uneasy and my hopes of any positive results sank. It seemed we had fallen at the first hurdle. This was going to be an audience with the patriarch and there would be an exchange of homilies but nothing of substance.

First the patriarch delivered a speech in a nasal piping voice. "These are difficult times. It is important to meet. When one member of the body is suffering, then all suffer; when one member of the body is good, holy and exalted, then all are exalted." The little man sat in the middle of a large sofa while we occupied armchairs on either side. In order to translate quicker and not have to shout, Lazar moved next to the patriarch on the sofa. It seemed quite natural here that this young man in a red lumber shirt, cuffs undone, brown jeans looking as though they hadn't been taken off in days, and dusty shoes should be leaning close to this eminent figure and speaking into his ear. I couldn't imagine this happening with the Archbishop of Canterbury. The patriarch talked about the close relationships between the Anglican and the Serbian Orthodox Churches in the past. They should remain close, despite changes in the Anglican Church. This sounded ominous. He was referring to the ordination of women. He then spoke of his ministry as Bishop of Kosovo for thirty-four years. "We meet with Muslims. We try to gather and witness love and dialogue between people. What is common between Muslims and Christians? It is faith in one Lord. So faith is coming to God who will pay us back for our actions..." He spoke of the communist system. "How can we express our belief to atheists? By serving truth and love we express our faith and help our brothers. We must always be open to all even to those with no faith. God gives us freedom, does not force belief. He gives us conscience, heart and understanding."

The words came simply, the old man's face drawn and pale, decades of experience in every line, yet his eyes were clear and round, like those of a child: a century in human form. It was hard to conceive the extent of history this man had witnessed and taken part in. His whole life had been devoted to the Church at a time when choosing such a path meant being an outsider, without the respect of government and civil authorities traditionally taken for granted in western European churches. He experienced at first hand the two World Wars, the Depression of the inter-war years, then the long period of communist repression, and finally the chaos of the post-communist years, the catastrophe of the last decade. When he spoke of his long ministry in Kosovo we thought of the laceration of that region by ethnic and religious hatreds and wondered how he had managed to survive. We sat before a man whose tiny physique made one underestimate a formidable determination and resilience. The quality of his spirit made him seem formidable and remote from ordinary human beings. His rigid adherence to Orthodox discipline irks a young free thinker like Lazar but it had helped him survive the century. But we detected no bigotry. His eyes expressed a soulful recognition of humanity in every person, however lost and corrupted. Though the meeting adhered to a formal exchange of opinions, his quiet dignity and tranquil demeanour made us feel at ease in his company. Pomp and ceremony means nothing to this ascetic person. He travels by bus, switches off the lights in the patriarchate at bedtime and orders the staff not to use the lift so as to save electricity and keep fit, like himself. One of the many anecdotes told to us illustrates the contradictions of his character, his rigidly old-fashioned morality and his natural compassion. Once, sitting on a packed bus with his chaplain, travelling through Kosovo, he watched an elderly woman enter with heavy bags, looking around for a spare seat. "Let's get off here," the patriarch whispered urgently to his chaplain. "But we're miles away from anywhere," said the chaplain, alarmed. "Never mind, get off, we can walk," said the patriarch. So before the bus moved off again they dismounted and finished the journey on foot. Eventually the patriarch explained his reasons to the chaplain. It was for the sake of the old woman's immortal soul. Being the patriarch no one would have asked him to give up his seat, even for the old woman, but he could see her getting angry. So to prevent her cursing he quickly left the bus. He wanted to protect her from the devil.

The patriarch displayed such a quality of wisdom and patience, of steadfastness and inner strength, that he serves as an example to other spiritual leaders. He has witnessed and assimilated the horrors of almost a century, always present, never looking away, and now represents a community, becoming a figurehead and spokesman in a time of political and economic chaos. He also had to deal with Milosevic and keep his integrity. It doesn't seem relevant that he is Orthodox. He might be a Catholic, or a Muslim, or a Buddhist, but it is the purity and dedication of his purpose that propels his ministry, and these qualities are demonstrated by an empathy for people, whatever their faith, even when they have none at all. It is as though having seen suffering at close quarters throughout his life, he simply cannot be anything other than this gentle, quietly spoken but resolute leader, looking both mournful and also determined, a frail man of few gestures. The sparsely furnished room with chairs lining the walls might have been a community hall in a suburb if it weren't for a cluster of ancient icons glistening in the corner.

Then Donald spoke. He launched into a description of the aims of the Soul of Europe and before he had uttered more than a sentence the patriarch's demeanour changed completely. He looked at Donald and suddenly a warm smile suffused his drawn features. It was like the sun coming from behind a dark cloud. Donald did not notice, being too busy trying to explain our aims. Everything depended on the goodwill of the patriarch, and though none of us had dared discuss this issue, the fear of failure lurked in the background of all our conversations when preparing for this morning's confrontation. I watched the patriarch while Lazar, concentrating hard, translated for Donald. The patriarch was not actually listening. He fixed Donald with a warm gaze that implied both affection and also indulgence, like the smile of a mother watching her child walk the first steps, or speak the first words. Something about Donald's manner, his eyes perhaps, or simply the intensity of trying to explain the purpose of our visit, nothing to do with the actual words, but a direct expression of the heart seemed to have won the old man over in an instant. From then on the atmosphere changed, light and warmth flooded the room. We had succeeded, even though nothing had been decided or even discussed. It is all in the emotions, in the direct communication between human beings, and language is no longer a barrier.

The conversation now became more animated. The patriarch and Lazar, the elderly wise man and the young dishevelled art historian, conversed rapidly together on the sofa while Donald and I exchanged astonished glances and the tall young man watched, not understanding anything. Lazar was filling in what Donald had omitted: many of the points that had been gone over so carefully the day before and had somehow been forgotten due to the stress and exhaustion of the night, so many points of Orthodox protocol, so many subtle implications to do with the difference of procedure. But though these were clearly of importance for us to get right, the patriarch had actually made his mind up. He agreed without hesitation to bring together the other religious leaders in Serbia and to host the meeting in the patriarchate. We should arrange this with the secretary downstairs. We had been there for about half an hour and a priest entered with a tray of glasses filled with tomato juice which we drank as though it were wine, toasting the future of the project. At this point the patriarch rose to leave for another meeting and we began to be ushered downstairs to the office. But before leaving, Donald, affected by the quality of this encounter, asked for the patriarch to bless him and our endeavour. The patriarch obliged and Donald knelt down and prepared to feel the hands of the old man touching him. He could not see the patriarch looking down kindly but also slightly embarrassed, as though not considering himself worthy of this significant request. Donald is a heavily built man, and so the patriarch looked even frailer in comparison, a man seemingly made entirely out of spirit.

The Refugee Camps

The issue of refugees in Serbia had arisen in the conversation. The Church occupies itself with providing food and lodging to the best of its abilities. Patriarch Pavle said that problems in peacetime are always worse after war. Even small gifts from visitors can help. We were told of a German businessman giving a hundred deutschmarks to provide milk for children, milk that the blockades had prevented from getting through. But now refugees run the risk of living in ghettoes and even landing in prison. Finally we spoke of the destruction of churches in Kosovo. Downstairs in the office, away from the patriarch, his pacific presence could no longer dam a tide of anger, and suddenly the gloves came off. The secretary and the priest taking us to the refugee camps attacked KFOR troops and their "disgusting behaviour", "adding insult to injury". Apparently after Albanians had burnt and destroyed up to eighty Orthodox churches in Kosovo, KFOR cleaned up the damage to remove evidence of the desecration.

The priest then drove us at speed through Belgrade, this rusting, decrepit city in need of attention to infrastructure. I expected to find the camps in Belgrade, but the priest drove us into the countryside. Apparently Milosevic had decreed that no refugees should be allowed into the city. This was partly face-saving, since he had declared Serbia to have won the battle with NATO, partly not to demoralize people living in the city. In common with governments everywhere in Europe, he doesn't like and doesn't want refugees. So they were stopped at the outskirts, and we would now see where they have to live.

We drove round suburbs of high rise flats and parks strewn with rubbish. Where no building stood, the ground had been turned into a dump. Eventually we arrived at a small town surrounded by orchards. In contrast to the fields of litter, the fruit trees stood in neat rows and had been expertly pruned and tended. In the town centre young people stood in groups at street corners, evidently unemployed. They looked like refugees, bored, hungry, and hanging around with nothing to do.

The first camp we visited stood on the edge of the town, a row of barracks surrounded by residential areas. A couple of scruffy children played in the mud and an elderly man turned his back and hurried out of sight. Washing hung on lines between the barracks. A young couple were in charge of about a hundred people who lived in barely adequate conditions, a roof over their heads, with shared kitchen and facilities. Several families appeared from behind closed doors and smiled, realizing they were being photographed. In one room we observed several children lying in one bed, grinning and stretching like kittens. The stale smell of unwashed bodies, that particular acrid, rancid odour reminded me of my childhood in a Lancashire mill town when my parents took me on visits to the homes of poor people, families where the mother had been too ill to take care of children, usually too many of them running around in rags, faces smeared with muck and the father absent, probably drunk. We were allowed to glimpse inside other rooms where whole families shared a cramped space. Even in these limited conditions each unit had been carefully decorated with a few prized possessions: homes created out of family snapshots on the wall, a cloth over a table with a vase and a few sprigs. This camp appeared to be in relatively good condition. The couple running it, a lawyer and his wife, had succeeded in attracting some financial assistance and voluntary work. In the kitchen a cook, who had left his job in the city to provide for these families, smiled at us and pointed at lunch, a vat of fried potatoes. Where would these refugees live eventually and what work could they get in a town where the inhabitants looked as destitute as the refugees? Some elderly people had already applied to live in the camp because the conditions were marginally better than in their own homes. They so desperately needed medical attention, food and clothing.

The next camp turned out to be in far worse condition. Here they were in need of basic facilities including toilets. These barracks consisted of dilapidated sheds. The people did not hide but came out in a crowd of despondent faces, mostly elderly. They looked at us expectantly as though we would immediately satisfy their needs. It became impossible to photograph their wretched plight. This was not simply because of the painful extremity of their desperation, but because young men hovered in the background and watched us steadily, with a quiet menace. Here were Serbs from Kosovo who almost certainly had committed atrocities before KFOR had driven them out. They stood apart and seemed ready to protect their dignity, observing our every movement: strong, heavily built men, holding themselves in readiness. Their wives did the work, cooking and washing in primitive conditions, a hosepipe being used to rinse the clothes. Despite the evident squalor, these women looked proud and self-possessed. I noticed how the young wives had taken care over their appearance. Even in the mud and cramped conditions, these attractive women were not permitting poverty to stop them dressing in skin-tight blouses and styling their hair. The elderly folk followed us around eagerly, not wanting us to leave without giving them some promise, some token. The people had only recently arrived and could not adapt themselves to their new existence as refugees, outcasts in a society which they had expected to help them. The younger men standing menacingly in the background were evidently prepared to sort matters in their own way. The filth of this camp, the inadequacy of the conditions, and the desperation can generate only resentment and a determination to improve the situation, in however nefarious a manner.

The priest spoke ceaselessly on our journey back. He deluged us with statistics as though we were United Nations officials needing to be informed of requirements: the cost of feeding dozens of families, church donations and voluntary rotas, immediate needs, and above all how much he himself was doing for the camps. He told us that his wife made vestments for the Orthodox clergy.

"We are late already," Lazar announced again. The visit to the camps had delayed our itinerary for the day. So the priest drove like a maniac along pitted streets, through the litter fields, past the carefully tended orchards and the crowds of young men hanging around street corners, back to the patriarchate. The priest shook our hands and his eyes burnt with zeal, as though he had been born and entered the Church just for this task. He told us how his daughter insisted on coming with him to the camps, sharing her dolls and toys with the refugee children, the poor helping the poor.

Bishop Ignatije

Making advance appointments is foreign to the Balkan way of life. Decisions are made and meetings arranged at the shortest notice. This explained the absence of a programme. Lazar spent the spare moments at the flat phoning people. His fingers danced rapidly on the telephone digits, skilfully juggling voices at the other end of the line, talking rapidly in Serbian, then announcing that "we are late already" and filling us in on the drive to the next appointment. When we looked alarmed, Lazar would laugh engagingly and clap his hand on our thighs, even putting his arm round our shoulders. "Don't worry," he would intone with an American accent, imitating a soap opera cliche, "Be happy!" These are not gestures of affection. He is signifying being in control and that we must follow and obey.

An important bishop had invited us to lunch after our meeting with the patriarch. He lived in Pozarevac, a town sixty miles from Belgrade near the border with Bulgaria. First we had to pick up Todor, Lazar's best friend. He stood waiting rather forlornly on a prearranged crossroads near an isolated tower block that bore the scars of NATO bombing, the upper storeys soot-smeared after fire, windows broken. Todor is a meek, kindly young man with a black, monk-like beard and a clammy handshake. Lazar was taking this opportunity to include his friend in the invitation to lunch. Todor is an icon painter.

We raced eastwards down the motorway, past orchards, hills, and forests, through an agriculturally rich countryside. Milosevic knew he could gamble on sanctions because as he kept telling the Serbian people, their land was self-sufficient. They wouldn't starve. Petrol and luxury goods might be difficult to come by, but most of the people had no need of these anyway. Lazar also pointed out that it's easy to copy western fashions, and so designer goods are cheaply available in Serbia. They are expert imitations, and certainly better value than in the West. Films get copied on video and are shown for free on television, even the most recent releases. No copyright is necessary, again because of the sanctions, and so Serbs can enjoy the latest Hollywood releases earlier and more cheaply than we do in England. In some respects, life is better in Serbia with the sanctions intact. As Lazar puts it, he would like to continue living in Serbia, but on a western salary.

We turned off the motorway and drove along a flat plain passing the fiefdom of Milosevic's son, a prosperous part of the country with thriving industries. The son had recently opened a theme park, called Bambiland, but from the road all we could see of it was the sign. Originally he had wanted to call it Disneyland, but once NATO began hostilities he changed the name. The houses looked affluent and Pozarevac resembled a busy English country town with crowded shopping precincts and supermarkets stacked with a variety of goods. No one knew how to guide us to the cathedral. Eventually a babushka in a kerchief, someone who looked as though she might light candles there, pointed us in the right direction.

After the muddy refugee camps the polished marble hallway and luxury of the bishop's residence came as a culture shock. The bishop greeted us in the reception room sitting on a throne, Donald to his right and Lazar facing, with Todor pretending to be invisible. Ignatije is a good-looking young bishop, smooth and quietly spoken. A thoughtful, cultivated man, supportive of Lazar and other young, more liberal-minded Orthodox believers, he gave us a warm welcome and listened attentively, speaking very little, stroking the cassock on his lap with gentle gestures of his small hands. Donald once again delivered his presentation, this time in a room furnished elegantly with velvet ruche curtains, thick pile carpet, drapes hanging over the windows and doorways, gold and crystal chandeliers, several cupid sculptured candlesticks, and rows of crimson upholstered chairs.

A mournful woman hovered outside the reception room

waiting for the bishop's orders, her demeanour constantly apologetic as though she were perpetually committing errors and begging forgiveness in advance. She served us fruit juices and rakija, her shoes clattering on the marble floors as she traversed the long distance between the kitchen and the reception room. After a lengthy audience, Bishop Ignatije graciously ushered us into the dining room next door where a table had been lavishly decked with dishes of cold meats, smoked cheeses, salads, and freshly baked breads. Todor and Lazar poured out wines from the episcopal vineyards. We piled our plates with delicacies, all of them home grown, home cured, or regional specialities. Particularly delicious was a cheese and herb flavoured bread, still warm and crusty from the oven, a cross between a quiche and a loaf. We had consumed enough for a whole lunch before noticing that each place had been laid with several knives and forks as well as soup spoons. We had been satiating ourselves on the hors d'oeuvres, the classical zakuska of Slav cuisine. A major meal would follow. We were being royally entertained and great effort had been expended on giving us this banquet. The refugee camps gave us the impression that Serbia had difficulty feeding itself. Bishop Ignatije's house existed in a different world.

The abundance of zakuska was followed by a bowl of light soup with a delicate lemon flavour. Then the woman with the mournful eyes served us a roast with vegetables, enough to satisfy the dedicated vegetarian Lazar, whom I noticed surreptitiously examining the food on his plate for any meat contamination. Wine and rakija lubricated the feast. Bishop Ignatije displayed all the qualities of a model host, forever attentive to our needs, pointing at the wine, giving orders to the maid, and keeping the conversation well oiled. After coffee and sweets, accompanied by more rakija, we adjourned sleepily back into the reception room where Bishop Ignatije sat on his throne and gave more orders to the sorrowful maid, who then hurried off obediently to another part of the house. She returned with two large and expensive looking art books on the frescoes of Kosovan churches which he presented to us as gifts in gratitude for our visit. The word

'Kosovo' reminded us of western interference in the Balkans, which had exacerbated a situation that inflicted so much damage on this priceless treasury of Serbian culture.

The books recalled Tarkovsky's *Andrei Roublev*, a film concerned with the life and times of a fifteenth-century icon painter. He witnesses a massacre when a church is burnt full of men, women, and children who had barricaded themselves inside, reckoning on sanctuary and the protection of God. Stunned and horrified, he picks his way over the corpses and rubble, possibly bearing the remains of his own paintings. An enemy soldier grins unconcernedly. He has performed his duty. The film deals with barbaric events long ago. But the catastrophe in Kosovo is still happening. The lifetime labour of gifted and inspired painters has been reduced to dust, the soulful gaze of saints and angels wiped out, and everybody killed. Hundreds of mosques have been destroyed too. Fingering the pages, choked with emotion and overwhelmed by his generosity, I tried to thank the bishop adequately, but the tears in my eyes might have been caused by overeating and too much wine.

We staggered onto the front porch accompanied by the bishop. Outside, the garden and the surroundings seemed dingy and more familiarly Serbian after the plush elegance of the interior. A peacock displayed its tail among bricks and stones on the front lawn, the view beyond of a nondescript housing estate and the back of warehouses. The house had only just been completed and the garden would eventually be turned into a park. We drove off leaving Bishop Ignatije standing alone, waving to us graciously.

I thought of him closing the front door behind him, stepping quietly over the polished marble floors, mounting the grandly curving staircase and retiring to pray in an upstairs room decorated with icons. Meanwhile the sad-eyed woman who had singlehandedly prepared the exquisite banquet would begin the arduous task of clearing the dining room.

It grew dark when we returned to Belgrade. Lazar stopped the car next to a tower block and looked thoughtfully at it. "I must see how my father is," he muttered reluctantly. We followed his eyes up to a window way up from the ground, half expecting to see an elderly man hanging from the balcony, or preparing to jump from it. Lazar looks after his father without the help of his two older married sisters. They have their own families and want nothing to do with him. The father is clearly a nuisance, but Lazar understands him. "He is afraid of dying." So the father frets and depends on Lazar, forever complaining and tugging at the heartstrings. Having been an atheist all his life, the father fears the finality of death, the nothingness beyond, the unknown. "He is like a child," Lazar says sadly. They have serious differences of belief. The father is a diehard Milosevic supporter, xenophobic and anti-religious. Occasionally he rings up the ambulance service, in a panic about his health. So perhaps the notion of him on the balcony is not far-fetched.

We waited inside a church nearby, but the blaze of colours on every inch of wall, all newly restored frescos, could not warm us and the bitter cold began to gnaw at our bones. As we left a teenager entered and made an elaborate show of crossing himself and praying. He wore chunky rings, bracelets, a designer jacket, and modishly baggy jeans. He then disappeared upstairs. He looked incongruous in this place of worship.

We then sat in the car and waited for Lazar. Waited and waited. Night fell.

Suddenly a new Mercedes screeched to a halt in front of us and several young men, teenagers dressed like the one in the church, sprang out shouting, swapping places so that another could drive, and all the while talking animatedly over mobile phones. Then with a squeal of sudden acceleration they shot off into the darkness. After this incident the silence became oppressive and eventually Todor sloped off to find Lazar, leaving us locked in the car, feeling not a little frightened. Lazar had been checking and answering his e-mails and had forgotten about the time.

We ended the evening at a restaurant on a cobbled street in the city centre. Though intended as a pedestrian-only zone, cars were parked everywhere. A drunken attendant allowed us to drive in for a fee which would be spent on another bottle. The restaurant was spacious and elegant, lined with dark mahogany walls and decorated with polished brass lamps, mirrors and traditional paintings. The tables were decked with white linen, the wooden chairs upholstered and the floorboards creaking. A wedding party was in progress in a neighbouring room. We ordered some soup and salad, including a Serbian speciality: cabbage cut in large portions and fermented in vats. The bishop had served it as part of the zakuska. It has a refreshing taste, slightly sour, tender and crisp. Serbia possesses a cuisine of considerable sophistication and variety and as yet relatively unknown in the rest of Europe. They also have a custom of placing a dish of pickled chilli peppers along with the bread rolls. The bishop had kept a small bowl of peeled raw garlic cloves mingled with chilli peppers on the table throughout the banquet earlier in the day. The raw garlic and the fiery rakija make certain that Serbian meals are completely disinfected. Waiters passed frequently through the doors into the wedding reception where a folk band played on fiddles and accordion.

We begged Lazar to take us home. I then settled on the two armchairs, Donald abandoned the room over the main road, sleeping in the small bedroom, and Lazar went home.

Breakfast

The phone startled us out of a deep sleep. "Lazar is down. Let me in." He had brought some pasta to add to the two dozen or so eggs rolling individually around the otherwise empty fridge, on top of which, unaccountably, sat a bag of about twenty lemons. The night before I had picked up some necessary toilet paper, tea bags, biscuits, chocolates, and juice from a local supermarket. We first had to change currency in a bar, a better exchange than the banks: we could get twenty dinars for a deutschmark (six in the banks), before being able to pay for the goods. "It's easy to cook, just boil it in water," Lazar said pointing at the bag of pasta. Clearly he has no interest in cooking. But the stove's oven knob had fused, black and broken, and I dared not touch it. The sour cabbage smell remained potent and although we opened every door and cupboard to identify the source, we found nothing and could only assume the smell came with the flat.

Lazar's fingers danced on the telephone dial while the machine peeped, burred and whistled back and he quaffed a pint of apricot juice, licking his lips that were bright red and encrusted with cold sores. "I am destroyed," he muttered to me. "If I don't have a rest I will get ill." While he talked to various people we would meet later in the day, "Lazar Markovic here!", we stood on the balcony and admired the wide panoramic view of Belgrade. The first impression is of rust and concrete, a shambles and general neglect. The infinite variety of brown, blue, red, and grey hues make the houses and offices appear to exist in some organic process of decline and decrepitude. In a flat opposite, a window opened on to a table with some flowers in a vase A cat leapt out and strolled on the roof, past a ramshackle chimney pot, before disappearing into a mass of twisted, rusted metal and some rubble. The offices and flats behind merged with tower blocks on the skyline, swathed in smoke and morning mist. On the right the River Sava flowed to meet the Danube, the bridges packed with morning traffic.

Breakfasting at the Hyatt Regency cost a fiver. This included a complete buffet, fruit juices, cereals, fresh rolls, fruit salads, cold meats, cheeses and even a cooked breakfast – a freshly made omelette with a choice of fillings. There were also a number of Serbian delicacies, special cheeses and cakes to tickle the most jaded palette. The other guests looked like Mafia or corrupt politicians. We remained on guard, ready to duck the bullets. Perhaps that explained why most tables remained empty. Even the solemn maitre d' only appeared now and then. In the distance a gigantic vase of pampas grass stood solitary in the marble corridor. The few other people breakfasting were also furtive and looked suspicious. At one table an important meeting was in progress, two older burly men in shirt sleeves giving orders and a young man in a grey suit, timid and obedient, constantly smiling and agreeing, while two smart men in dark glasses kept an intimidating silence.

The Mufti

The mosque stood tucked away down a quiet side road in an area of bomb damage. Two policemen guarding it observed us taking a photograph and immediately turned to each other. We pretended to be silly tourists and walked towards them as though we had done nothing reprehensible. They decided to ignore us. A smiling young Turkish-looking man took us into the building next to the mosque, after removing his shoes. A blonde Serbian woman working there contrasted with the other people, mostly Muslim women in veils and headscarves, dark-eyed and an unexpected sight here in Belgrade.

The mufti, a large man in a turban, greeted us with twinkling eyes and a beaming smile, arms outstretched. The atmosphere was pleasant and warm. Although we sat in his private room off the main communal hall, people kept walking in and out quite freely: the young man serving us coffee and veiled women dressed in black giggling and whispering before disappearing through another door, presumably to the mufti's apartments. We talked about the need to "love one another". "Without doubt!" said the mufti. He then introduced us to his son Mustafa, an imam, also a large and friendly person.

The mufti seemed happy with the aims of the Soul of Europe. He had attended Religion and Peace conferences in Amman and Melbourne, knew Sir Sigmund Sternberg, and believed in the example of religion and peace in practical living. He spoke of the pariah state of Serbia. He told us that he had himself initiated many practical projects. Without elaborating on these he assured us that in Belgrade there had been no cases of religious or racial killings. Even under Tito there had been a Sarajevo Association including Roman Catholics, Orthodox, and Jewish people all working together with Muslims. He was born in Bosnia but sees his country as Yugoslavian, which is the case with most Serbians, but not the general attitude in neighbouring countries, once part of the Federation. There had been good relations between the races and religions before the war, which is well known in Western Europe. Even during the war in the Middle East there had been a deal "not to attack each other". Brother Muslims were taught that all were brothers together. More Muslims came to Belgrade after the war than before, even after NATO's interference in Kosovo. There are no problems here, even though there are more than two hundred thousand Muslims in Belgrade. But there is just one mosque. "Thank God our people are normally behaving!" said the mufti. But there are many problems to solve: there is as yet no school (they are building it themselves without permission, hoping that the state will eventually support them), no graveyard dedicated to Muslims, and not enough mosques. Till now Muslims have been buried with Communists and Christians. The mufti spread his arms, beamed and smiled saying, "We understand, we wait. Be patient, no provocations, keep friendly with all religions, make no trouble. We manage to survive and to preserve our religion. There is no place in Serbia that is without Muslims."

It sounded promising, but I thought of the policeman guarding the mosque. If there was no danger, why were they necessary? And Bishop Ignatije yesterday had told us there were no Muslims at all in his diocese.

As to the meeting with the patriarch, the mufti not only had no objection, but was delighted. He would come whenever we asked. Apparently the religious leaders already meet regularly, but never all at once, just two at a time. And he supported all projects of collaboration with the rest of Europe. Of course. Serbia is now desperate and the period of isolation with sanctions has made all people victims. He then told us of his qualifications. He had been one of the founders of the Islamic Council in London and had been on the European Council for Mosques in Brussels and Madrid. He had contributed much to inter-religious relationships. "Muslims are flexible in this area," he assured us, explaining that he was trained in the Hanifid 'school' – a 'rational' sector of Islam. This apparently benefited a minority's situation.

The Soul of Europe will try to help overcome the isolation of Serbia. People in the West do not understand Muslims, the fact that they honour Christianity and Jews, that the faiths are intertwined. He then said: "Let all who follow the Holy Scriptures be together because there is one God." "Authentic Islam follows one God." Christians who are real are therefore good friends. "We have to cooperate." There is one God and according to the Koran, he wants us to cooperate "in love, not in war and hatred".

We thought of all the recent violence and of so many centuries of killing. Clearly those responsible did not read the Koran, just as Protestant and Catholic assassins in Northern Ireland have no time for the Bible. The hatreds are less religious than ethnic, race and class orientated. Access to territory, power, and wealth lies behind the perpetual massacres and vendettas.

The mufti then told us that Muslims are the poorest members of the community. There has been anti-Islamic propaganda for centuries, Muslims being seen as surrogates for Turkish invaders. When he came to Belgrade in 1967 he tried to teach that Islam was the faith of peace. Militants do of course exist but he added, "No crusades, no inquisition, no wars, no colonialism. We are for peace."

He had visited Kosovo. "I support all brothers, but they must behave properly!" adding, "I do not support aggression or throwing out anybody." This attitude brings him under attack and explains why he has no support, "except from God", and why two hundred thousand Muslims are coming to him. No nationalists will support him, however. "I am not afraid of anyone," said the genial mufti, continuing to smile. "We have good relations with the other leaders." But nevertheless he does feel isolated. "I am on my own."

We had heard reports about the mufti and his good relations with Milosevic, whom he saw regularly. Given his situation it seemed only politic to be friendly with everyone, including enemies. Who were we to judge anyway? The mosque felt like a toehold in this society and where else could the Muslims go? These were working-class people, rooted in their community and as unwilling and uninterested in moving elsewhere as their counterparts anywhere in the world. Why should they?

His son, the imam, then said: "Our first obligation is to learn. We believe in peace and in living together as brothers."

These words moved us. Our skewed impression of Islam in England is of fanatically fundamentalist communities with no desire to live as brothers with anybody different from themselves. Peace does not figure prominently in their vocabulary. The Muslims in England seem to create their own society and move as aliens in a country which does not understand them, nor has any wish to do so. So their reaction is to build barriers. Here in Belgrade the Muslims seem as alien as they might be in London or Manchester, with the added burden of a violent history of mistrust and mutual massacres, complicated by the periods of peace and intermarriage which then made it impossible to disentangle the ethnic groups. Nevertheless the mufti and his son expressed an open mind and heart. The Muslims' problematic position in Serbia could have more easily led them to be enclosed and defensive and their positive attitude struck us as brave and touching.

Finally they spoke about future developments, the building of the school, the buying of an ambulance, and starting a hospital. The mosque already runs a medical centre next door where we had come across women and children waiting. "We offer treatment to *all* poor people, of all faiths," the mufti explained emphatically. They also run a café for poor people. During the war they fed the poor, whether Muslim or Christian or of no faith.

"The poor always look after the poor," Donald said and the mufti's eyes twinkled, but they were also full of tears.

The imam then took us into the mosque where a number of men were kneeling, ready for worship. They looked small like mice, lost in the airy spaciousness of the light-drenched building. Apparently, because of us, the mufti was late. They turned and smiled at us, having been told of our visit, and seemed quite happy about the delay. The ancient walls of the building represented a beacon of light. It has survived centuries of bitter history and it had never been attacked or desecrated. The congregation of men ("the women are up there, out of sight," explained the imam pointing to the galleries above) sat comfortably on the floor in the warm space, a group of street cleaners, menial workers, and probably many unemployed, mostly uneducated men of all ages, leaning on their hands, toes twitching in their grey socks, and all of them stared at us, a mass of kindly eyes following our every movement.

Outside the sun shone down into the courtyard, kept neat and tidy despite the construction, with plant pots and washing on lines hung discreetly in corners. Men worked on scaffolding. The despised Muslim community of Belgrade is beginning the regeneration of the city.

The Empty Room with a View

Perhaps the most arduous task for Lazar was arranging meetings with non-governmental organizations. For a start there are about seven hundred listed in the directory. Donald specified the Women in Black, and Eileen Barker from the London School of Economics, and on our advisory council, had given us a couple of names to chase up. But what of the other six hundred and ninety-seven?

With Milosevic running the country, NGOs were in a curiously ambiguous position. They were able to express protest, and several, like the Women in Black, were successful. In a regime that was dictatorial, such protest might be seen as perilous, yet Milosevic permitted them to operate unharmed. This was not so strange once we took the trouble to understand Milosevic. He saw these forms of protest as fundamentally harmless, and by allowing them to happen he also gave the impression of being democratic and liberal. However, they all knew that the moment they threatened to loosen his grip on power, he would clamp down on them. Then they would be in danger. Even so, they might remain unscathed because they tended to be peaceful forms of protest that did him no harm. Only people with guns represented a real threat. Nevertheless there was always uncertainty: hence the ambiguity of their position. No one knew what would happen and the protesters had every reason to be afraid. Donald looked through the long list and discovered mostly insignificant groups occupied with weaving and flower arranging. NGOs cover a wide range of activities, hardly any of them political or radical.

In the afternoon, after meeting the mufti, we visited the Culture of Peace Centre. Had we bothered to think a little we might have been warned that this woolly title could mean anything and everything. And so it turned out. This may have been the least impressive of all our visits in Serbia, but the meeting turned out to be of crucial significance for the Soul of Europe's future. It was here that Lazar gave birth to the Bosnia Project.

The Culture of Peace Centre occupied a splendid office on a top floor of a high rise office in Belgrade's city centre. The view was spectacular. The great rivers could be seen meeting, and the city skyline including the Parliament and St Mark's Church was even more impressive than from our flat. My immediate question was how the young man who greeted us could afford an office in such a prime site. During the whole of our visit we got no answers to anything, even though we were given a cheaply xeroxed paper with a list of names of supporters. Not even the room told us anything. It was virtually empty. We sat on the four chairs available and apart from a computer on a small table, and a holy calendar hanging above it, not a single book or magazine or poster indicated what kind of NGO this might be, Most of the room was lined with cupboards. They reminded me of changing-room lockers in a municipal baths.

The young man looked embarrassed, as though we'd caught him unawares, his face quite red and his demeanour nervous as he sat in open-necked shirt and green jeans. Donald ploughed through his presentation again, which was a mistake. Since the young man had nothing to offer us in the way of ideas or proposals or action, he grasped onto some of our own. "We are similar to the Soul of Europe," he began, and we should have been immediately alerted to the danger of giving him any more hints and ideas. But we were tired and naively not expecting an NGO to be either without any policy at all, or possibly even to be a governmental set-up. As the meeting progressed we began to feel uneasy. Could he be a spy, sent to find out our plans? But why, and for whom? He was probably a desperate young man, someone unlikely to be in business like the Mafia, or qualified enough to be a teacher, or with enough chutzpah to be a politician, and so he had set himself up as an independent agency, probably receiving minuscule funding and maybe even persuading people to give money for the 'culture of peace'. We were a sign of hope in his wretched existence. But it didn't explain the splendour of his office – unless it had been borrowed. Afterwards Lazar discovered that the young man's brother ran another NGO with a similar unspecific title. Clearly there is a business in running NGOs and it's quite possible that these two men administered several, all from the same office. This would account for the lack of literature.

The meeting proceeded at a snail's pace. It felt like coming up against a brick wall and being thrown back. Every time we asked a question we were met with a barrage of words: tolerance, democracy, cultural heritage, common identity, awareness, humanitarian aid, cooperation, community, breaking barriers, long term views, catalysts for change, help, funding, etc., etc., in endless permutations.

Lazar lost patience with the conversation going nowhere. He launched into his 'big idea'. (Afterwards he regretted outlining the Bosnia Project to a person who might well pinch it and claim it as his own.) It began with some history, Lazar teaching us how the Albanians came late to Kosovo, that they never really belonged. They did not come as a religious community but as settlers from a neighbouring country whose aim was to populate a land lost to the Turks in battle by the Serbs. All the churches then were Orthodox. Only after the Albanian invasion did mosques begin to appear. The West needs to understand this basic historical fact which has so deeply influenced Serbian history to the present day. So we must launch action to persuade Europe that the Serbs are not all evil, and of course vice versa, that the Muslims are not all bandits. The Bosnia Project began as the Kosovo Project: to reconstruct one church and one mosque, from the ashes, to show that destruction is not the end of history. They would be built brick by brick. The inspired heart of the proposal was that the building work would be carried out by young people from all over Europe, representatives of all religions.

Lazar spoke with blazing intensity, as though to make up for the indifferent quality of the meeting so far. The red-faced young man sensed something important and Donald roused himself. A hand grenade had been thrown into the room with the pin taken out. This was not just a good idea, it would change the shape of the Soul of Europe for ever. We had hoped that such an idea might, with luck, come out of a year's travelling around Europe, bringing back shopping lists of small projects and needs after discussions with representatives from every country we would visit. But here suddenly, right at the start of our journeys, appeared a project which crossed every boundary, that encapsulated the principles and objectives of the Soul of Europe. Suddenly the words in our leaflet looked woolly and vague. Such words are bland: like the aims of the Culture of Peace Centre, they could fit any proposal. The Bosnia Project (the name changed because Kosovo is still far too dangerous a place, the situation there far from stable) means a gigantic workload: of funding to find, of people to interest, of politicians to persuade, let alone the task of actually making the project happen at all. The Soul of Europe's involvement meant that once the churches had been built, the work had only just begun. Here would be a new community representative of the whole of Europe, all its religions and ethnic groupings. The reconstruction signified only the first step in the project.

The young red-faced man became excited. "Yes, that was just the proposal we have been thinking about," he lied, referring to some invisible and possibly nonexistent body of collaborators, trying already to claim the idea as his own.

We conducted the rest of the meeting as though the young man were not even present. We talked excitedly about where the place might be, of how to accommodate the visiting Europeans, mostly young people, of employing local skills, builders, decorators, artists, and so regenerating an area that had been destroyed by the last ten years of warfare. Lazar had already been thinking about and had been hinting at this 'dream' in his e-mails to me. The destruction of the Kosovo churches had filled him with utter despair. For an art historian, nothing worse could be happening.

He accepted invitations to travel round Europe lecturing on iconography and listened to the relatively unimportant local disputes and problems of the affluent places he visited, like the controversy over having a lesbian bishop in Norway. "They are destroying our culture back home, and here they worry about whether a priest can be homosexual…" The task of the Soul of Europe became clear: to support this project and give it the priority it demanded.

As we left, the young man looked confused and desperate. "You have to let me know what happens," he demanded. "The idea was born in my office. You have an obligation…"

Art and Religion

The chapel in the patriarchate is on the top floor. Respecting Patriarch Pavle's instructions not to use the lift which looked ancient, rusty, and in need of service, we climbed three flights of stone stairs. The heady mix of incense, soft chanting, and the warmth of hundreds of bodies moving about added to our weariness. Everybody stands at Orthodox services, although there are chairs at the back for those who need to be seated – the elderly, the crippled, and the plain lazy. But most people are pressing forward to witness the spectacle being performed by priests and deacons against a sumptuously painted backdrop. The chapel is richly decorated, though clearly in a modern style, the images gaudy imitations of the ancient traditional ones to be found in old monasteries and churches. The predominant colour is cerulean, a pale blue which manages to be translucent and misty at the same time, not the clarion call of ultramarine. The censers swung, the smoke billowed over the shifting bodies, and two choirs sang alternately across the room. Elderly women formed only part of the congregation. A number of young men and girls joined the worship, all of them rapt and attentive. Eyes met across the room, and occasionally a young man would push his way through the throng to stand next to someone at the other side of the room. Meanwhile the priests intoned the ancient liturgy and processed to and fro, then disappeared and reappeared from behind the iconostasis, dressed in heavy robes and looking stern and solemn. The service lasted over two hours, never seeming to end: when it seemed a final chorus had been chanted, it began all over again. By now, the incense, the gentle chanting, the body heat, and the swaying crowds who occasionally joined in the chanting in a whispered singsong had combined to create a sense of shared rapture. Lazar moved through the crowd whispering to friends and acquaintances, his lips tickling their ear lobes.

Two murals faced each other at the back of the chapel. One on the right depicted Patriarch Pavle in a naive style surrounded by priests and crowds of people, who are worshipping him as a recently canonized saint. The other represented a censored version of the historic exodus from Kosovo when Bishop Arsenije led the battered remnants of the Serbs out of their homeland after their defeat at the Battle of Kosovo by the Turks. Here the artist could not portray a rabble of ragged men, women and children, wounded soldiers, and flocks of sheep moving forwards in a cloud of dust, as he had done in the original painting. The people, though clearly defeated, are defiant, moving in an orderly procession and in a mood of optimism, intending to return at a later time to reconquer their lost lands. In contrast to the mood of peaceful worship this picture, executed with scrupulous attention to detail in the tradition of nineteenth-century Slav painting, came across as an aggressive call to arms, a hymn of bloodthirsty triumph where the figure in the foreground of a wounded soldier, whiskers bristling and swaggering in bad tempered retreat, threatened menacingly. Religion and nationalism combine forces. The bishop rides at the centre of the picture, by his side a general decked in feathered cap and expensive cloak. A nineteenth-century patriarch had specified the content of this version of the painting which in its original form portrayed a mass of humanity on the move, a tragedy that has been visited on the Balkans for centuries at regular intervals with people having to tear up their roots and settle elsewhere. The bishop criticized the inclusion of livestock, which implied that the people were fleeing like sheep. But the sheep provide a necessary touch of compassion to the original painting, they draw attention to the plight and also to the resilience of human beings, who though now in desperate straits, must find a new home and rebuild their lives. In the patriarchate chapel all these humane details have been airbrushed out of the painting and what is left is a gesture of steely resolve, an unforgiving rage, a warning that there will be an eye for an eye, a tooth for a tooth, and a perpetual cycle of revenge and counter revenge.

Eventually Lazar signalled to us that we could leave. The service would continue for another hour and he had had enough too. As with all Orthodox services, people come and go. Outside it rained and the buildings looked cold and brutal.

Lazar had fixed up for us to meet an artist in the evening. He worked as an Orthodox deacon and specialised in icons. He lived with an artist wife and two young daughters in a salubrious part of Belgrade. We drove there passing through the district where Milosevic's cronies had built their expensive residences along tree-lined streets, in various styles, mock classical, mock baroque and American Dynasty – all ostentatiously protected with heavy gates, blinking alarms, and swivelling cameras.

We parked in front of a three-storeyed house. A tall, lean, and bearded priest with an expression of intense piety and wearing a black cassock waited for us at the entrance and led us up to the top floor, a converted attic. Modern icons and abstract paintings decorated the walls. The girls were watching television in a side room and peered briefly round the corner at us, like kittens, pretty faces in masses of black curls. The deacon's wife welcomed us formally. I sensed they were both nervous and ill at ease. Were we intruding? Were they worried about our reactions? Artists need so much encouragement. They practise the one art form which lays bare their soul for everybody to examine and reject. Often artists are not aware of how much they are revealing, and that is often when they are at their most communicative. Most people treat art as wallpaper. Apart from some discomfort or pleasure, the work passes them by. But other artists look differently and see to the core. They can be painfully critical. The icons were traditional and painted in bright colours. They reminded me of those Russian mother dolls you can buy on street markets, gaudily decorated in folksy style. The faces of the saints were facsimiles of Andrei Roublev, the slender fingers pointed in blessing, the heads expanding at the temples with long hair cascading around the shoulders and the folds of the robes executed in the abstract manner of a tradition going back centuries. The rules of icon painting are strictly adhered to: even modern saints have to be depicted in medieval style. The theory is to portray people in transcendent mode, characters seen at their best, faces being a distillation of their virtues, not human anymore, but divine. However, the old icons convey a sense of a world of suffering, of virtue being achieved at a cost. They depict a mystical view of humanity withstanding the batterings of a hostile world. These modern facsimiles deliberately avoid depth and social perspective. They are brightly coloured decorations.

The deacon artist watched us carefully, showing one icon after the other. But they all looked the same. Other pictures hung on the wall, warm, richly coloured compositions with sensuous shapes moving across the canvas. These turned out to be by the wife who was preparing hot punch for us in the kitchen. We sat for a while round the coffee table drinking the spicy punch, and eventually the girls came and cuddled around their mother, the three of them looking like gypsies with their strikingly beautiful faces, the large black eyes and tumbling hair. The deacon warmed to us, realizing we were friends, not critics. So as a gesture of trust he opened up his studio downstairs in a freezing garage. There stacked up stood large canvases, completely different to the icons upstairs. One theme dominated all the paintings: a female abstraction. He fixed her in the middle of the canvas, an emblematic female form lying on a couch, and each picture subjected her to unblinking scrutiny. Sometimes the figure was crossed out, sometimes assaulted by undefined objects. The colours were uniformly grey and dark, in contrast to the gaudy icons. The deacon artist showed us one picture after the other, all variations on this obsessive theme, and we were unexpectedly moved, observing his calm expression as he showed us the dark side of his nature, his evident fear of the female, his insistence at examining so honestly his anguished desires and thoughts. These pictures could never be sold. The icons, however, would always bring in a steady income, untroubling images to decorate some corner of a home. We thanked him genuinely for showing us his soul and left that cold cellar-like place for a few more moments of warmth upstairs before leaving.

He then invited us to a three-hour service with the patriarch at the Vavedenje Monastery nearby next morning. Even Lazar baulked at this offer. But we accepted, taking this as a cue to leave quickly and go to bed.

The Patriarch and the Students

We missed the service, attended mostly by Orthodox students, and arrived as the crowds of worshippers were moving from the church to a reception area where the patriarch already sat surrounded by priests and deacons. The deacon artist welcomed us kindly, assuming we'd been there for the last three hours, and we said nothing. The patriarch recognised Donald and immediately invited him to sit next to him, on his right side, then indicated that I should sit on his left. It meant that the priests already seated there had to make room for us. Neither looked pleased about this. It turned out that one of them was a vociferous Serb nationalist. The patriarch had difficulties with him and used Donald's presence as an opportunity to put the disagreeable man in his place. The room seethed with people, all eyes shining with emotion and gazing in adoration at the patriarch. Old women in overcoats and woolly hats craned their necks to watch his every gesture, and young people stood to attention, listening to every word as though it came from God. The patriarch repeated what he had said at our first meeting, about the Anglican Church and its long friendship with the Serb Orthodox Church, and he even aired his criticisms about women priests. Women have a duty and responsibility in this world, to bear children and look after the family. The saintly man explained that men were denied the particular blessings of womanhood: we could not give birth. So each sex must accept their particular responsibilities with joy, gratitude, and patience and not attempt to infringe on the other's. Perhaps he intended these words to pacify the Serb nationalist, still scowling from having to relinquish his seat to an English priest, because the patriarch then launched into a speech about the Soul of Europe, welcoming Donald and me warmly, putting his whole support behind our objectives and wishing us every success. The crowd looked admiringly at us and for a moment I felt what it is like to be worshipped. A smartly dressed young man served coffee and biscuits, which we consumed under the adoring gaze of several hundred onlookers. Then a fierce looking nun entered and announced that the patriarch should come to lunch. Dressed in an ill-fitting wimple and shabby dress she was the mother superior (or 'superior nun' as Lazar called her), and her gestures made it quite clear that we were not invited. That point being made we were ushered out quickly, the patriarch rising to his feet and bidding us farewell with such dignity as to inform everybody how much he valued our visit and the Soul of Europe.

We waited outside in the bright early spring sunshine, the air still nippy. Todor had attended the three-hour service and would join us for a meeting with a group of Orthodox students. Mafia houses stood beyond the Vavedenje Monastery, surrounded by high fences and security paraphernalia, fruit trees growing on every patch of ground. We then drove to a restaurant round the corner, one quiet room set aside for the students, music playing to accompany Sunday lunch elsewhere. The moment the young people entered the coffee house, they lit cigarettes and ordered coffee, yoghourt, and fruit brandies. Donald was in his element with an audience of eager and inquisitive minds, starting provocative arguments about politics and religion. The students put us on the spot with questions about NATO. Why were we so keen to shore up Milosevic? Why were we giving innocent Serbs such a hard time? The West and Milosevic were the two enemies, supporting each other.

The men sat at one end of the table to engage in discussion, while the women gathered at the other, not taking part, smoking like chimneys, laughing, joking, hugging and kissing one another. For them this was a social occasion, not to be spoilt by politics and arguments.

Suddenly we found ourselves being attacked on all sides. A heavily built Serb with clipped beard and coal black eyes blazing with indignation launched into an attack on the West. We were "buying" Serbia, keeping it weak in order to colonize them. A frail looking student, thin and anaemic, but with a zealous glint in the eye, began to expound Orthodoxy and the difference between the denominations. The arm of a friend sitting close behind him rested protectively on the back of his chair. Donald listened attentively and explained the purpose of the Soul of Europe and the possibilities of projects in the future. The hostile students smiled and warmed to us, having tested our mettle and gained some satisfaction from sharing their thoughts and opinions. Then they all left to join their families.

Sunday Afternoon

Lazar drove us into the woods surrounding the city for lunch in a popular restaurant, packed with families tucking into large plates of roast meats on beds of rice, with steaming cabbage and mounds of potatoes on the side. Afterwards we walked through the park. Lazar loosened his shoulders and announced that we could have the rest of the day off. As we strolled in the weak winter sun, talking about cinema, we came across an abandoned dog. The skinny creature stood near the garbage bin behind the restaurant, but did not appear concerned about food. It stared at us passing by, tail between its hind legs and ears hanging around two large sad eyes. It pined for company, missing a master. Perhaps it hoped the familiar face and figure would appear to take it home.

As we returned to the car, two young women passed us and must have overheard us speaking in English. They turned round and spat and swore at us.

We picked up Todor, waiting as usual on the busy highway near the bombed skyscraper, and drove to a suburb of Belgrade where we could walk along the Danube. Here the town buildings reminded us of Vienna and other central European cities with baroque church spires, attractive houses with window boxes, cafés along the river bank, and floating restaurants on the water. Judging from the crowds strolling along the pathways it is clear that Belgrade city folk come here for a Sunday outing. The river is wide and muddy, carrying its weight of pollution from Western Europe down to the Black Sea. In a car park a huge litter bin spilled mounds of rubbish, cans, paper bags, and bottles. Rubbish is not an issue in Serbia. As Lazar pointed out with some irritation, they have other matters to worry about.

As night fell we returned home to a telephone message which animated Lazar. His Greek friend Susanna would be arriving in Belgrade the next day and needed looking after. He dumped us at a cinema to see *Holy Smoke* before driving off rapidly to make arrangements. Suddenly we were alone in this strange city. "You will be safe," Lazar told us, impatiently, but we nonetheless felt nervous enough not to speak so that people would not know we were English. The large cinema was packed with noisy viewers, incessantly moving about, slamming the seats up and down, pushing the swing doors aggressively, talking, whistling, and commenting on the action in the film. When Harvey Keitel dressed himself in a tight frock and started stumbling around the Australian outback in a single high-heeled shoe, the men in the audience fell about laughing. This image was clearly too much for the average Serbian macho male. The women weren't laughing with them though. The antics of Kate Winslet's dysfunctional family were a different world from Belgrade. The audience seemed baffled by the camp gay son, his even camper boyfriend, the golf-playing dad, the frustrated sister-in-law, and her neanderthal husband. Lazar told us he identified with Harvey Keitel, a macho male being forced by a feisty girl to come to terms with his feminine side. Dressing in a skirt and putting on make-up is, however, a superficial perception of femininity.

The Jewish Centre

The synagogue and Jewish Centre turned out to be an ordinary old house along a side street. A disgruntled porter pointed us towards the stairs and a lift just large enough for two to squeeze in. A kindly old man and a grief-stricken young woman greeted us in the office. The peeling wallpaper, the worn carpet, and the partition dividing the office from the reception room gave the impression of a place under siege, a community being hounded into extinction. However, in best Balkan tradition, a round table stood in the centre of the room with an embroidered cloth under glass, and we were served coffee in delicate china.

The old man was standing in for the rabbi who had not yet returned from a visitation. He sighed and looked inconsolable, as though the grief of a century of persecution had exhausted every fibre of his being. Nothing we told him about the Soul of Europe could cheer his spirits, which seemed to have left his body long ago.

With a tired demeanour he informed us of the meetings in progress in Budapest and Amman where over six hundred delegates of the World Conference of Religion and Peace were having special meetings and making resolutions. Religious leaders from all the major towns, even from Kosovo, had agreed to meet and talk. The present Federation of Jewish Communities had always had good contacts with other religious traditions. In Belgrade there exists an Inter-religious Centre of Tolerance. The Centre meets occasionally to review problems such as the recent outbursts of anti-semitic propaganda, trying to gauge the reaction of Roman Catholic and Orthodox leaders. But these were political problems not religious ones. He added mournfully that no one religious group can have any significant influence on the political situation in the country. The atmosphere in the room became heavy with the weight of sorrow and hopelessness.

He then gave us some little known history. Though eighty-five per cent of Balkan Jewry died in the Holocaust, leaving only about three and a half thousand Jews now living in the whole of Serbia, and one active synagogue, the Serbs had never been anti-

Semitic. Rather they had protected Jews from the invading Nazis. Madeleine Albright herself recognized a debt of gratitude to the Serbian villagers who had saved her life as a girl. Only the Croats and Hungarians living in the Vojvodine region to the north of Serbia actively assisted the Nazis.

He told us about the situation in Kosovo, the synagogue that used to be in Pristina, how the whole Jewish community fled to Belgrade, one hundred and fifty of them, now living in the hotel opposite. Relations had always been good with both sides, Muslim and Orthodox. As soon as NATO came on the scene the Albanians began to persecute all those not Albanian, including the Jews. As there had been inter-racial marriages the situation became complicated. At this point the old man looked even greyer, contemplating the brutal repetitions of history, the perpetual cycle of persecution.

Donald outlined the Bosnia Project, the rebuilding of churches and the establishment of a centre for peace and reconciliation. For the first time we encountered pessimism. The old man agreed it was a good idea, but questioned its feasibility. Serbs are indeed being encouraged to return to those villages from which they had been expelled. Bishop Artemje, a critic of Milosevic, even had the support of Madeleine Albright to continue this resettlement, but the old man did not consider it at all workable, given the ethnic hatreds on the ground.

For a while we sat in glum silence listening to people moving about in the office on the other side of the partition. Then Donald stirred himself and decided to move the conversation into a different gear. He sat forward and fixing the old man with a glinting eye, reminded him of the passage in Jeremiah about the prophet buying a plot of land in Jerusalem just at the moment when the Jews were being taken into captivity having lost everything. Even when all hope has gone we are encouraged to make a gesture for the future. The man admired Donald's optimism but countered with a cryptic saying about people wanting to "jump first – then hop". He then reminded us of how the Jews have had a bad time as a people as well as individuals. However, Donald must have stirred a deeply buried ember in the old man because he roused himself, looking almost cheerful. But only for a moment. Donald asked what help the Soul of Europe might be to the beleaguered Jewish community. The old man spoke about soup kitchens, but said that spiritual help was needed as much as material. Suicides among the young were increasing. The rabbi believes that the problems are international and economic.

Lazar suddenly became restless, announcing that he had to make arrangements for Susanna. He began to bustle about, hurrying the meeting to its conclusion. This galvanized the conversation, as though the urgency of our visit had kindled a hidden spark of vitality in the old man. He admitted that though the religious leaders are friendly and speak regularly together, it is a different story in mixed communities who do not get on well: what is needed are workshops among ordinary people on the ground. Religious groups are actually weak to influence the killing and burning of homes, and the hounding of ethnic groups. Nationalism is now more influential than God. Just as we were about to leave we had come to the truth, and we were convinced that the Soul of Europe needs to succeed.

The old man accompanied us to the door and we observed his terminal greyness, a figure like the Patriarch Pavle who had lived through almost a century of wars and unresolved hatreds, surprised at surviving, but seeing no possibility of a creative and peaceful resolution, now just wanting to close his eyes, give up the ghost and rest oblivious in eternity.

Signing on with the Police

We remembered the border guard's command that we must register with the police in Belgrade.

The police station is a sinister place, unchanged over many decades, a decaying, grey, and concrete edifice with cold draughty corridors. Plain clothes police entered and exited rapidly. The passports and entry visas had to be examined in a small office on the ground floor, a tiny room with a desk and two officers looking at us with suspicion. The real police business happens elsewhere.

The cold winds outside had made it imperative to answer a call of nature and one of the officers directed me to the next floor. At the end of a long bleak corridor two men eyed me briefly before carrying on with paper work. The primitive toilet reminded me of the one I had to use once in the Moskva Hotel in Kiev, a place where no cleaners ever ventured, cisterns flooded, soiled paper everywhere, piss and shit smeared all over the floors and walls. The filthy bowl refused to flush. I sensed the history of the building, the decades of interrogation, of possible tortures committed on people in the rooms along the corridor. The place had the atmosphere of a horror film, the silent echo of the cries of victims, the slaps and shouting. Here nothing humane happens. Not even cleaners are allowed in.

Reuters

We needed to get as much publicity as possible for the event on Thursday 2 March when the religious leaders would meet at the patriarchate. So we decided to storm the Sky News desk at Reuters. This is situated in one of the modern buildings next to the Hyatt Regency. Donald, probably irritated by the pessimism of the old man at the Jewish Centre, was now in belligerent mood. "We have good news from Belgrade," he announced aggressively as we swept into the office. The staff looked at us in amazement. Donald's words sounded all the more effective for being uttered with such vehemence by a man dressed in a black cassock. Four men and a young woman were seated round a table waiting for news to happen and had to respond to a statement which came along with the unspoken tag, "So what are you going to do about it?" The men looked like those hardbitten journalists who have seen it all: women raped, children dismembered, graves packed with executed men, and swathes of country and town burnt to cinders. But even they looked astounded at Donald's chutzpah. The woman simply smiled dazzlingly at us, impressed and interested. Slightly built and looking frail in the company of the burly men, she ran the department and took to Donald immediately. From then on it was simply a matter of explaining the purpose of the Soul of Europe and giving the exact time and place of the meeting. She promised to be there with a film camera and a photographer.

Lazar didn't utter a word. He simply stared open-mouthed at Donald, and then laughed. He hadn't seen Donald in action like this before. We had been in the office barely five minutes when we were sweeping out again with a successful outcome. Even Donald, coming to his senses, realized we had achieved an impressive result.

The River

The rest of the afternoon we spent on the banks of the River Sava where Lazar made extensive use of my mobile phone, fixing meetings and making arrangements for Susanna. I assumed she would be sleeping with him at home, but he announced that she had to share with us, using the bed in the noisy front room. He would give her earplugs.

The view across to the centre of Belgrade was dominated by the baroque steeple of St Michael's Church. Old houses surrounding the church sloped down the hill towards the promontory at the confluence of the Sava and Danube. Here the ancient barracks still stand isolated from the rest of the city, looking out over the rivers, as they have done for centuries. The harsh architecture of Communism spreads beyond the centre and into the distant suburbs. On our side of the river, the bridge looked to be sinking into the water. Even some scaffolding holding the structure up had bent under the weight. A kiosk stood nearby, every pane of glass shattered, and litter strewn all round.

Having rung several people, Lazar began to throw the mobile contemptuously into the air as much as to indicate he would not allow himself to be ruled by this piece of gadgetry. He then parked us at a restaurant for a couple of hours while he fetched Susanna.

She turned out to be an attractive young woman, married to a Greek musician. She had personal problems which she needed to discuss with Lazar. This would mean a drain on his energies and resources.

The Women in Black

Of all the NGOs we intended to visit, the Women in Black were the best known internationally: a group of women with branches all over the world, who show their solidarity with the oppressed by staging dramatic protests in the street, dressed in black. Because of their fame, this NGO in the Balkans existed at considerable risk. Their office stood round the corner from our flat, difficult to locate, as it does not register an address or advertize its existence. We were ushered into the warmest, cosiest, and most beautiful room of any we had yet visited. Posters, paintings, and photos covered the walls, and the room was furnished with sofas, carpets, and armchairs. Several young women sat with us while in the next room another woman spoke loudly and impatiently over the phone, continuing to do so for the whole of our visit, sometimes shouting angrily.

We were made to feel comfortable. Donald was in his element, sitting forwards on the sofa and engaging in serious conversation as he used to do years ago with the women of Greenham Common. A young man joined the group, possibly the son of the leader. But they introduced him as a solicitor working on papers for conscientious objectors. Handsome with angry coal-black eyes in a pale face, slender and delicate looking, he refused to be drawn into the conversation but listened intently.

The Women in Black established themselves in October 1991 to express their protest against war and violence. That must have been at the start of the Balkan conflict, that decade of the worst fighting, killings, atrocities and destruction in Europe since the Second World War. They saw themselves as witnesses, 'voices made visible'. They protested about once a month and particularly on the International Day for Women on April 8. Now it is a worldwide network. The Women in Black are pacifists. Between 1992 and 1999 conferences of autonomous women's groups met annually to share their experiences. In the Belgrade group there is usually a topic of the day. Women from all over Yugoslavia come, including Kosovans and Albanians. The work of each year is gathered in a book, printed in four languages, available in

Italian, Spanish, and German. Women's groups from wealthier European countries support the Women in Black financially.

The NGO now concerned itself with projects, including workshops all over the country and small networks in villages. They supported initiatives and encouraged activities in five areas of the former Yugoslavia, including other cities. Every six months they met to keep contact. This NGO would be of crucial importance to the Bosnia Project once we are established, and so we valued this friendly contact with the Women in Black.

They were generally ignored by the government and allowed to continue their protests as evidence that Serbia was a democratic country. Nevertheless their active protests had to endure organised attacks. Vigils were disrupted and posters defaced.

Donald asked how they 'kept on keeping on'. They admitted having less and less time to celebrate together, though from the feel of their cosy room sisterhood nourishes a loving home atmosphere, whatever the problems. They have no links with the Orthodox Church, which on the whole took the Nationalist side throughout the wars in the Balkans. And since the women believe in free choice (abortion) the Church is bound to be hostile. They told us that Serbs in general see women as 'machines for birth', in fact the Albanians less so.

The history of the Women in Black started in Israel. It is not however an international organization, although they did have contact with the Greenham women. They cooperate with ecological groups and even with some churches interested in discussing political issues.

The conversation continued amicably. Teddy bears lay scattered round the room. Flowers filled vases standing between piles of books. On the walls, next to photos of the women in action, hung reproductions of paintings by Picasso and Frieda Kahlo. The women were not at all as wary and defensive as we might have expected considering the danger of their situation. However, their constant smoking, lighting one cigarette after the other, indicated how much they existed on their nerves. Despite the evident tensions they were in good spirits and gladly posed for a photo, falling in a heap on the sofa, one on top of the other, laughing and cuddling.

Lazar was now in a hurry to pick up Susanna and a priest whom we had invited out for supper that evening. He rushed out and Donald followed rapidly behind. A familiar looking face pinned on the noticeboard in the hallway had featured in a recent issue of *Gay Times* concerning the leader of the Serbian gay and lesbian community who had allegedly been murdered by his lover. Zorica, the leader of the Women in Black, confirmed the suspicious circumstances of the murder, though no one knew for certain whether it had been a politically or personally motivated killing. He had been a vociferous leader and an embarrassment to a country so machismo in its attitudes to gay people that to 'come out' here is still dangerous and possibly fatal. It would have been interesting to hear Lazar's opinions, but he had gone. The young man came up to join in the conversation, his manner completely changed, clearly longing to talk further, but outside Lazar beckoned impatiently.

The priest turned out to be Lazar's boss on the magazine *Iskon,* and he eyed us with suspicion. We were responsible for taking Lazar away from his duties. Lazar drove us out to the restaurant in the woods where we had lunched the day before, and we engaged in a stilted discussion about Orthodoxy and intellectual issues remote from the grassroots problems of survival and protest we had just been engaged in with the Women in Black. The evening ended with Lazar dropping us off at the flat while he took Susanna off to a nightclub.

The next morning when we asked whether they had lived it up last night, Lazar answered that they had spent the time talking and added, "We are intellectuals. We do not dance."

The Catholic Archbishop

Archbishop Perko lived on a busy narrow street in an elegant but rundown building in the style of the Hapsburg Empire. He stood waiting for us in the vestibule as we came through the front door. Dressed in a red skull cap and cassock, he appeared out of the darkness, stretched his arms out in welcome and smiled at us. We had been warned that he suffered from lung cancer and was terminally ill. When he spoke his voice came out loud and clear, but uncontrolled. He could not speak quietly, but though the effort clearly cost him, he always smiled, his good nature triumphing over pain.

He led us into a dimly lit room, elegantly furnished with a crimson carpet, wood-carved and upholstered armchairs, and crimson drapes over the window, half hiding the dusty net curtains. Bookcases lined the walls and large candlesticks stood on shelves. The residence looked prosperous, newly decorated and tidy. A crozier hung on an elaborate coat hook. He immediately offered us coffee, which a nun served ceremoniously, carefully placing a spoon of foam in each decorated cup before pouring. On the coffee table before us several dishes were piled high with biscuits and sweets.

The gentle and friendly old man listened attentively and politely to Donald, nodding and evidently moved by our proposals. By now Donald's presentation had become smoothly polished. The archbishop supported our initiative. There was a need for it in the Balkans. Though good relations between the religious leaders have existed for many years, based on personal friendships, there were as yet no common projects. He had proposed at the start of the year 2000, Jubilee year for Christianity, that all the leaders would issue a common statement. But nothing happened. He is still waiting for an answer. Perhaps in mid-May, before the Orthodox gathering, he might get a response. Donald suggested that at the big meeting the following day in the patriarchate he would ask: "What are you doing for the Millennium?" The archbishop smiled ironically and talked of the variety of opinions in the Orthodox Church, and therefore how difficult it is to form a common statement about common projects. Patriarch Pavle is a collegiate leader: therefore no decision is made. It is difficult for him. But the archbishop agreed that there really does have to be a common project.

Catholics are in a tiny minority in the Balkans – just two in every thousand. There are only eighteen priests. But being a minority is in fact a useful position. The archbishop expressed sorrow at the explosion of hatred in recent history and that Christianity could not do anything about it. The situation in the Balkans is very complicated to grasp, even for insiders. He spoke of a 'satanic' influence, big atrocities being committed by all sides. But how to solve the problem? The Pope had been against the bombing of Belgrade.

Towards the end of *War and Peace*, after the Battle of Borodino where the subtle tactics of Marshal Kutuzov defeat Napoleon, Tolstoy writes of the inevitability of history. Leaders come and go, even those as forceful and charismatic as Napoleon, but it is the mass of people who decide the fate of countries. In other words there is nothing we can do to alter the human condition, except to inspire and nudge along changes for the better. Milosevic made inflammatory speeches, but ordinary people from villages all over the region themselves planned and carried out the atrocities. Our project might provide a different inspiration.

Suddenly the archbishop became cheerful. Clearly delighted with our visit and seizing any opportunity for celebration, he stood up, fetched a bottle of liqueur from a hidden cupboard and, laughing loudly, offered us a drink consisting, as he put it, "of a hundred herbs, a hundred prayers and a hundred rosaries". Pouring this potent potion into delicate green glasses decorated with gold leaf and figures painted in white glaze, he continued with a joke about optimists and pessimists. "Optimists are saying everything is very good because peace will come: this is the Last Judgement Day. Pessimists are confirming this, but only in the afternoon!" We did not understand the joke, but laughed anyway. It was difficult not to admire this man approaching the end of his life in such good humour, despite the pain of an illness which was killing him and the bitter disappointment at the terrible situation in his country and community.

Donald began to outline the smaller projects, package holidays to monasteries, young people helping with restoration work, opening Serbia to the world again. The archbishop talked about the poverty endured by the majority of Serbs. People have to survive on thirty pounds a month and pensioners get just ten pounds. Only ten per cent of the population earn more than this, and only ten per cent of humanitarian aid actually reaches where it is supposed to go. Even though the Catholic charity, Caritas, helps the Catholics in Serbia, ninety-five per cent of this charity goes to others. So he welcomed any new initiatives like ours, saying, "Symbolic help is important. It creates a new atmosphere." At this point he suffered a prolonged coughing fit, painful to listen to. He then commented that it is not easy to have concrete action in this area because, although Caritas has helped many people, receivers of the charity are suspicious: "Why are the Catholics helping us? There must be an ulterior motive." Over the last ten years most of the young people have left the Church and only older people are left in the Catholic community with just one priest to care for them. It's a difficult ministry.

He then talked about his illness. Now seventy-one years old, he will retire in two months and go to Lyublyana to be cared for by "lots of doctors". "But no one can send me to God," he sighed and smiled, shrugging his shoulders. He would like to die, but God won't be hurried. What's the point in fretting? Perhaps he still had some task to perform. So he waits patiently. However, the last ten years had made him desperate. "There is no joy living in such surroundings." And he added how when in Rome reporters had asked him to describe the situation in the Balkans briefly, he told them, "It is a madhouse." Twenty-eight years ago he had donated a kidney to his brother. Since then he has undergone three operations for cancer, all in the last three years. But he remains cheerful about his condition. He believes in intercession, the potent power of prayer. Thoughts of death, though unspoken, dominated the final moments of our meeting. We talked about prayer, which seemed appropriate. The Orthodox apparently do not approve common prayer though the archbishop pressed for it. In 1993 the Pope offered to pray for peace in Bosnia with the Orthodox. The archbishop personally approached Patriarch Pavle who said immediately, "We can't; church laws forbid it." No representatives from the Serbian Church went to Assisi to discuss this proposal. "We must not hurt the feelings of the Orthodox Church," commented the archbishop, to which Donald countered: "The Orthodox Church must not hurt the feelings of the Catholics." At which the archbishop laughed out loud and suffered another painful coughing fit. He then told us he had been a professor of Ecumenical Theology and knew all the other professors, which is why he understands how it is possible to hurt without intent. He asked Donald whether the Soul of Europe would become a movement. Donald said he had no intention of becoming a pope, just to be a spiritual initiator. The archbishop then told us that he used to initiate interfaith meetings between young people, also in Bosnia. In Kosovo this had been even more difficult. The Catholics and the Orthodox have leaders there, but not the Muslims, a fact which came as a surprise. Such initiatives are difficult to establish. The Catholics and Orthodox were prepared to meet with Muslims, on condition that no terrorists be present from either side, Serb or Albanian. So far no luck. The Soul of Europe seemed more important than ever.

Donald repeated his Jeremiah story. "People *will* return. God will be faithful to his people." "There's a lack of Jeremiahs here," said the archbishop, but assured us that there are indeed good Christians among the Orthodox. We should remember that for decades there had been no religious teaching and atheist propaganda had influenced most people. However the Catholics always continued education in the churches, though not in schools. No one objected to the Catholics teaching, but Orthodox teaching was forbidden. The Orthodox bishops used to complain to the government about this, saying, "It's not fair! It's OK for the Catholics but not for the Orthodox." The archbishop smiled and added that the Catholics were a harmless minority, while the Orthodox on the other hand would have fomented rebellion.

We talked briefly about Milosevic. "Milosevic will not leave," said the archbishop, who occasionally saw the president socially for cocktails. At the end of November 1999 he had attended an official party and met Milosevic. The archbishop told him, "God bless all nations." Then he added pointedly, "And to you personally all blessings!" Milosevic looked suspiciously at him as though the archbishop had actually cursed him. The archbishop's opinion was that for good or bad Milosevic was president and therefore he had to communicate with him.

Before we left, the archbishop insisted on pouring us some more liqueur and couldn't resist another joke. Commenting on the healing qualities of the potion he added, "The bigger the sinner, the more drink is necessary," and laughed loudly again. He accompanied us out of the building and told us its history. The course of the twentieth century had been decided here. The building used to be the Austrian Embassy and the First World War officially started here. The Russian ambassador had precisely five minutes to prevent the ultimatum from reaching the enemy, but suffered a heart attack and died in the vestibule where we were standing. The first victim of the war fell here. Five minutes that might have changed the course of history.

The archbishop had welcomed us alone, with no assistant to open the door, and now bid us farewell, smiling in the shadows of the dimly lit hallway, a solitary figure with arms outstretched.

Nemanja and Memories of Vukovar

We spent the rest of the day visiting more NGOs. The Centre for Democracy, off a busy road in the middle of Belgrade, is a smart hi-tech office with black furniture and a large curved desk topped with computers and screens. Professor Eileen Barker had recommended we meet its leader, Nemanja, and I expected an older man. Nemanja could have been a university student, young, wiry, a handsome face under masses of black hair, nervous, chain-smoking, and looking tired to the point of collapse. Strikingly bold abstract paintings hung on the walls and a massive rock sculpture occupied a whole shelf. A young man with a head shaved in an intricate pattern served us coffee.

The Centre for Democracy organizes conferences on issues of politics and society, and as such must have been a thorn in Milosevic's side. Recently ninety people from abroad, mostly scientific institutes, joined representatives from Serbian churches at a conference on Church, State, and Civil Society. The media covered it. All issues were treated, engaged in, and acted on, but religion was not a priority.

Immediately Donald wanted to know about the Centre's relationship with the government. We were told that a training programme for judges had recently been the object of repression. Suddenly no judge could afford to take time off for it, but Nemanja still intended to run the programme.

Looking around the smart office I wondered where they found funding. About a thousand NGOs competed for funding, although in some regions, such as Montenegro, it was considered a betrayal to accept money from the government. Nor was there legal support. The Soros Foundation and the European Union funds supported the project, though no money had yet appeared. We learned nothing new at this meeting, just a confirmation of what we already knew about the standing of NGOs in a country ruled by a dictator, cleverly masking his authority by seeming to tolerate democratic procedures.

Nemanja, though polite and friendly, seemed to wonder at first what we doing there, and then began to tell us his history. In 1991 he fled from Serbia to avoid army service during the escalation of the war with Croatia. Lazar became excited. He had also, for the same reasons, decided to flee to Bulgaria. Otherwise both of them might have met in Vukovar. The mention of Vukovar reminded me of my first exhibition in a London West End gallery, where I devoted a series of paintings to the war in Yugoslavia. Ostensibly the pictures illustrated each song from Schubert's *Winterreise*, but as I painted, press photographs and reports from the Balkans filled them with images of soldiers, massacres, and devastated towns and bridges. The ruins of Vukovar appeared in a number of these paintings. It seemed an age ago, and yet the destruction and murders still continue in the Balkans. I had intended the exhibition to be a meditation on the century which had given me birth; it had been dominated by the image of a soldier, usually a young man barely out of adolescence, smooth-faced, frightened-eyed, and disguised in army uniform. These images of violent disruption to everyday life provided a political and social perspective, a contemporary counterpoint to the themes of individual alienation and despair running through Schubert's song cycle, that mountain range of Western music which has been a central influence and inspiration all my life as an artist. Now I sat in the presence of two men who, had they not been clever and determined, might have ended up witnessing and taking part in the atrocities which I included in my paintings. The conversation became animated as they exchanged opinions and told us that the reason they refused to fight had nothing to do with being conscientious objectors or even out of fear for their lives, but because they both knew what would have been expected of them, and neither could bear the thought of the terrible psychological scars they would have to endure for the rest of their lives had they survived and been compelled to witness the atrocities carried out in places such as Vukovar. They were two among many intelligent and sensitive young men who simply fled the country to avoid this catastrophe. They waited in safety until their families told them the coast was clear and they could return. I then thought of my last series of paintings in which I put my soldiers to sleep. Sleeping soldiers are harmless but also vulnerable. The issue of macho masculinity still occupies my mind, and I keep trying to express in my pictures ways in which this destructive force of human nature can be pacified and transformed. Eventually I stripped my soldiers naked, and they now lie under showers of blossoms surrounded by ruins – like sleeping beauties waiting to be awoken with a kiss. But when I painted all these pictures I never imagined I would ever visit the part of the world which inspired their content. Here were two young men I had been painting long before I even knew of them.

We spoke about the bleak situation for NGOs. Most work independently, particularly the feminist organizations which, though always present in strategy and resources meetings, prefer to cooperate only with women. The approaching election might bring them together and even hard-core feminist groups were opening up. The next steps for the Centre for Democracy needed to be networking, providing an advisory service for legal counselling, fundraising, working with other NGOs, schools, and student clubs, and providing a forum, strengthening the voluntary sectors, organising human rights meetings, etc., etc. There is a long history of NGOs in the Balkans, going back over a hundred years.

As with the Women in Black, it became clear as the meeting progressed that this NGO would be of help to the project. And we would be of help to them also. Because of the problems of surviving and of having to spend time on administration, and therefore becoming too centralized, grass roots initiatives tended to be neglected. So our project with its specific grass roots objectives comes at the right time. However, the churches are frightened of NGOs and need to be wooed. Not once had we mentioned them in our meetings with the religious leaders. Nemanja made an important point about the Centre for Democracy, that they were in a position to teach churches, leaders and other people how to 'talk', how to deal with issues such as enabling former enemies, Serb and Muslim families, to live side by side again.

Nemanja had warmed to us considerably by the end of the meeting and we looked forward to meeting him again on the project, just hoping he survives Milosevic.

Most (Bridge)

Like the Women in Black this NGO is run mostly by young women and is situated in an unspoilt, beautiful part of old Belgrade, behind the cathedral. They welcomed us into another attractively furnished, warm, and cosy room, full of pictures, books and posters.

Most (Bridge) is a centre for anti-war action, concerned with non-violent conflict resolution, demonstrating against war by helping refugees, in particular children, to restructure their lives. Since 1993 Most has been a collective of psychologists. They print manuals, posters, and educational pamphlets. They were always in fear of Milosevic, who constantly threatened them for being NATO slaves. Yet they persisted and assisted people in prison, as for instance a professor, recently arrested for 'treasonable information' and being interrogated about his activities. They were funded by UNICEF and a Swiss evangelical church who supported their debates and initiatives.

The three of us sat on a long sofa faced by three attractive, lively, intelligent, and vibrantly purposeful women. Donald and I felt quite at ease. Lazar did not enter the conversation. Occasionally the leader looked at him quizzically, eyes widening, smiling, and sensing his ambivalence.

We spoke about our various projects, they telling us of peace studies, being facilitators at conferences, and about their links with the Mennonites and Belfast. Once the Bosnia Project gets under way it will be important to involve Most and their skills in community relations. As in Russian, the Serbian word 'most', means 'bridge'.

As we left, a woman from Denmark entered to discuss a Danish initiative, Next Stop Serbia, in which from June to September, two thousand people will come to Serbia to break down barriers with western Europe. She smiled brightly at us, and it occurred to us that dozens of do-gooding groups must now be descending on the Balkans, feeling righteous and fulfilled, while the people here have to endure their goodwill, but simultaneously trying to extract as many funds as possible out of them. Were we just such another group?

The Big Day

After the expected nerves about whether all the leaders would be there and whether Zorica and Sky News would bother to turn up, it came as a relief to find everybody already at the patriarchate. The mufti and his son, the imam, wore their best turbans, the archbishop looked neat and pressed, accompanied by a rotund monk straight out of Chaucer, and the youthful rabbi arrived in skull cap and sweater, in a more optimistic frame of mind than his elderly assistant who had poured cold water on our project.

Zorica was installing the camera crew and the patriarch himself stood at the door to the reception room greeting everybody with a kindly smile.

As the meeting progressed it became clear that this event was of more importance for the Soul of Europe than for the leaders, who evidently knew one another well personally and were actually laying on this show specially for us. The patriarch gave the first speech, followed by the archbishop, the mufti and finally the rabbi. All spoke about the importance of collaboration and supported the project in Bosnia. The rabbi made a special point of reminding them that all the religions had experienced persecution. He then paid tribute to Donald, saying that what moved him most was the fact that Donald had retired from his duties as a priest to establish the Soul of Europe and had taken the trouble to come to Serbia and see for himself the situation here. The Sky News cameras were ushered out after the first few minutes to wait on the other side of the door. The morning sun sent slanting rays across the wide spaces in the centre of the room round which the guests and speakers sat in a circle. On the walls hung several large portraits of former patriarchs, all upright and aggressive, the cloth on their white hats flapping in the wind of their zeal. Patriarch Pavle, sitting beneath the largest portrait, looked a complete contrast, modest and humble, his frail form dressed in black. He turned occasionally to look kindly on Donald, while fixing the others with a sharp and watchful stare as they spoke. The voices echoed across the chamber, in particular that of Lazar, who gave a virtuoso display of interpreting, sitting forwards on his chair, hair tousled and sticking up at the front, hanging on to every word and aware of the significance of the occasion, not only for the Soul of Europe but for us all personally. In the corner sat a scribe, a young bearded man like a character out of a Kafka story. He scribbled without pause page after page of minutes, head never lifting for an instant. Another young man served us tomato juice in small glasses. Chaucer's monk swallowed it contemptuously, smacking his lips noisily while the patriarch was still speaking, then folded his plump hands over his belly. The patriarch's secretary bustled about twice during the meeting, and after the rabbi had finished he announced that the patriarch had to leave for another engagement and asked everybody to move to the throne room for more photos.

Zorica and the crew were waiting for us, and after the formal line up in front of a large mural depicting the conversion of King Lazar, she interviewed Donald. At that moment the leaders shrugged off their formality and greeted one another with affection, laughing and joking. There was clearly no animosity between them. What a pity that their relaxed friendship could not be transferred to the communities in Kosovo and elsewhere in the troubled region. The large mufti almost lifted the little patriarch off the floor to plant kisses on his cheeks. The mufti glanced nervously at the television cameras now trained on Donald, wondering what he might be saying. His eyes twinkled at people he knew, but hid their sparkle from strangers. Because of his dealings with Milosevic, people did not trust him, but the Muslims in Serbia were a minority and always at risk. All the leaders treated the young rabbi with particular affection, like a son who needed protecting. It would have been interesting to understand what they were busily saying to one another.

Just as we left the patriarchate the priest who had taken us to the refugee camps on the first day of our visit came up excitedly to tell us that a large group of refugees were waiting for food and donations round the back of the building. The crowd stretched like a cinema queue, families of mostly young people standing patiently, chatting and staying close together. Sky News hurried to film the scene. Lazar approached them to find out whether any would like to be interviewed by us, but they refused. He mentioned the possibility of money that we might be able to raise for them and they doubted this. "Where is this money?" they demanded. They knew about the ninety per cent of donations not reaching refugees. Lazar returned angry: "These people just don't want to be helped!" But I understood their pride. Fate had dealt them a bad hand. Some months ago they had driven out their Muslim neighbours in villages in Kosovo; then the tide turned and now it was their turn to suffer. They held their heads high and huddled close together against the rest of the world.

To celebrate the success of our mission Lazar took us to a popular and fashionable restaurant behind a bus stop under one of the main roads through Belgrade, a most unlikely and almost inaccessible spot. It was situated down a flight of steps and disguised its unattractive location with a vine-clad pergola over the entrance. Inside it was smart and comfortable, with a fleet of waiters skimming between the tables, pouring wine and being attentive. The rich people of Belgrade came here, mostly businessmen and politicians, but not many Mafia. For about twelve pounds we enjoyed an extravagant meal for three, but all the time we could not forget the refugees at the patriarchate. The contrasts in Serbia were crass and unavoidable.

The Decontamination of Culture

We found our next NGO in the middle of a built up area, old town houses stood cheek by jowl with modern flats. Traffic and crowds of people surged along the street, surrounding a quiet and secluded courtyard with sculptures and potted plants on outside staircases. These lifesize sculptures created an eerie and fantastical atmosphere: they were of naked men, shaven headed and with their genitals uncovered, seeming to be leaning against the railings on the stairs or walking about. The sculptor had left some decapitated stone heads lying like ruins on the steps, surrounded by herbs and climbing plants. I felt a sharp pang of recognition. This artist shared my view of the world: these are the figures who march through my paintings.

Before arriving at this haven we had experienced difficulty parking the car. For all the sanctions and scarcity of fuel, the city of Belgrade is packed with cars. Parking space is almost impossible to find and for a few moments we stopped by the entrance of an office building. Immediately an armed guard approached and ordered us to leave. When Lazar asked why, the young man became quietly threatening. "You ask too many questions!" he said in a low voice, shifting his rifle.

The Centre for the Decontamination of Culture hosts a programme of concerts, plays, and exhibitions. It is situated in the area of foreign embassies, and we passed several queues waiting for visas to Germany and Scandinavia on our way there. Once inside the courtyard, the arts and the imagination take over and ordinary life carries on outside the charmed space. A woman with long grey hair tied in a loose bun and wearing a pearl necklace took us into her office, a library with floor to ceiling shelves of leather bound books printed a century ago. She sat at a large table in the middle of the room, threw her head back, and heaved a huge sigh. "The army is concentrating in the north of Montenegro," she announced and shook her head sadly as much as to say, "What next?" "Milosevic is probably just sabre rattling," she added, but in the Balkans the presence of an army rarely means that nothing is going to happen. "Another Kosovo?" We spoke about the importance of church buildings and how we judge a culture through them. She described the destruction of buildings, even without people in them, as a 'metaphor', and much appreciated our project. She spoke passionately and furiously about the whole situation in the Balkans, about Milosevic and support for the Sanjak Muslims in Bosnia, compensating for the destruction of Muslim architecture there. She told us that the big question involved the relationship between the Orthodox Church and the Nationalists, which had played a complex role in the war. She knew much about this subject since her father had been a Professor of the Sociology of Religion.

Her face looked deeply sorrowful and tears began to pour from her eyes. Her voice cracked with grief. Perhaps the tragedy of the Balkans had finally become too much for her. It turned out that she was simply suffering from a bad cold.

"Building is affirmation," she said. "We are a critical institution," probably meaning that the existence of the Centre was of critical importance. Architects and sociologists were already meeting to understand the social significance of building projects, beginning to think about the restructuring of Belgrade in the future. A century's history had to be understood: how Marxism became the State religion, and then at its passing, Orthodoxy took over and that in turn became a form of Nationalism. The Church has to take responsibility for precipitating the war in the Balkans. Then there was the problem of property, the land that once belonged to the Church, taken by the State and how should it be returned.

The woman saw herself still as Yugoslavian, not Serbian. There has been such a mixture of races in the Balkans through intermarriage between ethnic groups and religions that the new borders and divisions are artificial and for political purposes only. The brief of this NGO is to shed light on this situation, to clarify through the imagination, by 'shocking' rather than talking. "Catharsis by art," she exclaimed. They employed between ten and a hundred people receiving funds from Sweden and Finland, anti-fascist organizations and the Soros Foundation for Opening Society. Norwegian People Aid provided money to build the roof over the theatre and smaller grants come from French Catholic organizations. Her husband worked as a human rights lawyer and they hardly see each other.

"We must build the three churches!" she exclaimed, rousing herself, almost in desperation, but wanting to encourage us in case we lost heart. We then discussed how the Centre could be of help, and wanted to learn the significance of the phrase 'decontamination of culture'. It was a form of resistance and protest but Milosevic cunningly used the same rhetoric, which was how the government countered their influence. "It's a mess," she said. But she had found a soul mate in Donald. "Powerlessness is a big power," he said and she perked up at this. They began to talk about the process of rebuilding, and she reminded us of the Gaudi Cathedral in Barcelona, a place where participation is the key. Then we began to dream about all the activities around the project. We should get hold of sympathetic stars, people like Erland Josephson from Sweden.

She then quoted Lenin's dictum about "a battle in the Central Committee; schism in the Church", leading to cleansing. Then she took us to see the theatre across the courtyard. The programme of performances and exhibitions was arranged for the year ahead. We stood for a while in the hall, empty apart from seats raked at one end and spotlights hanging from the ceiling. Her face became transfigured, radiant like a Beata Beatrix. I looked round the bleak and featureless space, for a while not comprehending its significance. Then suddenly I realized why she stood speechless with ecstasy. This was Temenos. Here existed a space devoted to the imagination: a blank page, an area with specific dimensions around which people could sit, watch and partake in the world of possibilities, of mirrors being held up, of grief, rage, contemplation, laughter, and all the senses. Apart from its dimensions, the space had no definition right now, but because it was empty it invited anything and everything to happen in it. Donald walked around deeply moved and silent. St James's, Piccadilly, used to be like this, a space offering defiance to the apathy of the world outside. Here in Belgrade such a space represents an alternative to despair in a country locked in a perpetual cycle of crime and retribution. The space's emptiness bristled with hopes and dreams.

Via: a New Age Group

Lazar had been pestered for the last few days by a woman insisting that we come to check out her organization. She rang on the hour every hour, leaving messages. So we couldn't get out of it. Lazar's energies were being sapped on all sides. He had to take care of Susanna between ferrying us round Belgrade. He had to search out unlikely places to change our currency, such as a baker's shop and a photographic studio, where we could benefit from a better rate of exchange than in a bank. Then he had to fit in meals and sightseeing, such as registering NATO bomb damage: dramatic falls of rubble which gashed buildings along the main roads. Finally Susanna packed her bags and had to be taken to a bus station as trains no longer ran between Belgrade and Vienna, as the main bridge across the Danube north of Novi Sad was still half submerged in the river. Later in the evening we had been booked to meet two journalist friends of Lazar, a young married couple, and we drove in our usual haste to an outer suburb of Belgrade and hoped to get this last visit quickly out of the way.

We arrived as dusk fell, and Valerija, the head woman of Via stood waiting for us on the street. The rest of the group had long been gathered inside a spacious suburban house situated at the rear of a large front garden and next door to a police station. Valerija took us indoors, her children taking my hands and skipping along. Lazar had given us no clue as to the kind of NGO we were visiting, perhaps because he didn't know himself, except that it involved craft work, jewellery, woodcarving, and painting. Valerija, petite and determined, with teased black hair, seemed to be in charge. Two slender and handsome young men were dominated by a group of women with intense expressions on their faces. Our arrival somewhat restored the balance of male and female. The room had been furnished and decorated as a communal area, the seats arranged so that we could watch a performance they had been rehearsing specially for us. The purpose of our visit remained unclear. We asked about their funding and support. Basically they sold craft work on the streets, specializing in stained glass ornaments which they proceeded to show us. They did not seem to be poor, perhaps coming from wealthy, middle-class families and wanting to live an alternative lifestyle. They opened a thick photo album which recorded their various activities, like holiday snaps, the scantily clad men smiling and pitching tents, the women playing with children on the beaches and in pleasant country surroundings. The pages turned slowly, showing the same group beaming with happiness. The sun was shining and all of them appeared to be on a perpetual vacation. Gradually we learned that one of their tasks as an NGO involved organizing holidays for groups of children from war torn regions of the Balkans and poor areas in Bulgaria and Romania. Donald spoke about the refugee camps and suggested they visit the people there and share creative activities with them. But would those menacing men and fiercely defensive women take kindly to these New Agers? The idea fell on deaf ears. This group exists for itself, creating a new family with distinct but unspoken hierarchies. Attractive Valerija ran the community, and we detected a pecking order with the uglier, fatter women lower down and the two men floating around. This group of people seemed to have cut themselves off from the reality of life outside, taking no interest in politics. But who can judge how young and sensitive people in Serbia chose to survive the wars and a corrupt government?

The house opened at the back on to another stretch of garden which sloped steeply down to the Danube, flowing quietly past in a wide stream, the opposite bank far in the distance. Lazar looked at me and shook his head smiling. He dreams of living in a house boat floating on the river.

After some herb tea, the performance began. The young man not married to Valerija crouched in front of three drums, and two of the larger women prepared themselves, the taller one standing up barefoot, the other crouching on the other side. It began in silence. Then the drums started to beat softly and the large upright woman threw some marbles across the floor at us. The other woman began to hum. The beating and humming continued for a while and gradually we felt relaxed, realizing how busy we had been these last few days and how right it was just to be sitting and being an audience. The drumming grew louder, the humming turned into a raucous song, and the large woman in the middle began to dance, stubbing her toes on the floor. She stamped her feet alarmingly and banged a tambourine. The singing became louder too, turning into a wail. Then the dancing figure approached us one at a time. The woman wanted to express something individual about each person, perhaps an unresolved conflict with a colleague, perhaps a gesture of forgiveness to another. I dreaded her approach. Lazar was first and her gestures became provocative, coming close to him with voluptuous gestures, then quickly withdrawing as though hiding fearfully from the possible dangers. Lazar's lips curled slightly and she quickly turned to Donald. Fortunately nothing sexual or provocative there, though she seemed to be mocking him slightly, making gestures of obeisance, showing exaggerated respect for his position as a priest. When she turned to me I smiled encouragingly, wanting her to know how much I appreciated her performance but also wishing her to move on quickly. She didn't seem to know how to react to me anyway and turned to Valerija, the presiding priestess of the group, giving her a deep, respectful bow. Valerija's handsome husband received an affectionate greeting, as though in gratitude for favours done in the past. Meanwhile the singing grew even louder, the crouching woman lifting her head and keeping her eyes shut as though in a trance. Folk melodies crescendoed into a banshee howling. This touched me, hearing a cry of grief for the last ten years in the Balkans, all those raped women, the dead babies, the massacred men, the burnt villages, the destroyed mosques and churches. As soon as the dancing finished and the large woman sank to her knees between the drummer and the singer, the shrieking stopped and the drumming subsided slowly into silence. We applauded them enthusiastically, grateful for the entertainment and that it was over. We promised to put them in touch with New Age groups in England and left.

A Beautiful Couple

Lazar told us that the couple of journalists we had arranged to meet for supper, a husband and wife, were famous in Belgrade. The man fronted a news programme on the independent television station, a kind of Jeremy Paxman, and his wife was an anchor woman on the same station. Lazar indicated that he and the woman often crossed swords. She was apparently difficult and even shrewish. The couple were beautiful, the woman tall and slender with long flowing blonde hair, the man a heartthrob, muscular, dark-haired, and with soulful eyes. We met outside a restaurant where an abandoned dog lurked near the entrance. The couple had just received a grant to visit England to learn more about media studies. Here they looked like stars, but when they told us how little cash they would have to live on in London, we thought of them being treated as aliens, two more in a tide of asylum seekers, and their beauty faded. A young Pole once travelled to Vienna with me from Katowice by train. He was a tall

Adonis with blonde curls, athletic physique, and the arrogance of someone accustomed to being admired. While he waited for a connection at the Sud West Bahnhof, crouching by his baggage, wealthy Viennese passed by and eyed him with suspicion. Suddenly he looked deflated and poor, all self-confidence vanished, no longer beautiful.

A Day Off

We suggested that Lazar take time off from us, but he told us that once we had gone he would have plenty of time to rest. When we picked up the tape from Sky News, Zorica and the camera crew had been called away on an assignment, but an assistant assured us that the item had been broadcast. We passed the gauntlet of gypsy children in the car park and drove off in the direction of Bulgaria to visit a monastery.

We looked forward to getting out of Belgrade and not having to worry about the 'big meeting', and the day began well. Outside Belgrade we noted the road leading to the refugee camps, hidden from view. Beyond this point Milosevic had forbidden the refugees to enter the city, yet a number of them had managed to reach the patriarchate yesterday.

Clouds covered the sky and it began to rain. We discussed plans for the day, first visiting the monastery of Manasija where we could look at some fifteenth-century wall paintings. Bishop Ignatije had already alerted the nuns to our visit and they were to provide lunch. Afterwards we would search out a spa specializing in mud baths and sit for a couple of hours with our heads sticking out of a bubbling black stew. On the way we would enjoy the countryside, the rolling fields, forests, hills, and orchards of Serbia.

Manasija

First glimpses of the monastery took us back hundreds of years. The road becomes a track and thick woods cover the hills, and then suddenly the sturdy grey walls and towers of a fortress rear up in a clearing above a bend in the river. There had been a time of Turkish invasions in what was then a remote area of the Balkans. Inside the impregnable walls the church stands like a pearl framed in iron. By now the weather had deteriorated, rain poured steadily, and a bitterly cold wind blew from the forested hills. The grounds of the monastery inside the fortress walls looked well tended but deserted. Around the chapel stood the living quarters for the nuns, timbered structures probably unchanged over the centuries. Despite the wind and rain the place looked a haven of peace and beauty.

After much knocking on doors and calling out, a little elderly nun appeared, a black habit enclosing all but her face. It only needed a yashmak to make her a devout Muslim. They had indeed been warned of our visit and were preparing lunch for us. First we must look at the murals. Nothing prepared us for their wild grandeur as we entered the dimly lit church. After centuries of neglect they had survived invasions and assaults, the walls crumbling and mildewed, the paint peeling and fading. Recent preservation simply ensured that no more deterioration could destroy them completely, and they remain monumental scarred remnants that depict warrior saints, tall figures with sturdy limbs, wielding swords and staring out under tousled hair, eyes blazing with conviction, terror and menace. Angels, saints, and Jesus himself are all dressed and ready for battle. In their pristine condition they must have filled the invaders with dread, but now with the paint blending with the colours of the ancient stones they spoke a different message of mortality, like a harmony of distant trumpets fading into eternal silence. They recalled the warrior patrons depicted in the highest windows at Chartres Cathedral, figures only seen from the high vantage point of the organ loft. These medieval leaders also express menace and fear, eyes wide and fanatical, as though they had only just emerged from a blood bath and had witnessed as well as committed atrocities. The Church then needed protection so that the vulnerable members of the community could survive enemy invasions. Over the centuries these buildings survived intact despite regular vandalism. Only at the end of the twentieth century, in the last few years and continuing in Kosovo, are they being systematically destroyed. These warrior saints cannot protect any longer. Their bodies rear up more than life-size, stretching muscular limbs, faces staring, garments swirling. The artists had worked urgently, inspired by danger and the need to preserve faith. The paintings express both the sensitivity and violence of the Balkan character, the extremes of human nature. The nun pointed out a detail, a painting in the vault of a low arch between the sacristy and the nave. It depicts the hand of God. "This is famous," commented Lazar. A large hand cups a huddle of little figures in swaddling clothes, like babies. It is a small but striking image, set against a square superimposed on a circle, which both imply the divine nature of the hand. The sensitively painted tiny, frail human beings resting safely in the palm of God's hand are surrounded by massive angels holding wands or spears, and these winged people turn into warrior saints who then cover the rest of the walls, rising up into the cupola.

The nun spoke in a monotone, having uttered the same words to visitors for many years. We moved across the mosaic floor with its bold pattern of abstract shapes reminiscent of Islam and its cultural influence in a region where Turks were at the same time massacring the people.

Much to Donald's relief, his capacity for admiring murals being limited, and constantly complaining about the cold, the nun took us to a small dining room set aside for guests, with portraits of recent abbesses wearing white wimples. Another nun helped serve lunch made up of a variety of dishes with meats, cheeses, salads, fried new-laid eggs, soups, and vegetables, each accompanied by fruit brandy, distilled by the nuns. Most of the time we were left on our own, but eventually the little nun sat with us, her face looking sadly up from her black wimple. She then told us that she had been a nun in this same place for over fifty-five years, since being the fourteen-year-old daughter of a local peasant family. She smiled for the first time at our astonishment. I thought of a life parallelling my own, but spent in one and the same place, remote from the rest of the world, a quiet and regular existence taking care of the livestock, digging the vegetable garden, tending the orchards, extracting honey from the monastery hives, milking the cattle daily, and collecting eggs, alert to the passing seasons and witnessing scarcely any changes. The monastery had been modernized, but only with the minimum of amenities. Heavy stone sinks and a nineteenth-century range stood in the kitchen. The furniture in the dining room and guest areas was of more recent vintage, about fifty years old. Priority had been given to the redecoration of the heated domestic chapel used by the nuns instead of the church, and their refectory. Here were impressively extravagant murals in the brightly coloured imitative style of contemporary iconography. For all the isolation of her existence the little nun implied that she had seen and learnt much, her countenance heavy with sadness for the wickednesses of the world, eyes looking upwards and rarely directed at us. She sighed and shrugged her shoulders, but we could not elicit from her any response to world events or to what was happening in her country. Nor could we find out why she had chosen to be a nun so young, at a time when religion was virtually outlawed in that part of the world. However, she told us that only recently had she experienced fear for the first time. NATO bombers would gather, flying low in the skies directly above the monastery, preparing for raids on Belgrade. The stealth bombers, black and menacing, had circled the low forested hills, and we felt guilty at the way these nuns had been pointlessly terrorized. The nun refused to be photographed. Her face recalled Rembrandt's portrait of his mother, each line and wrinkle speaking of a life's accumulated wisdom, patience, and acceptance; a simple yet extraordinary life, polished into a pearl.

As we left Manasija, the Monasteries Project took shape, and we visited the hotel in the nearby town to investigate the possibilities of groups of young and not so young visitors coming to learn about the Serbian way of life in a remote region of the Balkans, the monastery itself being the chief cultural interest. Clearly the nuns would not be able to accommodate so many frequent guests, but the hotel, though smelling strongly of sour cabbage, would be able to provide cheap beds. The bedrooms in fact were more than adequate at the price – about six pounds a night – with fresh bed linen and en suite bathrooms. The hotel manager offered a deal of nine pounds for full board. The project now looked a serious possibility and Lazar offered to find other monasteries so that people could visit several at a time. The bishops would be happy to support this venture, to open up an Orthodox traditional way of life to people from western Europe.

We drove away looking back towards the fortified monastery of Manasija, now hidden by thick forests, a torrent of a river rushing from the hills past the hotel. The wild remoteness of the place reminded us of how little we knew about this region of Europe.

The rain continued to pour and the afternoon grew prematurely dark. We headed westwards towards a spa town, about fifty miles away, where we might find a mud bath in which to submerge our weary bodies. The road became narrow and pitted, the car bumping and shaking along mile after mile. We drove across country with fields and hills stretching in every direction but with barely any human habitation. Darkness fell and we seemed no nearer to our destination. The terrible road shook every bone in our bodies and tempers began to fray. We stopped for a while by a meadow, listening to the cold wind soughing in the trees and imagining some other similar region of the country not so far away where soldiers had only recently arrived along bumpy roads, jumped out of their vehicles, and torched villages, leaving bodies lying on the wayside.

Eventually we arrived at the spa hotel which had closed for the winter season and we decided to return to Belgrade, continuing along a slightly less bumpy road, but still forced to travel slowly. Lazar wanted to show us a large and apparently spectacular church on a hill outside the town of Topola. It boasted a famous mosaic floor. We could not enter, the doors being bolted shut. Lazar knocked on the door of the caretaker's house. The lights shone inside but no one answered. Eventually a young man walked over from behind the church looking scared, but refused to open it for us. It was meant to shut at six o'clock. "But it's only half past five," said Lazar. The man shrugged his shoulders and couldn't give a damn. The hotel nearby had not changed since communist times. It smelt powerfully of stale frying fat. Three people sat around disconsolately and glanced at us, while two waiters eyed us indifferently. After a lengthy wait, they deigned to serve us some mint tea. Sixties pop music played through crackling loudspeakers and echoed around the vast spaces of the otherwise empty dining area.

Lazar felt that he had let us down, disappointed at the failure of his last two treats, no mud baths as promised and he couldn't show us the church. Now it was late and we were tired and miles away from home. The driving rain, the glare of oncoming traffic refusing to dip headlights, and the greasy filth on the windscreen, misting inside and out, meant that Lazar could not see to drive. "I'm blind!" he kept saying, desperately trying to keep the windscreen clean with his hand. We prayed that Belgrade would come over the horizon. At last we came to a garage, but the attendant told us he didn't have any window cleaning fluid. He pointed us to the other side of the motorway, which we crossed, dodging the speeding traffic, only to find that the salesman in the garage opposite had taken a dislike to us, and although the cleaning fluid could be seen quite clearly on the shelf, shrugged his shoulders, glared at us menacingly, and refused to sell us any. But Lazar can be intimidating too and although the salesman, sitting immovable behind the counter, became truculent to the point where I expected him to leap over the counter and beat us up or take a gun out of the drawer and shoot us, we eventually persuaded him to sell us a bottle, and then made a rapid exit. While we had been fetching the cleaning fluid, several vehicles had parked themselves around our car so we were wedged in. Lazar shouted at one of the drivers, who climbed out of his seat, a stoutly built labourer rolling up his sleeves for battle. Lazar's eyes were now cannonballs and he too began to climb out of the car, at which point the labourer thought better of it, grudgingly let us through, and we completed our journey home without further incident.

The evening ended around midnight at the flat with a television arts presenter and a crew of three men interviewing me about Andrei Tarkovsky. The Russian filmmaker's films have a devoted following in Serbia, and when Lazar discovered I had actually known the filmmaker personally, he informed his media friends who seized the chance to film me. The interview could have continued uninterrupted and been put under wraps, had the batteries in the film camera not run out. After half an hour the crew shrugged their shoulders and arranged to come and complete the interview next morning before we returned to Budapest.

The lift broke down on our last morning in Belgrade, but undaunted the film crew hauled their heavy equipment up six flights of steps, smiling and assuring me that "this is quite usual here". The sun poured into the living room as the director questioned me about the lecture Tarkovsky gave at St James's, Piccadilly, in 1984 on the Apocalypse, the theme of an arts festival we organized that year. Tarkovsky had agreed to attend the festival because of the theme. All his films deal with the Apocalypse in one way or the other, an awareness of the world as we know it coming to an end, the need for understanding and radical changes to make it a more humane place. Apocalypse means 'revelation'. In the Bible the revelation refers to God's new order when the end comes. For Tarkovsky revelation means uncovering the human condition which has brought about so much suffering and destruction in the world. His films deal with the extremes of human experience: war, love, and death. These themes are understandably close to the heart of all people in the Balkans who are still experiencing the extremes of violence and suffering.

In Tarkovsky's first major film, *Ivan's Childhood*, war corrupts innocence. Children become soldiers and die. What makes the film extraordinary is the contrast between bleak, cruel, and inescapable reality and the boy Ivan's dreams of an idyllic childhood, his mother washing and feeding him, water gushing, fruit tumbling in abundance, children playing and horses galloping. Reality is the aftermath of Armageddon, houses burning and a few crazed survivors wandering across a smouldering landscape reminiscent of Breughel's painting, *The Triumph of Death*. But the film begins with a dream of flying, the freedom of the human spirit soaring above the horror, and the dreams punctuate the grim narrative of what happened to just one of millions of people who fought and died, the numbers so inconceivable that Tarkovsky sought hard to illustrate the mind-boggling truth, coming up with a final image of a snowstorm of names on bits of paper flying through the ruins of Berlin.

The film crew had tears in their eyes as they recalled the images in these films which mean so much to them now, reminding them of the need to hold on to dreams in the midst of chaos.

For thoughtful and sensitive people in the Balkans art has become particularly significant and necessary. Lazar wanted to see the El Greco paintings in Budapest's National Museum of Art. We sat for a long time in silence in front of half a dozen large canvases including the *Agony in the Garden* and *Mary Magdalen*. The paintings are monumental: the vivid colours, the massive abstract shapes, the false perspectives, and the flowing lines unite all the figures in one elemental stream. El Greco's vision encompasses the unity of the mystical and physical world, the soul become sensual, the senses become spiritual, human beings striving for transcendence and yet occupying natural space, at ease with their heavy corporeality.

Lazar the art historian couldn't resist pointing out some details and went up to the *Mary Magdalen* to show me the way a breast nipple pushes through her clothing. He almost grazed it with his finger and an attendant moved sharply in our direction. "I'm not touching!" Lazar shouted, indignant that she might think him capable of soiling a masterpiece.

Postscript

In the Gellert Baths in Budapest, families sat in groups and young men eyed one another across the steaming waters, queuing to crouch under the fountains spouting from the mouths of two stone lions. Beyond stretched the elaborately decorated hall with its columns and tiles, the stained glass and cupolas dwarfing the people of every shape, age, and size wandering around in towels.

A distant memory came back to me here. Thirty-five years ago as a nineteen-year-old student I had once travelled through Yugoslavia. I hitched several lifts and remember in particular a smartly dressed middle-aged man driving somewhere on business. Generously he invited me for a substantial lunch of local delicacies in a small town, and spent time patiently educating me about his country. As he deposited me once again at the roadside, he delivered a warning which puzzled me then, the year being 1965. "Look around, you see a beautiful country, people working together in peace. But don't be fooled. There will come a day when people will be enemies. It will be terrible. Just remember I told you this."

LONDON, FINLAND AND COVENTRY

17 March – 12 April 2000

DIARY – PETER PELZ

LONDON

The visit to Serbia changed our thinking about the purpose of the Soul of Europe. The journeys to western European countries taught us that they could respond to us only if we came with practical proposals and ideas that would be turned into projects. Our contacts were already making it clear that they did not understand the vague wording on our original publicity material. What exactly were our intentions? Once we talked about the Bosnia Project they became interested. But we also knew that the two of us could not be expected to organize such projects. We needed to find friends and supporters across Europe who would be prepared to collaborate and help turn our vision into reality. This was particularly so in the Balkans where the needs wait to be urgently addressed. As Donald says, "Some things you can't turn your back on." We needed to consult our Council and work out how to proceed. The contrast between Serbia and western Europe made it seem that the countries were not in the same continent. We call ourselves the Soul of Europe and the issues we encountered in Belgrade are not unrelated to the rest of Europe. The Bosnia Project demanded attention. How should we proceed? The following meetings and journeys gradually began to clarify our thinking.

Stephen Wenman lives on the Thames, in a block of flats which overlooks the Globe Theatre and the Tate Modern. There had been a power failure. A man with a torch let us in and then lurked in the darkness waiting to let us out again later. I'm not used to being greeted by a butler at the door and began to think I had lost my mind, not recognizing Stephen and wondering why he'd changed so drastically. Stephen was upstairs, preparing for the meeting. The flat looks out on the Thames in two directions, a view to transfix the eye. Graham the butler served us coffee and homemade biscuits and Stephen sat on a low chair listening enthusiastically to our Serb adventures. He supported us in everything, but campaigned for more use of the Internet and our web site. The problem is that not many people on our Advisory Council or among our supporters know how to use communication technology.

Our visit to John Banks in the afternoon became traumatic. Normally he is amenable and encouraging. But he now expressed serious doubts about the development of the Soul of Europe. He had presided over its genesis and advised us how to make it succeed at several meetings in his Baker Street office. Now it seemed we were forgetting the initial aims of developing a network of 'good practice' churches and communities across Europe. "Don't lose the plot," he told us. He also seemed to be in the middle of a crisis, and halfway through the meeting while he was reminding us of what we ought to be doing, he took a long telephone call. "Saudi Arabia, Dubai, litigation, off to New York, million and half pounds…" He ended abruptly with a throw away, "See you on Monday", at which point he put the phone down and without drawing breath continued to tell us what he considered the Soul of Europe was about. He rejected our involvement in the Bosnia Project, suggesting that we concentrate on organizing a conference of world religious leaders, politicians, and businessmen who will support our projects, not just one of them, but a whole sackful, from every country we visited. "You've a lot of work to do. You're not project managers," he told us sharply. We should go around eastern Europe finding a lot of projects, and bring back shopping lists to put before the conference and let others deal with them. We reeled and tried to grasp some sign of encouragement. He then told us that we had succeeded wonderfully in Serbia, and therefore could do the same everywhere else. Our strength is in persuading leaders and important people to come together and initiate big projects. Forget the small ones and concentrate on organising the big conference. "It's going to be hard," said John Banks, "But then who said it was going to be easy?" Then he added in a more conciliatory vein, "But you can do it. You got the religious leaders in Serbia together..." Donald pointed out that the leaders in Serbia are desperate. They were only too happy to meet for our benefit. When we mooted that the conference could be in Sarajevo, John Banks surmised it would be too dangerous. Berlin is better. He has a branch of his office there and could help us organize the conference.

Far from clarifying our thoughts, this meeting had confused them further. Perhaps things look different from behind the desk of a managing director of an advertising agency. We had been somewhere totally different from anything anyone in western Europe can understand unless they've actually been there. So this book has a purpose. People should know how it is on the ground. We needed to explain how it is impossible to go around eastern Europe like humanitarian voyeurs, picking up sensational projects that give poor and desperate people hope, only to relinquish direct responsibility while we get talking heads to meet in grand surroundings and decide their future.

However, John Banks did support us. He clearly admires what we've achieved and simply wants us to be clear about our strengths and what we can do. Our skills lie in networking, and we should keep a clear view of our overall objectives, which cover all of Europe. Nevertheless we also have to work at the grass roots.

"Where do you get all these ideas?" Donald had asked John in a conciliatory vein as we left. John suddenly looked humble, as though we'd caught him off guard with a compliment. The skilled manager with a large respectful staff, a man with a mind like a scalpel, and with an infallible instinct for good business, leaned across the table with a shy smile on his blushing face, and seemed genuinely not to know what we were talking about. We were the ones with the great ideas; he was simply encouraging us and telling us to get on with them, using our skills to best advantage.

REPORT TO ADVISORY COUNCIL

DONALD REEVES

In view of the Bosnia Project the purpose of the Finland visit changed: from discovering inspiring examples of ministry to seeking partners from the Orthodox Church of Finland and the Lutheran Church of Finland. The anticipated outcomes have been just about successfully realized, though much follow-up work has to be done.

The Orthodox Church

The Finnish Orthodox Church is a small church, some 58,000 in a population of five million. But it could be a significant partner. We visited the Archbishop of Karelia and all Finland in Kuopio, a five-hour journey from Helsinki, near the Arctic Circle.

This was a courtesy visit. The archbishop promised to find a 'contact' for the Soul of Europe. We also met Teuvo Laitila, the editor of the fortnightly review of the Finnish Orthodox Church, *Aamun Koitto (The Rising Sun)*. He interviewed me for the magazine. Back in Helsinki we met Fr Heikki Huttunen, a parish priest in the suburbs. He has met Lazar Markovic, who once interviewed him for his Orthodox magazine in the Balkans. I preached at Vespers; he presented me with a reproduction of a beautiful Serbian icon and provided much information about European Orthodoxy, since he has worked in Geneva for the World Council of Churches. It is possible that he will mobilize some of the local parishes to support the project financially. He is clearly an important figure in the Finnish Orthodox Church; everyone knew about him and respected him, including people from the Lutheran Church. In Helsinki we met Metropolitan Leo who was also enthusiastic about the Soul of Europe. He told us that the four bishops of the Orthodox Church in Finland were meeting in a fortnight, together with a minister from the Foreign Office (whom we met) and the Soul of Europe was going to be on the agenda, specifically the matter of a representative from Finland and becoming our partner. We learned that the Orthodox Church in Finland is establishing

Orthodox Aid for places of need in Europe. I would hope that the Soul of Europe will benefit from this initiative.

We also met Father Markku Salminen, Chairman of the Orthodox Youth Association. He is ready to invite young people to take part in the Monasteries Project and to participate in the Bosnian Project.

The Church of Finland

The established Church of Finland is Lutheran and is a formidable institution. There are two thousand students of theology at the University and most will be ordained. There are many organizations for social welfare and social responsibility. The fact that fewer and fewer people actually attend church does not seem to be of any concern because as we were told: Finns are born Lutheran and anyhow fifty per cent of the population comes to church at Christmas!

It was not possible to meet any of the eight Lutheran bishops. They were on a skiing retreat in Lapland.

However, we discovered a firm advocate for the Soul of Europe and the Bosnia Project especially, in Juhani Forsberg, the Ecumen ical Officer for the Church of Finland, whose remit also covers Foreign Relations. He is a significant bureaucrat, is one of the architects of the Porvoo Agreement (where Lutherans and Anglicans recognize one another's ordinations as valid), and is active in much else, a highly respected figure, known to everybody. Juhani fixed up several meetings including one with the minister at the Foreign Office responsible for the Balkans, where he vigorously advocated the Bosnia Project. He also introduced us to Helena Manninen-Visuri who is the Programme Officer at FinnChurchAid, a formidable person who found the objectives of the Soul of Europe "most attractive" and will help us. Juhani Forsberg will act as 'post box' for us, pending the identification of a permanent contact person.

Meetings with Elsi Takala and Helena Manninen-Visuri

These were important conversations since both women work in Kosovo and Bosnia. Their reaction to the Bosnia Project was at first cautious. Was this just another scheme for humanitarian aid? But when I explained the organic way in which the rebuilding will take place with local people together with young Christians and Muslims from all over Europe working together, when I emphasized the idea of establishing among the ruins the centre for reconciliation and peace, and when I stressed the need for employment and economic regeneration (where the Soul of Europe will try to act as a catalyst), there was much support and enthusiasm. We were told about designated towns as 'United Nations Open Cities' where all ethnic groups are moving back together; we were warned about only rebuilding churches because Saudi Arabia and Croatia are now funding the building of 'big, fancy churches' as a form of aggressive political action. But our organic and multi-faith project with young Europeans across all denominations taking part has a different dimension which appealed to the women. I also made the point that we will collaborate with anyone who shares the same vision, particularly with the World Conference for Religion and Peace which is active in Sarajevo. I have asked Lazar to be in touch with both these women. He will gather useful information, they are happy to help him, and they will also benefit from his native perspective once he has visited Bosnia.

We also had a brief meeting with the Deacon of the Roman Catholic Cathedral (there are only five thousand Catholics in Finland, mostly foreigners). I preached at the Anglican Eucharist and received some informed and enthusiastic interest from British and American diplomats, and also from Diana Webster, the European Representative on the General Synod. We will keep in touch and they also want to help.

We learned that seeing the appropriate and influential bureaucrat or bishop as well as lively parishes takes care of the networking. The Finland people want us to address the question, "What does partnership involve?" Everyone appreciated the effort we made coming to Helsinki. Personal contact is more effective than e-mails, sending material through the post, or telephoning. People need to hear us talk, to discuss, ask questions, and share their doubts and own opinions. We gave them time and attention and they became supportive and committed. Every meeting became the basis of a future collaboration.

FINLAND

DIARY – PETER PELZ

There are two seasons in Finland we are told: winter and July. While the Baltic is frozen over and snow covers the forests the cold is bearable, but in late March when the ice breaks and metal grey waves lap against the coast the cold intensifies. Perhaps this accounted for the reactivation of our hibernation instincts. Every time we ventured outdoors, walking to meetings, we returned to our hotel rooms exhausted and had to lie down. The moment our heads touched the pillow slumber took over. Even writing my reports each day turned into a battle with sleep, my head dropping and the pen slipping over the page.

Nature gives Helsinki its character. The city stretches round bays and wooded peninsulas along the Baltic Sea. The trees stand upright as though frozen against the sky, their stillness contrasting with the shimmering sea and movement of clouds. Beyond, forests stretch into the distance, their darkness bringing to mind the music of Sibelius, icily monumental with long, slow climaxes. At first glance the city centre is not strikingly beautiful, seeming dull, and apart from the Lutheran cathedral rearing above a grand flight of steps, no extravagant gestures alert you to the fact that this is a capital. In fact the understated art nouveau architecture gradually exerts its own quiet charm. It is rather like the Finnish character, at first forbiddingly indifferent, then becoming friendly and dependable. The elegance of Helsinki is expressed in its simple design, uncluttered by decoration. Tiny art nouveau motifs and symbols appear almost apologetically above doorways and windows, serving to underline the simplicity, as unfussy as the Finns themselves. Yet startling city sculptures punctuate the monotone, as though August Strindberg, that Nordic expert in fraught human relationships, had been commissioned to interpret the national psyche in public. Three naked men swing hammers and genitals at one end of the city centre, while at the other a languid, heavy-hipped naked woman attracts the attention of four louche seals, stretching their phallic necks towards her, unable to reach the object of their lustful attentions because their flippers and fins prevent them. This sculpture caused public outrage at its unveiling. To my mind this is not because of the nude female figure. She is passive; it is the four seals that are menacing. Their tense muscles express fury and sexual frustration. Their immobility makes men feel uneasy, yet the woman is trapped. It is a dark and uncompromising depiction of the battle of the sexes.

This preface may help explain the undercurrents of our visit to Finland. After the explosion of activities in Serbia and the enthusiastic welcome given to Donald on a first visit to Sweden, Finland seemed lethargic and sluggish in its responses. People there resist immediate reactions and we hope their reticence does not mean indifference. That all remains to be seen. So far only the Orthodox Church has shown interest and appointed a representative. The comfortably powerful Lutherans are biding their time, cautious of involvement and jealously guarding their own interests in the Balkans. They are proud of their political influence in Kosovo. We have come to expect nothing from the powerful: their concern is primarily for themselves. It is the weak who welcome and support one another.

On our first day, we took the train to Kuopio, a five-hour journey half way to the Arctic Circle, in order to pay our respects to the Orthodox archbishop of Finland. There is nothing you can do with the Orthodox unless you have the blessing of the hierarchy. Archbishop Johannes was touched by our efforts and gave us a warm welcome.

The Hotel Anna in Helsinki where we stayed is simple and functional – it is run by the YWCA – but at least everything works. The beds are narrow but comfortable. The showers distribute a steady stream of warm water, but there is scarcely room to turn around in, let alone swing the proverbial cat. However the breakfast is substantial. It combines all meals in one. Apart from the usual juices, cereals, and variety of breads, a bewildering display of smoked and pickled fish, sliced meats, salads, and thick fruit compotes stuffed with forest berries make a confusing assault on the digestive system at the start of the day. We had to rush this feast on the first morning because our English contact in Helsinki had ordered us to attend the eight o'clock morning service in the Anglican Chapel. We trudged through the biting cold to the cathedral, the gold cupolas gleaming in the blinding sunlight. The chapel happens to nestle, like an elegant garden shed, to the side of the cathedral, half way down the steps. But first we entered the cathedral to find this out. The interiors of Finnish Lutheran churches are a striking contrast of Protestant denial with suburban aesthetic: expensively upholstered pews under massive, gaudy candelabras, but few works of art.

After the service, Rupert Moreton, the Chaplain, took us to a coffee house opposite the cathedral. He was embarrassed and burdened by our presence, a task he had taken on out of duty. He played devil's advocate by questioning our naivety in trusting the Serbs. Weren't we being used by them? Clearly he was not an ally. He seemed to be busy with many commitments, which meant that he had to rush us to the first of our two engagements and drop us off half an hour early outside the Catholic Church offices, saying, "You don't mind going for a walk do you?" and then driving away in haste, leaving us stranded on a bleak stretch of highway with one of the long-haired girls.

Mr Pentti Laukama, Secretary to the Catholic Church in Finland, immediately phoned several contacts for us, including the Orthodox archbishop, and promised to support the Soul of Europe. The Catholic Church in Finland is weak and without influence. But we appreciated his kindness. We sat in his office, and since he offered us no hospitality we assumed he preferred us to be quick and leave.

The visit to Finland was almost a planning disaster for the Soul of Europe. Not a single person we met had any idea who we were, despite our correspondence, daily e-mails and attachments being sent both over the net and by snail mail, to make sure they would be well informed. In the West we pay scant attention to e-mails and post. Not only that, but each person looked at us wearily as we arrived and sat down, smiling wanly as they admitted to not having a clue about us, even though I could see a file full of our correspondence on the table in front of them. Each meeting turned into yet another assault on the North Face of the Eiger. Being reticent and uncommunicative, the Finns needed at least half an hour before allowing us a response. That half hour became a formidable challenge at each successive meeting.

Our next meeting was the one exception to the rule. Our main contact in Finland, Juhani Forsberg, welcomed us not only warmly and enthusiastically, he also took us out for an excellent lunch at a well known Russian-style restaurant. He brought with him two formidable women who administered Finland's Aid to the Balkans, to Kosovo in particular. Juhani Forsberg, a kindly and gently spoken man approaching retirement, is well known for having negotiated the Porvoo Agreement, which is entirely to the Anglican advantage, since it is the Lutherans who are generous with money, and at least in Finland provide the Anglican chaplains like Rupert Moreton with office space, staff, and proper salaries. Juhani had already taken the Soul of Europe on board and offered to help us in every way, fixing up meetings for the rest of our stay in Finland. However, the women watched us climb the North Face of the Eiger as we consumed an authentic borscht soup (with plenty of grated beetroot and sour cream) and reach half way up it during breast of duck with buckwheat on the side. This was not as arduous a climb as it became later on when we had to overcome resistance and scepticism and, most difficult of all, avoid 'treading on toes'. It seemed that everyone we met ran Bosnia projects in the Balkans. They questioned why they should be interested: there is nothing unique about ours. After all they were doing fine, thank you very much. (So why is the situation there still so bad?) Mrs Rantakari had been in Kosovo only a week before and seemed to spend most of her life there. The Finns are foremost in administering aid in the region.

The last stages of the climb to the Eiger summit were particularly hazardous because we needed to clarify that we are not encroaching on their activities in humanitarian aid, that we only seek to create a symbolic gesture, to bring hope, not just to the region, but to a fractured Europe as a whole, to bring young people from the West in particular to the Balkans (not only to Bosnia, but to Serbian monasteries as well) and that the objectives of the Soul of Europe cut across all religious and traditional ethnic divides.

This last point became more desperately urgent at our meeting with another formidable woman, Elsi Takala at the Foreign Ministry, who painted a sinister picture of Bosnia where each religion is pouring money into building churches and mosques as defiant political gestures, the theological equivalent of arming with tanks and cruise missiles. In Mostar, for instance, an imposing new Croat Catholic church and a shiny Bosnian Muslim mosque now challenge each other across the river which divides the town and where an ancient bridge was destroyed, a bridge that once linked the ethnic communities and gave its name to the town. We talked about economic regeneration of the region, of young Muslims and Orthodox sharing the labour, of the project being for our children and grandchildren. At this stage of the meeting the panorama began to spread beyond the mountain peak. Mrs Rantakari suddenly understood that we weren't treading on her toes. She even smiled and allowed that we had a 'beautiful' project. Others expressed a more grudging opinion, sceptical in a typically comfortable, well-off western European way that we could achieve anything so fraught with problems.

Juhani Forsberg was moved by our objectives, particularly at the way we handled the formidable women who had initially expressed serious doubts about the extent of our experience in administering such a project. Rupert Moreton's eyes rounded in amazement at the rapidity of doors opening, and before we left for Kuopio Juhani had fixed enough meetings to have made the visit to Finland worthwhile.

The train passed frozen lakes, snowbound fields, dark pine forests in the distance, and avenues of silver birch trees, slender and supple, their light grey bark creating an ethereal effect against the white drifts, seeming to float, insubstantial and dream like.

Kuopio is reminiscent of mid-Western towns in the States: identical concrete blocks of buildings on a grid plan. We passed the archbishop's house several times, not believing that the pre-fab bungalow, looking like a long, low-roofed warehouse, could be a residence. It also contains the Orthodox Church Museum. A young man greeted us formally at the door to the archbishop's apartments. Inside, the comfortable rooms were elaborately furnished and decorated with masses of icons, mostly modern imitations, painted wooden eggs, folk-style embroidered cloths, and other Orthodox ornaments, interspersed with landscape and flower paintings in garish colours. However, a large oil painting in the study gave a grand and peaceful impression of the landscape in Karelia, the Orthodox heartland. Tiny monasteries peeked out from wooded hillsides surrounded by large stretches of lake.

Archbishop Johannes may appear elderly, but he kept a sharp eye on the proceedings, judging when to lighten the mood with a joke and when to keep a distance. So although Donald managed to extract an assurance about finding a Soul of Europe representative in Finland, he refused to be rushed on the subject. "Yes! Yes!" he frowned every time Donald mentioned the representative. "I will do it! I will do it!" Mostly he spoke about his own life and good works, ranging from noisy fifties New York to the frozen wastes of Lapland where he inaugurated a slalom, on which at that very moment a gathering of Lutheran bishops were skiing and socializing. Back then the area belonged to Laplanders and reindeer. He had converted to Orthodoxy from Lutheranism. Instead of the traditional bushy beard he sported a raffish goatee, carefully trimmed. A man of refinement, he kept the conversation going at a leisurely pace and entertained us with tea and biscuits served from elegant porcelain at a table laid specially for us. Afterwards he allowed me to snap a photograph and he signed two hardback catalogues of the museum collection, mostly vestments and artefacts, but including a few ancient Russian/Finnish icons. He didn't commit himself and we left disappointed, but clearly the archbishop needed time to chose a representative.

Before leaving Kuopio, Teuvo Laitila, the youthful editor of the Orthodox magazine, cornered us in the hotel for a couple of hours. Like all journalists he drained us of information and gave little in return. But it turns out he will be our Orthodox representative in Finland.

We touched base with an Orthodox priest, Heikki Huttunen, a lively, good looking young man, who is building up a strong congregation in Tapiola, a suburb of Helsinki. Scouring the area for a cup of coffee I noted the overcrowding of high rise flats, a labyrinthine shopping mall, and the lack of vistas or any points of interest. But the church itself provided an oasis of calm and beauty, even though the familiar new frescoes were not finished. Large scaffolding with platforms straddled the central part of the church, the artist having been given three more years to complete the painting.

Again we climbed the North Face. Heikki seemed tired at first, patiently trying to understand why we had made an effort to see him. But once the summit had been reached the panorama stretched for miles around with barely a cloud in the sky. He did however express a fear of becoming too involved practically, as he clearly had his work cut out in this crowded parish. And the church attracted many new worshippers from all round Helsinki. But even as we scaled the higher reaches of the rock face he came running with ropes and assistance, pouring out names and contacts from all over Europe who might support the Soul of Europe. He looked at us kindly with warm attractive eyes (he must have constant trouble with admiring worshippers), and he wasted no time, finding names and addresses while preparing for Vespers and dealing with parish matters. He managed to bear us and our problems in mind while he calmly and efficiently attended to the details of the worship. This grace informed the whole of Vespers where he performed all the priest's duties, moving swiftly behind the sanctuary screens, singing the responses in a clear baritone voice, processing with the incense, remembering to give Donald a service book, attentive to everybody else as well and keeping the rhythm of the service flowing smoothly. Vespers is a relatively short service, not a three-hour marathon. The congregation were attentive, standing still most of the time, but occasionally shifting from one leg to the other and taking every opportunity to cross themselves on cue. An assistant priest gave a clear lead to the choir of five. He skilfully hummed each note in the split chord before conducting and singing confidently in a light baritone. Two little girls in kerchiefs, worn proudly as though for a party, sang in the choir, legs crossed and fidgeting occasionally, but generally well behaved throughout the hour-long service. Several latecomers would light candles ostentatiously, kissing several icons, tapping the girls approvingly on the shoulder, smiling at friends, and nodding in welcome at strangers. Next to me a tiny elderly woman in jeans paid close attention to every word of the service, every gesture. The scaffolding and the incomplete painting did not interrupt a tradition so honed and familiar that each worshipper knew and hung on every moment.

Finally Father Heikki introduced Donald, who spoke about the Soul of Europe to an interested and approving audience. When he spoke about young people helping with the Bosnia Project, the father squeezed his two girls who had just sung in the choir. Heikki then presented Donald with a fine reproduction of a Serbian icon, framed on wood. A ferocious Christ looks out, more warrior than saviour. The gift implied support for our work and we were moved by the generosity of the gesture. We felt we had at last made grass roots contact in Finland.

No other meeting in Finland had the same depth of response as with Father Heikki, who although clearly not having the time to be an active partner in the Soul of Europe, will definitely be associated with it, one of the first parishes to illustrate that quality of 'best practice' we talked about a year ago, when the idea was being born. The Soul of Europe candle definitely burns here.

We visited Metropolitan Leo, the Bishop of Helsinki, someone clearly with his eye on Archbishop Johannes's job, friendly and attentive, though he implied that he knew about us already and had nothing more to say than add his support. Both these bishops had once been married, and the death of their wives made it possible for them to be elevated. In the Orthodox Church only priests and deacons are allowed to have families – in fact they have to be married for the job – but bishops must be unmarried. But if priests can lose their wives, then they too are qualified for the episcopacy. A dazzlingly good-looking boy greeted us at Bishop Leo's flat while his attractive young mother hovered in the kitchen area. We enjoyed the traditional hospitality of tea and biscuits which the bishop consumed with a hearty appetite while observing our climb up the North Face. Then he was in a hurry to get rid of us, and we left without a sense of having made much impact. But at least he was friendly.

An Orthodox priest youth leader met us after the Sunday service, friendly and also non-committal, and the following day we visited a hospital run by the Deaconess Institute, which seemed an unlikely partner for the Soul of Europe until we had talked with its leader, Birgitta Rantakari, who made our final assault on the Eiger relatively easy by understanding and supporting our objectives without reservations. A lively woman, not so formidable as the others we met, but even more capable and experienced after years of working in Africa among the poor in dangerous conditions. The most formidable woman of all worked in the Foreign Ministry. Elsi Takala administered the Balkans Desk and she made us climb the North Face in blizzard conditions. Her fears and suspicions concerned our plans to rebuild churches. But once we had explained the pan-European nature of the Soul of Europe, the multi-faith aspect, and the economic regeneration of the region, she warmed slightly but remained non-committal. We sat round a huge polished wooden table in a featureless room. Two paintings of Finnish peasants gathering the harvest and carrying baskets of apples decorated one wall. Their healthy robust bodies, strong arms, and plain rustic clothes contrasted with the sterile atmosphere of the office. The minister grilled us thoughtfully about the practicalities of our objectives in Bosnia. Juhani Forsberg supported us firmly and we took that as a gesture of his future interest. We thanked Elsi Takala for sparing time to see us. "It's my job," she said, which though a modest observation, actually made her even more formidable and unapproachable. The case is simple: she feared we might ask for money, and it is the duty of all people in charge of the pursestrings to resist such demands. The richer the country, the less chance of the strings loosening. We were constantly being told that Finland was a poor country. Poverty is a relative issue in the West. Go south and east. Witness real poverty.

COVENTRY

DIARY – PETER PELZ

The rebuilding of Coventry Cathedral after World War II has become a worldwide symbol of reconciliation and peace between nations. Germany bombed the munitions factories there and destroyed the old cathedral. The greatest artists, sculptors, and glass engravers in post-war Britain joined creative forces to create a modern place of worship, leaving the ruins nearby as a sacred and public place where memorial sculptures and plaques are a constant reminder not only of what happened but, more significantly, of the possibility of forgiveness. There is a prayer displayed on a wall of the cathedral thanking God for the disaster because it presented an opportunity for people to learn about peace and reconciliation. Strong links were then forged with the German city of Dresden which suffered some of the worst British bombing of the war. Over a hundred thousand citizens were killed there in the hellish firestorm and one of the most beautiful cities in Europe was reduced to rubble.

Paul Oestreicher was instrumental in forging these links between Germany and Great Britain. Now he urged us to visit his successor in Coventry, Andrew White, who is reckoned to be the 'Richard Branson' of the Church of England. He is a man able to translate vision into substantial action. The task of reconciliation between Germany and the rest of Europe has now been achieved, and Coventry wants to take its message of peace throughout the world to all places where conflict is still far from being resolved.

The example of Coventry Cathedral is an inspiration to the Soul of Europe, particularly in its appeal to the imagination as a source of bringing people together. It also has a network of communities worldwide, all devoted to reconciliation and initiating projects. We want to get in touch with these, make ourselves known, and gain their support. Andrew was eager to meet us, and he suggested we attend the first conference of this network later in the year. The network is called the Cross of Nails. The morning after the bombing of the cathedral, the provost, surveying the ruins, caught sight of two huge nails, used in the Middle Ages to secure the beams. They happened to be lying in the shape of a cross. This became the symbol of reconciliation and all members of the Cross of Nails network wear it.

Andrew White is astonishingly young for his position and reputation, though it is easy to see how his direct manner allied with natural charm and an ability to put you at your ease makes him an irresistible force. There is something of the potentate about him. He was lordly in his welcome, smiling and holding out his arms, offering us seats on sofas and ordering tea and coffee. When the tea came he sent it back. "Go and make a proper cup of tea," he ordered the timid assistant who looked alarmed, although Andrew was being good-humoured about it. "This is undrinkable!" Then he flung himself onto a swing chair, throwing one leg over the other knee and looking at us both steadily while talking, taking us in, working out what we were doing and what business we could have together, all the time gesturing, swinging around on the chair and dealing with phone calls and people intruding with questions.

He invited a young German pastor-in-training to join us, and though this student turned out to be more knowledgeable than his years might have suggested, he seemed quite cowed by the three of us. When invited to join us for supper he declined politely.

Andrew's office is both functional and comfortable, with much of the space laid out for hospitality, with a large coffee table, sofas, and armchairs, while his desk is set diagonally across one corner of the room. The purpose of this design reflects his genius at doing business. Most people would make the desk dominate, so as to establish protocol and status. In his own way Andrew makes everybody feel important, whoever it is, whether archbishop or secretary. Pictures, photos (including snaps of Andrew accompanying famous people, such as the Pope), and books line the room and make the atmosphere cosy. He does not sit behind the desk but pulls the stool into the orbit of the central hospitality area, which gives him space to gesticulate and move around the room at ease, not bounded by the desk. For all his ease of manner, as though he were making things up as he goes along, the room has been carefully organized, and its appearance and proportions do almost all the work for him. This is exactly the way an office should be. In such a setting a man can achieve any objective.

Amidst the gossip about church matters, and Donald's managing to fit in some explanation about the project, despite Andrew's mind being on several other matters at the same time, we learned much about various organizations of significance to us, the World Conference of Religion and Peace, the Balkan Regeneration Fund, the Mostar Project (where Croat Catholics were making it difficult for the Germans, who are not used to coping with areas of stress and having their carefully constructed bureaucratic and official structures ignored), the Annual Peace Prize, and various charitable trusts and foundations with Jews and Muslims. We talked about the Cross of Nails Network and he readily gave us the list of addresses.

He then told us about the dangerous journeys he undertakes regularly in such hot spots of the world as Nigeria ("where people are still chopping one another's legs off") and Iraq, driving for fourteen hours through the desert in bullet-proof cars. He had just entertained Iraqis in Coventry. "We gave them the full-goat treatment," he said, and we tried to imagine a goat being roasted on a spit in the cathedral courtyard and wondered who would have been offered the eyes. Over supper at an Indian restaurant with lavish self-service he gave us considerable advice about handling local politicians, about always being respectful of one's own government however disagreeable, and about the importance of having 'juniors', a proper staff on the ground, people to rely on who can keep the infrastructure solid. 'Juniors' keep their heads to the ground and concentrate on organizing trips, keeping the machinery oiled and running. We will need just such a saint quite shortly if and when the Soul of Europe really gets off the ground.

The handsome young German with the floppy blonde hair and sky-blue eyes had left us for engagements elsewhere. In his place came the man who had served us tea, also young and gifted, and able to speak several languages including Swedish and Serbo-Croat. Andrew invites everybody into the conversation but concentrated on Donald, wasting no time in burrowing for the significant link between Coventry and the Soul of Europe.

Our connection with the rebuilding of ruined churches in the Balkans has to be in the spirit of Coventry, a way of building bridges between communities who have been enemies. Coventry is important for us, and our significance for Coventry will be in the projects that we initiate.

SWEDEN AND DENMARK

March and May 2000

There were two visits to Sweden. Donald went by himself in March 2000 to set up meetings for the next visit with myself and Lazar Markovic in May. He wrote two reports, one after each visit.

FIRST REPORT

DONALD REEVES

I had a useful meeting with the Archbishop of Uppsala. The archbishop is elected as the first among equals of the thirteen bishops. He is a most significant public figure in Sweden. He has been in his present office for three years and he is regarded as a 'real leader' (that is how people describe him to me). He successfully negotiated the Church of Sweden's change of role as the established Church of the nation to an organization which, potentially, has much more freedom.

The archbishop knows me well. He had attended a day's seminar I led for clergy when he was Bishop of Lund. He visited St James's Piccadilly and wrote a testimony for my last book (in the paperback version).

The archbishop was really enthusiastic about the Serbian project (the monasteries) and particularly the Bosnian Project. He said that Europe urgently needs the sort of symbolic action which is now being proposed. He was enthusiastic about the name of the project and encouraged us to work with all religious traditions so that "we move beyond the fears of syncretism".

We did not discuss questions about funding and organization, but it is clear that the Soul of Europe has arrived on the Church of Sweden's desk at just the right moment. (The chairman of the Swedish Christian Council next year, for example, will be a Serbian Orthodox bishop.)

I had a meeting with Hans Engdahl, Ecumenical Relations Secretary and Maria Hamarstom, a theologian who runs the office of the Church of Sweden Youth Department and also Birgitta Rosen, EU Cooperation officer of the Church of Sweden. Birgitta Handog, the European Secretary of the Church of Sweden, was in Romania. These officials were as enthusiastic about the project as the archbishop and gave me some useful advice about the process of starting projects. The meeting was called at very short notice by the archbishop who wanted me to meet as many people as possible in one day!

Two major parishes were represented at the conference, one in Malmo, the other at Helsingborg. The clergy and lay staff of these parishes were also enthusiastic about the project. Both have agreed to set up meetings in their towns, together with a church in Copenhagen (which is only twenty minutes away by ferry and even less when the bridge between Copenhagen and Malmo is opened). The details have yet to be worked out, but Peter and I will go for five days or so at the beginning of May. One of the parishes has promised to raise some funds for us. They will set up all sorts of meetings as well as bringing the leaders together in Malmo from the Muslim, Croat, Serb, Jewish and Catholic communities. This has never happened before.

I have good reason to believe the Church of Sweden will become a major participant in the Soul of Europe.

SECOND REPORT

DONALD REEVES

We visited Sweden from 13–19 May. This included a brief visit to Copenhagen.

The purpose of the visit was to secure interest in and commitment to the Soul of Europe and particularly to the Bosnia Project. Lazar Markovic joined us from Belgrade and made significant contributions to our presentations.

The Revd Pelle Lidbeck of St John's Church in Malmo invited me to preach on Sunday 14 May. He also set up a meeting of other churches in Malmo. As a result of our meetings and conversation, we have four or five parishes in Malmo who will become partners in the Soul of Europe. Once the Bosnia Project is grounded, most of the Lutheran churches of Malmo will become partners.

In Stockholm we visited the Ecumenical Centre and had meetings with Peter Brune of the Swedish Peace Movement, Margareta Ingelstam who has worked in Croatia, Michael Ellnemyr and Father Michael Sundkvist, both of them from the Swedish Orthodox Church which has around 100,000 members (Michael Sundkvist also represents Finland who are now committed to supporting us), and Anna Karin Hammar, Director of International Development in the Diocese of Lund and Chairperson of the Swedish Churches Work in Israel/Palestine.

The question I asked each person was: "What would it take for the Churches in Sweden to become partners in the Soul of Europe?"

This was their answer:

a) Present a proposal to the Swedish Christian Council. The fact that the Archbishop of Uppsala has agreed to be a patron will be in our favour. The proposal should be as detailed as possible about the Bosnia Project. If we are 'adopted' it will be possible to have the collections in Swedish Churches once a year given to the Soul of Europe. The Scandinavian Orthodox Churches are looking for a project in Bosnia to support.
b) Before a proposal is presented to the Swedish Christian Council, the Soul of Europe needs to have the support of another ecumenical Council, Churches Together in Britain and Ireland.
c) The Soul of Europe needs to be set up in such a way (in issues of governance, accountability, financial transparency etc.) that it is in a position to receive substantial donations.
d) The same points were made by the Revd Ane Hjerrild, the Secretary of the Danish Inter-Church Committee in Copenhagen. Her word counts and as we were leaving she said, "I am already thinking of people who can help you."

Lazar Markovic had just returned from Bosnia. He visited Sarajevo. From there he visited Bihac in Western Bosnia. The region of Bihac is one of the few areas of Bosnia where all three communities, Muslim, Serb and Catholic, had developed a tradition of living together in harmony before the war in 1992 shattered it. Bihac would therefore be the most appropriate place for the Project to happen. We will be visiting Sarajevo and Bihac in the next two weeks. On our return we will write a detailed report for the Council and if all goes well I shall ask the Council at its July meeting, at which Lazar will be present, to endorse our recommendations formally.

Visits

Question: Is it worth the energy, time and expense to meet busy people (whose lives are dominated by meetings)? After all it could all happen by e-mail. The answer is that our visits have been worthwhile every time. People appreciated the trouble we took to visit them, were impressed by our presentations and inspired by meeting us. As a result of our visits, the Soul of Europe is now part of the bloodstream of the Scandinavian Lutheran Churches and the Scandinavian Orthodox Churches. We learned that people had been talking about us and checking us out on their networks, even before meeting us. This would not have happened if we had engaged in correspondence alone.

Anna Karin Hammar

This was our most constructive visit. Anna Karin (I met her in Lund five years ago) also happens to be the sister of the Archbishop of Uppsala. She is formidable in her intellectual clarity and has much experience in the area of peacemaking and development. She also knows Bosnia. She made it absolutely clear that we must be "Catholic, Orthodox and Muslim" from the start, at the highest level in our Council as well as on the ground in Bihac, where partners in the project must have the support of their respective hierarchies. She underlined what we had already been discussing with Lazar on his return from Bihac, when we realized he would get nowhere without the trust of Muslims and Catholics, an alliance based on friendship. It will not be possible to get this representation in place immediately but we shall work towards this as quickly as possible, inviting the Catholic and Muslim hierarchies to suggest people. It is a priority. Lazar already has the blessing of his Orthodox bishop and is talking with the Muslim and Catholic leaders there whom we will be meeting when we go in the next two weeks. Trust and friendship between the faiths and communities are vital to the project, even before it gets off the ground.

Funding

I am haunted by two off-the-cuff remarks: Redmond Mullin said, "We must not run out of money." Anna Karin Hammar said, "Rushing is of the Devil."

In other words, at this crucial founding stage of the project we need donors who will be sympathetic to Anna Karin's observation that we have to get the process right and that this takes time. It cannot be rushed.

Our immediate tasks are: to prepare for Bosnia and July; to rewrite and publish a new leaflet; to develop a fundraising strategy; to search for sympathetic donors and covenants during this period of development; to prepare a 'proposal' for the Bosnia Project for Swedish, Danish, Finnish and Norwegian Christian Councils; to visit Churches Together in Britain and Ireland and the Orthodox and Catholic leadership, and establish contact once the proposal is in place with Conference of Europe Churches and European Catholic Bishops Conference; and, most urgently, to establish links with European Muslim leaders. They are to be represented on the Council and should be familiar with the Balkans.

Personal Comments

I celebrated my birthday in Copenhagen. As we left Stockholm I told Anna Karin Hammar that her brother had agreed to be our patron. "Well," she said, "He likes people like you!" She had also said earlier when committing her support for us: "You have a beautiful project." This is the second time that the word 'beautiful' has been used to describe the Soul of Europe and the Bosnia Project – quite specifically 'beautiful' as opposed to 'interesting', 'nice', or 'worthy'. This pleased us, because we want most of all to inspire and enthuse people and hope that the Bosnia Project will be born as a gift to the whole of Europe. Certainly Anna Karin's comments and others we are receiving validate the Soul of Europe. We have a long way to go but they encourage us.

The Soul of Europe. Who are we?

As the possibilities of the Bosnia Project materialize, the question, "Who are we?" needs to be addressed and answered.

Now we function under the auspices of a registered charity – CAFE – and we are served by an Advisory Council. Decisions about the development of the Soul of Europe have so far been taken by myself in consultation with Peter Pelz and Lazar Markovic, although I have always kept the Council in touch with developments and welcomed comments. I have taken or been given the freedom to begin the Soul of Europe.

However, we are about to approach substantial foundations and the European Union for funding. To be successful in our applications we need to start developing proper structures of accountability and financial transparency, and address issues around our governance. We are applying for charitable status but that is not enough.

There are of course legal matters to be considered. But there are also prior questions. What, for example, should be the relationship between the satellite projects and the centre? By satellites I mean the Bosnia Project, the Serbian Monasteries Project and other projects as they come on stream. How are decisions made? To whom, for example, are the employees of the Bosnia Project accountable? What is the role of the Chairman and Council?

I am not clear how we resolve these matters in an organic way. The trouble is that it all takes time and it is important to start the Bosnia Project as soon as possible. Donors will not be interested in an idea, however laudable, and at the same time we have to get our organization into shape and raise the necessary funds.

President and Chairman

The Soul of Europe is developing quickly. Lord Plumb feels he is not able to meet the inevitable growing demands on him as Chairman. I have therefore invited him to be our first President and he has accepted this invitation. I am most grateful to him for his encouragement and assistance in the early days of the Soul of Europe. He will continue to help us when he can.

The Rt Reverend John Austin, the Bishop of Aston, has agreed to be our Chairman. He will chair the Council Meeting on 10 July. I am most grateful to him for taking on this task.

SWEDEN

DIARY – PETER PELZ

The new bridge from Sweden to Denmark appears to stop halfway across the Baltic Sea and disappear into the water. Apparently it leads into a tunnel for the rest of the way. However, the impression of incompleteness, of stopping in mid-breath, reflected our mood about the Soul of Europe. The idea had sprung into life, full of possibilities, then suddenly found itself airborne but stuck in mid flight and staring with alarm at the ground far below. In Malmo, Pelle Lidbeck, the priest organizing our visit there, looked at us both wide-eyed and coolly detached, as though astounded at our confidence but expecting us to hit the ground with a bump and realize that the project in Bosnia could not possibly happen. For the first time I saw us as some others do, a perplexing trio consisting of a renegade priest, a Montenegrin bandit, and a crazy artist. So the first days in Sweden became a struggle to combat depression, sensing failure and the pointlessness of our mission. But by the end of our time there, particularly after the meeting with Anna Karin Hammar, certainly the most formidable of all the women we have met so far, her support, sympathy and understanding becoming a vindication of the Soul of Europe, we began to feel more positive about the future.

It turned out that most of the people we met had already talked about us before our arrival, with the Swedish Orthodox in touch with the Finns and clergy ringing one another up in between meetings. So the final assurances became a summation of our whole visit, and only as we left did we understand the process that led to their support, the behind-the-scenes discussions fuelled by the momentum generated by our talks, encounters, and journeys.

Crucial to our credibility in Scandinavia would be the quality of the work of the Soul of Europe. Archbishop Hammar of Sweden had already told Donald on a previous visit that our original leaflet left him cold: it was vague and woolly. But as soon as Donald had outlined the Bosnia Project the purpose of the Soul of Europe became clear and the Archbishop became enthusiastic, even agreeing in principle to be a patron. His reaction warned us that people in Scandinavia required concrete proposals, not just good intentions. On this visit we came with our Balkan colleague, Lazar, and also the name of a place where the Bosnia Project might happen. My reading of northern Europeans is that they pride themselves on their 'good works', spending money on humanitarian aid. Their money and active concern in the Balkans has become a gesture of moral defiance towards NATO, so that they feel no one can teach them anything. They are rebuilding the area. However, they come as outsiders, wealthy Europeans deciding and choosing where to bestow their largesse. Elsi Takala in Helsinki expressed this arrogance, particularly when she criticized the notion of rebuilding churches. She knew best what the Balkans needed. Of course she observed correctly how the erection of big 'fancy' churches and mosques in places such as Mostar had become politically hostile gestures, claiming high ground and further fanning the embers of ethnic hatred. But in the manner of pragmatic politicians from wealthy countries where business and money are paramount issues, she could not grasp the notion that, after a terrible war with so many atrocities, people might need spiritual sustenance and a new more human identity. Western Europe can bring money and expertise, but is unable, unqualified, and ignorant about helping to restore human values or bringing former enemies to live together in peace. Such values are of small concern to countries whose priorities are security and the preservation of wealth. So Lazar's presence is significant. He is not a recipient of charity but an initiator of a project which sets out to deal with all the important issues of reconciliation and reconstruction, on every level, human and practical. People from Western and Northern Europe may look at Donald and myself with indulgence, feeling no need to respond, but they cannot ignore Lazar. He represents what they are lacking. His presence might even sting their consciences and persuade them to support us.

Lazar had found a suitable site for our project, in the region of Bihac in Western Bosnia. He was bringing photos. He dismissed other areas with a wave of the hand: "Forget Brcko!" These places have the disadvantage, from our point of view, of having only two of the three ethnic groups living there, often with one group dominating. "Forget Sarajevo!" he said, telling us that this city is now overrun with agencies and humanitarian aid. Bihac is a remote area, on the whole neglected though we have since discovered that a right-wing Catholic organization is bringing aid there. What makes this place so special for the Soul of Europe is that the three main ethnic groupings in the Balkans, Muslims, Catholics and Orthodox, had lived at peace together there before the war and were now beginning to return. A tradition of mutual tolerance and even harmony has been shattered over the past decade, but at least the people are apparently prepared to start again. The only issue preventing the return of the weakest parts of the community, the Serbs and the Catholics, is lack of work. But Bihac happens to be an agriculturally rich region with potential for economic regeneration, trading with neighbouring Croatia and providing food for the resorts on the Adriatic coast. This will also be of benefit to the Soul of Europe: we can build a centre for peace and reconciliation there which will be self-financing. Farming and tourism will help to make the region thrive again.

Lazar also told us that Bihac is a beautiful area, with mountains, clean air, unpolluted rivers full of fish, waterfalls, "nature and all that stuff"!

We sailed across the Kattegat to Malmo in the late afternoon, the sun unseasonably hot so early in May, feeling confident with such a substantial project to present to the Swedes. Lazar would join us later next day – perhaps from Stockholm, perhaps from Copenhagen. The process of organizing visas for him had taken days of our time and exhausted our energies, the countries of Scandinavia no longer being signatories to the Schengen Agreement which allows travel for people from poorer, eastern European countries. Donald spent most of the week preceding our journey chasing up consulates, embassies, officials and dignitaries, generally finding they were 'out', in particular a Mr Bobic from the embassy in Belgrade, whose assistance was crucial. Most of the day we were informed he was "at a meeting" next door and would be back in "ten minutes". That legendary 'ten minutes'. Of course we never spoke to him. He remains a Kafkaesque figure, someone perpetually out of reach, although apparently only in the next room. At the end of each day Donald would be informed, triumphantly, that "Mr Bobic has gone home; please ring tomorrow." Lazar seemed to have no idea as to the complications and kept telling us blithely over the phone "not to worry – it will be all right!" If necessary he would smuggle his way into Sweden, an idea which only fuelled our stress. Even now, on our way to meet him for the first time since Serbia, we could not be sure of his arrival.

Malmo is a prosperous looking city, the streets crowded with young people socializing and cruising, spending their earnings. Once the new bridge is open, easy traffic with the continent will make the place even richer. Apart from a bizarre public monument depicting three naked men spouting water from every part of the body except the expected orifices, each hanging limp and dry, Malmo has no striking features. Robust blonde girls roam the streets in gangs, wearing short dresses and heavily soled shoes.

Pelle Lidbeck met us outside the station, his bald pate emphasizing the roundness of his eyes as he stared at us trying to understand why we had bothered to come to Sweden. Immediately my confidence vanished. Here in Malmo the Bosnia Project seemed irrelevant, the Balkans on a different planet of small concern to these affluent northern Europeans.

He settled us in a small, clean, and expensive hotel, and we looked forward to supper, having been travelling since crack of dawn. But Pelle insisted on taking us first round the city. The walk became a route march through shopping centres, across several large squares, everything looking identical. We worried about finding our way back, searching in vain for striking landmarks. Eventually we arrived at a busy square where young people filled a row of outdoor cafés. Here Pelle bought us a welcome beer and wine and we talked to him about the project, at which he smiled benignly but without committing himself. Behind him, athletic and well groomed young males moved around in large groups, eyes shining and looking expectantly for entertainment. I noticed how despite Pelle's remark about the ethnic groups being segregated in Malmo, the younger generation seemed to be well integrated, the world community equally represented. From the generally stylish clothes and grooming, affluence is what unites the disparate groups. There is no sign of poverty in the centre of Malmo.

Pelle glanced at his watch, as he would throughout our stay, anxious about his children, alone at home. He does not live on the job, as vicars do in England, but commutes to a neighbouring town, Lund. There his wife, a journalist on a woman's magazine, expects him to take care of the family while she works. She does not attend church. We discovered that no one there had ever met her. For Pelle, as for so many Swedish clergy, church constitutes a job, not a calling. The hours are set and at five o'clock the church closes like an office and the staff disappear beyond reach. We were therefore extramural work for Pelle, and we rapidly felt guilty at encroaching on his free time, particularly as his children needed attention.

Pelle left us. We were hungry and disorientated. We guessed the direction back to the hotel and as we crossed several squares and walked down pedestrian precincts we felt our spirits decline even further. How could we possibly interest the comfortable people of Sweden in the needs of another part of Europe?

On one of Donald's previous visits to Sweden, he met Archbishop Hammar and sensed positive and enthusiastic support. It had even been suggested that the combined collections from all the churches in Sweden on one particular Sunday should be donated to the Soul of Europe. Attending a service in Malmo next day and sitting alone with about forty souls scattered among the pews, it occurred to me that this kind proposal would yield only a meagre offering. And hearing the chink of small coins being deposited in the collection bags from a mostly elderly congregation I realized we would be lucky to afford even a secondhand bike for Lazar, let alone a car for his Bosnia journeys. Apparently the churches are only guaranteed to be full at Christmas.

St John's Church in Malmo is a classic example of art nouveau, as perfect in its unity of vision as a gothic cathedral. Substantial expense, imagination, and effort had gone into this now celebrated building. Three murals of severe, black-gowned Lutheran worthies, including Martin Luther above the altar, look out of place surrounded by a blend of fin-de-siècle decadence and piety. Angels striking camp poses are surrounded by thick foliage, twining branches, and heavy blooms; roses crown the low pillars, a richly ornamented organ case with much gold leaf in evidence towers at the back, and elaborate chandeliers hang from the high roof. In the extravagantly framed altarpiece adoring crowds surround a pre-Raphaelite Christ. The elegant lines of the curving architecture lead the eye up the wide windows to masonic symbols including a staring eye: God returning our gaze with fixed, unblinking intensity.

Half a dozen women and two men including the organist were rehearsing pieces with scrunching post-Grieg harmonies, when the back door opened and a disturbed woman shrieked at them. They stared at her in polite silence, the Swedes being clearly adept at remaining detached and cool in times of crisis. When she had finished raving and left, they continued with their ethereal music.

The sun shone through the expanse of glass and though the service was about to start hardly anyone had arrived yet, despite it having been well advertized because of Donald and the Soul of

Europe. Pelle had warned us about Sweden being a secular society. When the service started there were more people in the choir than in the pews. The shocking truth was at last sinking in that no one goes to church here. This beautiful space remains mostly empty. The question is: Why should people come? What might inspire them? And what were we doing here? Why should any of the elderly couples and several isolated women trying to remain invisible in the mostly deserted ranks of pews, be remotely interested in Bosnia? Tragic events happen to other people elsewhere in the world.

While Pelle apologetically greeted the scattered souls, as though fearing that the few people already seated might rise and leave, suddenly remembering more interesting commitments, the bells rang on the hour and a young man aged about twenty entered in haste and sat at the front. He glanced round at me shyly and smiled in greeting. I wondered why he had bothered to attend. He later introduced himself, and he turned out to be a theological student, training to be a priest and interested specifically in the Bosnia Project.

Throughout the service a disembodied voice spoke from the middle of the central candelabra, the sophisticated sound system making the proceedings seem remote, unreal and artificial. As Donald pointed out afterwards: "God has withdrawn from the Church. Everybody else has too!"

Donald also correctly surmised that no one would remember his sermon except for a joke, and that not even his own. His customary presentation is now polished to a shine and a young woman translated it into succinct Swedish. But despite the care and the fact that everyone had a translation to read, only the joke captivated everyone – and that one courtesy of Rabbi Lionel Blue, famous for his endearing self-deprecation, for instance describing his bouts of depression as "sitting alone in churches, weeping into my ice cream". He warns against long sermons and tells the story of a rabbi observing a man leaving the synagogue in the middle of his sermon. "Why are you leaving?" he asks angrily. "I'm going to have a hair cut," the man replies. "You should have thought of that before the service," scolds the rabbi. The man says, "I didn't need one then!" The solemn Swedes laughed out loud. Donald regularly preaches long sermons and Pelle had purposely restricted him to ten minutes. Hence the joke.

Afterwards Donald stood at the back to talk to anyone interested in the Bosnia Project. With the exception of one woman and the young man, who took a Soul of Europe leaflet and told us he wanted to be involved in our work, everyone else sidled out in embarrassment, eyeing Donald fearfully as though he might bite them. Before the service began, Pelle had announced that coffee would be served afterwards, but apparently the person responsible for brewing it hadn't turned up. Pelle then told us he had to return home to look after the children. We received the strong impression that his wife had no interest in or patience with his duties as a priest, probably considering his job as an indulgence and an irritating hindrance to his main responsibilities at home. Sunday is generally accepted as the priest's main work day and her demands struck me as particularly unreasonable. To make up for abandoning us, Pelle gave the organist and several members of the choir enough money to take us out to lunch. They informed us that they had never seen Pelle's wife and that priests on the whole keep their family lives separate from the church. They had no interest in the Bosnia Project whatever but spoke continuously about music, singing, and concerts in the church, giving me the impression they preferred the place to be empty so long as those continuing to worship were old people who needed consolation, an opinion which struck me as patronizing, conservative, and outdated. Our spirits plummeted further. With the exception of the young man whom we could not reckon on seeing again, no one had the slightest interest in our plans. We were silently and ruefully counting the cost of this journey and the bleak prospects of being given any financial assistance by the Swedish Church, when the organist proceeded to tell us that they were going to get rid of the present organ. It had been installed at great expense only ten years earlier but fashions had changed.

This baroque-style instrument, which sounded fine to me, could not perform late romantic organ music, now all the rage, to his exacting standards, so the church was now raising three quarters of a million pounds to install a new organ. Without discussion or consultation, a member of the parish council had gladly taken responsibility, and there would be no difficulty raising the money. We thought of the dwindling congregation, of the fact that only the choir and the organist were interested in the new organ, and also of our attempts to interest people in the Soul of Europe and the needs of Bosnia.

After recovering from the initial shock at this evidence of priorities, Donald channelled his fury into several meetings with important officials in the Swedish Church later in the visit. He spoke about God abandoning the Church and the officials who initially were treating us patronizingly, suddenly found themselves under judgement, sat up in alarm, paid attention, and became sympathetic.

The rest of the afternoon we waited for Lazar. We had invited Pelle to supper so that he could learn about the Bihac project and hopefully feel part of the team. First he had to look after his family, which meant a trip to the seaside in the afternoon. He agreed to join us at the dockside.

Added to the disappointing lack of response in Malmo, Donald felt depressed that a number of his Swedish friends and supporters failed to attend the service. Some of them are assistant priests at St John's, but when they aren't actually taking a service, they don't bother to attend. They are not compelled to and so they spend the weekends with their families. On the other hand, Donald's visit was a unique event and we would have expected them to be there.

Apparently several priests in Malmo found out later about Donald's visit and rang Pelle up complaining that they hadn't been told.

Two meetings had been organized for the next day. Pelle had written letters to different communities in Malmo, the Croats, the Serbs and the Muslims, inviting them to one in the morning. It occurred to me that a letter might not have been sufficient. Considering the hostilities between these communities, we would have had to visit each in turn, explaining the Soul of Europe in detail and gaining their confidence. Only we could have done that and Pelle could not be blamed for the lack of response. Lazar had arrived the night before, bearing several bottles of rakija and in high spirits about the project in Bihac. The three of us stood outside the parish office waiting to greet anyone who would turn up. A woman cycled past leisurely, her long skirt blowing in the warm breeze. Otherwise the streets remained empty as though there had been warning of a nuclear attack. Upstairs in the meeting room dozens of coffee cups stood in readiness, several flasks waiting to be poured, and large dishes piled high with homemade biscuits. It reminded us of the parable of the banquet to which no one comes, all having an excuse. But we could not even see a tramp or beggar to drag off the streets.

The afternoon meeting fared better. A dozen people turned up to listen to Lazar's slide lecture about Bihac. We looked at hilly landscapes with forests, waterfalls, and uncultivated meadows. The only ruined church on show happened to be Serb Orthodox, with Muslim graffiti sprayed over the walls and the local bishop standing outside next to a broadly smiling Lazar. No Catholic ruins, no mosque. We hoped the Swedes were not sharing our suspicions that the Orthodox intended to look after their own interests and ignore the other communities. On reflection we realised that Lazar did not have access to other churches, and that he needed the support of the bishop and his four monks, just as they welcomed his presence. It would be up to Donald and me to break the barriers once we arrived there.

The young man from the service attended the meeting and seemed to take a serious interest in the project. He wore shorts and had an exceptionally muscular pair of legs for a theological student. He then introduced himself as Philip Dagerklint and revealed that his hobby was flyweight boxing. He intended to bring some of his Muslim boxing mates to Bosnia. Suddenly this one enthusiast lifted our spirits. Philip spoke about his enthusiasm for theologians such as Paul Tillich. His intelligence, idealism, and youthful energy gave us hope.

After the meeting we celebrated the emergence of interest by eating the untouched biscuits. Then at 4 o'clock Pelle announced he had to go home. The office closed, and away he went.

DENMARK

DIARY – PETER PELZ

Our brief sortie across the water to Copenhagen before heading north for Stockholm coincided with a match between Arsenal and Galatasaray football clubs. Groups of young Turks swaggered noisily through the city while the English fans skulked in the aleys. The atmosphere could be cut with a knife and camera teams were as ubiquitous as the fans, everyone waiting for trouble.

We met Ane Hjerrild, another formidable woman who would be our most important contact in Denmark. She was the Secretary of the Danish Inter-Church Committee. After politely preparing the ground, telling us that we should send our proposals through a recognized ecumenical agency and that the Danish Church is ruled by the bishops because there is no other body like a synod, and so our proposals would have to be sent to her, she then suggested various other names to contact. It seemed as though we were being diplomatically rejected, but Donald and Lazar together made an equally formidable duo. Both spoke eloquently and Donald told her the story of the organ in Malmo. "God has abandoned the Church, etc." Ane Hjerrild stiffened respectfully, sensing that Donald meant business and would not leave without some substantial response. People have to meet Donald and engage in discussion face to face to realise that he has thought things through thoroughly and practically. He is not a weak clergyman. Nor is he woolly in his thinking. Once people learn that, they respect him and begin to think more positively about helping him. So we left Ane Hjerrild with the assurance that the Church of Denmark would support us, even financially. All we had to do was submit a concrete proposal that she could put before the Council. She will help us if she can.

As we returned to the boat for Malmo Donald bumped into his friend, the organist Gillian Weir, who happened to be giving a recital in a church in Copenhagen. "We really must stop meeting like this!" she beamed, embracing him. This had happened in Vienna some years ago, accidentally meeting in the Stephansdom, where, dressed in an elegant and spangly sheath, slit along the sides, she had captivated both the ears and the eyes of an astounded audience. She gave us an impromptu recital in the church, the organ sounding splendidly through the aisles, all packed with wooden sculptures, like a museum. Denmark is proud of its organs. They have a tradition of building these extravagant instruments going back centuries. Her fingers skipped lightly and effortlessly over Bach's Toccata and Fugue in D Major, modestly expressing her fear of tackling this music for a concert she had not realized would be transmitted live all over Europe the following evening. Musicians travel everywhere sharing a common language. People appreciate the moments of stillness, beauty, and absorption they provide.

Music is often the first messenger of reconciliation between peoples. When the Second World War ended, Yehudi Menuhin wasted no time in visiting Germany to perform violin concertos with Wilhelm Furtwängler. Being Jewish this gesture became particularly poignant as at the same time evidence of the atrocities and murders committed in concentration camps was being uncovered. Musicians were among the first to start the process of peace building in the Balkans. The American soprano Barbara Hendricks sang in Dubrovnik during the war in Bosnia and the Bosnian pianist Ivo Pogorelich played in Belgrade after the NATO bombing. Music calls on the basic humanity in all people. It can however also inflame nationalism and camouflage a regime of terror and violence. Orchestras played Strauss waltzes to drown the screams of victims in concentration camps. But when wars end, people turn needily to music first, and former enemies come together as friends and colleagues.

SWEDEN

DIARY – PETER PELZ

The Ecumenical Centre in Stockholm is smartly furnished with kitchen facilities and a dining area on each floor. The offices surround this public space and people meet and congregate here. The atmosphere is conducive to relaxed, unhurried, and friendly discussions. For private meetings we only had to move to one of the office rooms. When we arrived it became immediately apparent that we had been talked about already. The decision to support and help us had already been taken. We came weighed down by the disappointment of Malmo, only to find the weights lifted from us one by one.

The meetings increased in importance as the day progressed. First the coordinator of the Swedish Peace Movement, a young man called Peter Brune, tall and willowy, eased our tensions by declaring his support for everything we were doing. He then introduced us to a smiling woman, Margareta Ingelstam, who discussed the Bihac Project with us in depth, from her own experience with a similar project in Croatia, in the city of Ocijek. We would need to draw on the experience and wisdom of the people involved in that project. She gave us books and leaflets about it. She had a gentle laugh and seemed to be completely unfazed by any stress. When a woman approached as we left, clearly a stranger, and accosted Margareta with the tiresome reproach, "You don't remember me!" Margareta simply smiled even more sweetly and made out as though she did, then added softly and kindly, "Please wait a moment while I say goodbye to my friends!" I admired her handling of a tricky moment.

Later we met the Orthodox contingent, two young men, one of whom was a priest and looked barely twenty years old, but turned out to be the lynchpin of the Orthodox Church in Sweden in its connections with Finland. He had in fact been sent to communicate with us. Both of them, Peter Elnemyr and the priest, Mikael Sundkvist, stated categorically that they would support us in every way. They had been waiting for a project like ours. Again, as with Ane Hjerrild in Copenhagen, they needed a concrete proposal to set before their various councils.

Finally we met an extraordinary woman. Robust but with a gentle expression, eyes looking seriously straight at you and smiling warmly, Anna Karin Hammar happens to be the sister of the Archbishop of Sweden, but is clearly a formidable presence in her own right. She brought our peregrinations in Scandinavia to a most positive end. Having introduced herself as a 'contextual feminist' she questioned us closely and sharply, evidently wanting to reassure herself that we were not idle dreamers, woolly thinkers, or generally incapable. Lazar spoke in English for about a quarter of an hour without stopping, explaining the Bihac Project from every dimension, political, theological, ecological, sociological, and even bringing in the imagination. Afterwards he told me that he realized how important this meeting might be, and how influential and qualified Anna Karin was, and he knew he had to be absolutely at his best. Now I understood what she meant by context. She underlined the crucial importance of "taking our time" and "not rushing" (quoting the Latin tag, "Rushing is of the Devil"), of making friends and gaining the trust of Muslims in particular, and of all three communities at every level, from top to bottom. In other words we had to find allies and friends right away, amongst ourselves. We had been discussing this already. Lazar would first have to join forces with at least one Muslim in the area and also a Catholic before we even began to plan the project. And that takes time, even if it is a realistic possibility. But Anna Karin now encouraged us.

For a moment Lazar was put on the spot. She questioned his Serbian allegiance (hinting at 'denial') and though he did not even attempt to argue, he acquitted himself well by reminding her of history, of the lack of evidence on every side, and that she must not judge the situation only from one side. Lazar never crumbles and his honesty is disarming. So even Anna Karin softened. When we left her she kissed both Donald and me once, but Lazar she embraced warmly and kissed him three times.

We ended our visit to Sweden with jokes and laughter. When Donald, slightly self-deprecatingly, spoke of himself as being a maverick, she countered, "That is why we love you!"

So feeling valued and encouraged in every way, we also parted from Lazar and took the next train to Malmo and a boat to Copenhagen for the flight home.

On that flight we witnessed a fight between the English and Turkish fans on their way back to London. The English were needling the young Turks until a confrontation became inevitable – fortunately not until they had been thrown off the plane at Heathrow. Violence generates a sexual intensity: men love it.

BOSNIA

June 2000

REPORT – DONALD REEVES

"I asked the general why he was destroying our churches. 'Churches,' he replied, 'are the heart of your life and identity. If we destroy the heart – your community will be shattered.'" Bishop Franjo Komarica, Catholic Bishop of Banja Luka. From 1992–1999 in his diocese, ninety-eight per cent of the churches were either destroyed or damaged and some ninety per cent of Catholic congregations were displaced. Six priests were tortured and killed.

"I am very happy to be in your country. I have always wanted to visit Bosnia…" There followed an interruption by some hundred students heckling in good humour. One shouted back: "We are the Srpska Republic!" Donald Reeves speaking about the Soul of Europe in Banja Luka to a group of students studying mechanical engineering and computer technology and attending a lecture on the part Orthodox Christianity played in the recent war.

"I am a mufti without a mosque. There were sixteen in Banja Luka. Now there are none. All were systematically destroyed at night in a military operation. We can never forget but we have to try and forgive." Mufti Edhem Camdzic, Banja Luka, in his office, the only Muslim building left in the city. Only a week before our conversation, on 30 May, attempts had been made to set fire to this building. The doors remain heavily charred.

"Do you know the name Omarska? The concentration camp? I was there. When they came to take me away, in front of my children, they put a knife against my throat and asked them, 'Would you like to see your father's throat cut or shall we take him to prison?' I was there for two months. They beat me every day. I was then an imam. I used to meet with a group of religious leaders. None of them visited me in the camp. I begged for help. One Orthodox priest said to my children, when I sent them to inform him and ask him to help release me from the camp: 'If mufti is innocent nothing bad will happen to him. If he is innocent they will let him go.' " Mufti Hasan Makic of Bihac. He was understandably reluctant to meet us.

"Canadian engineers saved us and the building. The mines had been laid in such a way that if we had opened the door we would have been instantly killed and the whole building destroyed." Brother Sophronje, one of three monks still attending the fifteenth-century Orthodox church at Martin Brod, south of Bihac. They wait to rebuild the destroyed Rmanj Monastery next to it.

"I encourage my people to return – but if they have no work they will leave." Bishop Chrysostom, Diocese of Bihac. He still has no home or office. He lives in a hotel in the town of Shipovo.

"We are like fish on dry ground without water. We need help now. We cannot wait while people talk and promise." Father Anto, Bihac Catholic community, responding to my statement that we need time before the Soul of Europe can make concrete proposals.

"Give us this day our daily bread… Deliver us from evil…" Donald Reeves was invited to say the Lord's Prayer by Bishop Komarica in his chapel beside the photos of six murdered priests and a nun. By the altar stands a sculpture of the Madonna and Child, the only statue left undamaged in a destroyed church.

"You have fine ideas. Please keep them going until our next meeting. Religious practice is increasing, but we have to base it on proper foundations because we are aware that no religious person can live from faith alone. You bring faith, dialogue and discussion together with especial emphasis on economic reconstruction. That is the beauty of your project. The centre for peace and reconciliation should bear the three symbols of the three faiths. Your work and personal contacts will help bring Bosnia into Europe as a democracy. If someone has work he will learn to love other religions, other people. But without work, his future is without hope." Ifet Sisic, First Minister in the Department of Trade and Industry, Una Sana Canton, Bosnia, welcoming the Soul of Europe unreservedly and intending to share our proposals with the President of Bosnia and Herzegovina, because our objectives "cross the boundaries of different ministries and is of national importance".

"There is much darkness here. Even the smallest candle gives us hope." Bishop Komarica responding to our visit. He may have been referring to our logo.

The Situation

This brief, highly condensed and over-simplified background may help to make sense of our visit to Bosnia.

As reports of atrocities during the recent war there began to disturb the western conscience, attempts were made internationally to solve the conflict. The Peace Conference began in Dayton, Ohio in November 1995. The final agreement was signed in Paris in December.

It was agreed that Bosnia would retain its pre-war external boundaries but would be composed of two parts. The Federation of Bosnia Herzegovina would administer fifty-one per cent of the country including Sarajevo. The Bosnian Serb Republic of Bosnia Herzegovina including Banja Luka (now commonly referred to as the Srpska Republic) would administer forty-nine per cent of the country. The federation is predominantly Muslim, especially in western Bosnia, the main city of which is Bihac, where our first project will be based. The Srpska Republic is almost entirely Orthodox.

The signing of the Dayton Agreement brought to an end the wholesale bloodshed. But it has failed to lay foundations for a lasting peace. The Serbian authorities in Banja Luka have blatantly failed to comply with the provisions of the agreement. Non-Serbs are prevented from returning, and the present authorities continue to refuse even the most minimal protection for all non-Serb minority groups in Banja Luka. There are similar difficulties for the non-Muslim groups in the Bihac area.

The Report

Our visit to Bosnia tested us intellectually, spiritually, and emotionally. So what follows is written in a more personal style, to attempt to convey a sense of what we experienced.

No one can visit western Bosnia without being struck by the beauty of its landscape. Valleys, rivers, waterfalls, forests, hills, and meadows full of every species of wild flower provide a poignant backdrop to the sites of destroyed villages and memorials to the dead.

Banja Luka and Bihac are typical central European provincial towns. We encountered people who had survived the war of 1992–1996, still scarred by the witness and endurance of suffering on a scale impossible for us in the West to imagine. But we also noticed the new generation strolling through the parks and along the street in the early evening. Young women dressed stylishly and young men carefully groomed themselves, ignoring the muezzin call to prayer from the central mosque in Bihac. Their self-assurance, poise, and friendliness suggested a positive change of attitude. Perhaps, just perhaps, the war represented the final destructive death throes of a repressive and corrupt totalitarian regime. The old guard, once high ranking communist officials, turned militantly nationalist and fanned the flames of ethnic hatred in order to hold on to power. Many are still in power, but once this old guard have passed away, the majority of the new generation will build a new and more tolerant society. There will always be minorities of resistance and resentment, as there are in the West, but everyone we encountered expressed a genuine desire to live in peace and welcomed the possibilities of peaceful coexistence and reconciliation.

As we drove from Zagreb to Banja Luka, I wondered, not for the first time, what we were doing in this part of Europe. The

Soul of Europe is such a young, fragile organization that to think of working in the Balkans seemed just foolish. I also wondered what kind of welcome, if any, we might receive. I was therefore clear that whatever might emerge from our visit, we would hold on to five principles:

1. We will become a European organization. Whatever project emerges in Bosnia will involve young Europeans from all over Europe.
2. We will assist in rebuilding ruined churches and mosques. Such reconstruction has to be an integral part of a wider social, political, and economic restructuring. An essential factor of the rebuilding is that it will be undertaken collaboratively with the different religious communities.
3. We will develop, as part of the above, imaginative, ecologically responsible opportunities for small businesses to flourish.
4. We will create opportunities for peace-building and the long hard work of reconciliation.
5. We will nourish the imagination. We will see that whatever projects develop they will have an incomplete, ongoing, open quality which will say to the rest of us in Europe: "This is how we are trying to live together."

Visit to Banja Luka

The most significant visits were with Bishop Komarica and Mufti Camdzic. I have invited both to be our patrons for our work in Bosnia. The bishop saw us for two hours. His theological and political reflections on 'Reconciliation, Return and Reconstruction', a lecture given in Rome in January this year, are essential reading. I sense he is naturally gentle, shy, and compassionate, but circumstances have forced him into a more prophetic role. He is also a courageous man. He welcomed us kindly. At the end of our meeting we prayed in the chapel and he blessed me, embracing me warmly. We have a friend in Bishop Komarica. He was also sharp in his comments on our proposals. He appreciated the time we were devoting to our assessment but said that "we must always seek out the truth".

Mufti Camdzic of Banja Luka was an angry and bitter man. He told us that there had been no fighting in Banja Luka during the war because the Serbs were the dominant majority. The destruction of the sixteen mosques in the city was a planned military operation. Overnight these centuries' old beautiful buildings were razed to the ground and nothing was left to indicate their presence, not a single stone. Just a bare patch of land. The mufti alerted us to the scandal of his being a mufti without a mosque. Imagine the Bishop in Exeter without a cathedral or a single church. There is nowhere for the 4,700 Muslims still living in Banja Luka to worship. This denial of the basic human right to be allowed to worship is a flagrant breach of the United Nations Declaration of Human Rights.

I am therefore going to seek out the Muslim leadership in the UK, to ask them to invite Mufti Camdzic and the other muftis in Bosnia to London to seek public support for the rebuilding of the mosques in Banja Luka, and then to take this matter to the European Union, and wherever it will help, to put pressure on the politicians in Banja Luka to allow this rebuilding to take place. It is not only the least I can do, but any success we achieve in this objective will naturally open doors for our own project in Bihac, a predominantly Muslim region of Bosnia.

The Orthodox Church

I met a deacon working with young Orthodox people who invited me to address a gathering of students in Banja Luka. I sensed a genuine openness and willingness to participate in our multi-faith proposals, including their cooperation in the rebuilding of mosques in Banja Luka.

I had the good fortune to meet Professor Radovan Bigovic, a well-known theologian from Belgrade who was giving a series of lectures on spirituality in Banja Luka. He has a considerable following among young people, being radical and unpopular with the authorities because of his condemnation of Serb atrocities in the war. He told me that the Serbian Orthodox Church would like to know more about Anglicanism. He asked me to suggest books about Anglicanism which he would arrange to have translated into Serbo-Croat. He would also like to explore the possibility of exchanges between Serbian Orthodox ordinands and Anglican ordinands. I asked him if women ordinands would be welcome. He said, "Absolutely!" In fact many women are studying Orthodox theology in the Balkans. I will be in touch with the Bishop of London about these matters.

Visit to Rmanj Monastery and Bihac

We arrived half a day late and missed the Liturgy of the Ascension to which we had been invited. Renting a car in Bosnia is no easy matter, because of the refusal of companies to offer insurance, and the difficulty finding a suitable and affordable vehicle. Our first car had faulty brakes! The second one also had several faults. Eventually we arrived in Martin Brod, a remote village, and met three monks in their early thirties together with Bishop Chrysostom and an ordinand. We came away with a long shopping list. The bishop needs to rebuild the ruined church in Bihac and the monastery in Martin Brod. He also wants help with setting up businesses. Without work people simply cannot and will not return to the area. The communities have a need for plumbers, farmers, and public transport. At present there is no way at all for people without a car to travel between villages. The bishop said, "If we fail to find work for them, the few people still remaining will leave." The monks are determined to remain. They welcomed us warmly with much generosity despite their evident poverty. They continue to say their offices in the church. Towards the end of the war, mines had been attached to the front door in such a way as to destroy the whole building and kill the monks at the same time. A Canadian unit from SFOR found these in time and saved their lives.

We were invited to a shortened Vespers and I was asked to say the Lord's Prayer. The words: "Give us this day our daily bread", "Forgive us our trespasses as we forgive those who trespass against us" and "Deliver us from evil" take on a special urgency in these circumstances.

I have asked the bishop to be a patron of the Bosnia Project. I wonder how the young Orthodox in Banja Luka could support the work of their churches in Bihac. Helping first of all to rebuild a mosque in Banja Luka will certainly open doors for them there.

Bihac

We met Mufti Makic, whom I quoted at the beginning of this report. He met us reluctantly and offered us initially ten minutes but did not hurry the meeting. In the event we had half an hour. He evidently and understandably mistrusts all Christians. But he indicated that though we could not expect him actively to support our multi-faith proposals, he made it clear that he would not stand in our way. He would also be happy to come to London with the other muftis if he were invited. In fact he expressed a strong desire to visit England. The meeting ended cordially.

We met the Catholic priest of Bihac, Fra Anto, who is trying hard to keep his small community together and works on a range of welfare projects with hardly any resources.

We also met the secular authorities of Bihac in the persons of the Head of the Department of Trade and Industry, Mr Sisic, the Education Secretary, Mr Trgic, and the Minister for Small Businesses. They were most welcoming, as can be gathered from the quote at the beginning of this report. They clearly want Bosnia to become an integral part of Europe and want to be kept in touch with every aspect of the work of the Soul of Europe as it develops. Their support will be crucial for us and of course we will cooperate with them.

We are still working out the next steps of the Soul of Europe. Our visit to Bosnia brought the first year of its existence to a conclusion, full of possibilities for the future. We will first visit Sarajevo and meet our Muslim contacts there including the Reis ul Ulema, Dr Ceric, the Chief Mufti, the High Representative, ambassadors, and our friend, Saba Risaluddin. Then we will resume contact with Bihac and begin the long, slow, and painstaking process of discovering what we can do together there and hopefully establish a Centre for Reconciliation and Peace. Donald Reeves will proceed in mobilizing Muslim communities in Europe to put pressure on the politicians in Banja Luke to allow the rebuilding of mosques there.

BOSNIA

DIARY – PETER PELZ

Going to Bosnia

"Don't forget your flak jacket!" Baggage attendant at Heathrow.

Entering Northern Bosnia from Croatia, the road narrows and crosses a plain towards Banja Luka. Family houses line the road, each surrounded by a plot of land cultivated with vegetables and fruits, most with a small vineyard, poultry scratching under the trees, and a cow or a tethered goat grazing the lawn. Peasant women in kerchiefs mop their brows on the roadside, leaning on pitchforks, and men sit on carts laden with early summer hay and drawn by donkeys. Young people lounge in roadside cafés watching the traffic pass.

There is no sign of ruined villages, damaged churches, or the debris of war.

This is the Srpska Republic, the half of Bosnia firmly controlled by the Bosnian Serbs and apparently untouched by the events of the last decade. We arrived at Banja Luka in the early evening, the hills rising behind the town, thickly forested, the scene reminding me of the lower foothills of the Alps in Austria. There is no sign of tourism and farms and small villages are scattered over the slopes. The sun set behind the western hills and the streets teemed with young people socializing in the cool of the evening.

Banja Luka is mostly a twentieth-century town with typically plain communist architecture, concrete tower blocks standing in rows against the wooded slopes. The wide, deep, cool River Vrbas flows through the town centre. A castle with a restaurant perches on a rock immediately above a bend in the river, providing a splendid view. In the *Guide To Eastern Europe* Banja Luka boasts the alarming qualification of being the least desirable place to visit in Eastern Europe. For all its neglect and the terrible history of the last decade, including the destruction of all its mosques and the persecution of Muslims and Catholics, the evidence of this deliberate policy of obliteration has been comprehensively erased and the town gives an impression of peace and activity. But appearances can be deceptive, and though the town has charm and the mostly young people are friendly and hospitable, the question remained: Who are the people who committed these outrages, where are they, and why is it so easy to remove evidence of destruction? We know that the leaders and main perpetrators are in hiding. But looking at the amicable young people strolling down the streets and making us warmly welcome in the smart new hotel, it is hard to imagine that this generation would have anything to do with the crimes and atrocities of their parents.

First impressions of the people in Bosnia turned out to be accurate, not deceptive, as can often be the case. We came expecting ruffians, armed and vengeful, living among ruins and resentful of critical foreigners. The destruction and the atrocities became evident soon enough, but rapidly we learnt that on the whole, human nature, even after outbursts of extreme depravity, yearns for civilized coexistence. People everywhere have basic and simple needs: to get on with life, find enough to eat, and feel protected under their own roof. After talking to representatives from different sides, the picture sketched in the first impressions became clearer and universal. The divisions in Bosnia are clearly marked. The majority in each area have total control and the remaining minorities suffer powerlessly. Forests of minarets proclaim the Muslim majority in their part of the Federation of Bosnia and Herzegovina; signs written in the Cyrillic script proclaim the Serb majority in the other half, the Srpska Republic, to make it clear that it does not consider itself part of the Federation. As for the Catholics, they control small pockets and towns but are invisible elsewhere. However, it is not religious or ethnic intolerance which prevents the people from moving back into mixed communities and living together, but crucially the lack of work. This beautiful region of Europe is economically stagnant. Naturally the majorities look after their own first, which inhibits cooperation and collaboration between the different groups. Survival appears to be a rapid healer of wounds, but clearly people have not yet begun to deal with the atrocities and destruction of war. They are still demanding basic requirements, homes, jobs and security. Humanitarian aid agencies have moved to Kosovo and were anyway chiefly based in Sarajevo, so that other regions of Bosnia remain neglected. It is basically a secular society, a heritage of Communism, yet wherever the faiths are in a minority, they help everyone in need, of whatever persuasion. But after the deliberate destruction of churches and mosques during the war, these minorities no longer have buildings to worship in. Freedom of worship is a basic human right which urgently needs attending to in Bosnia. Money seems to be in plentiful supply to build large, gaudily decorated Orthodox churches in the Srpska Republic and the towns and villages in Muslim Western Bosnia bristle with shiny new minarets. Most of the people on the streets show no interest in these buildings and are secretly resentful that money can be found for them, but not for improving their lives. Young Muslim girls parade the streets of western Bosnia dressed in the latest fashions, resembling Spice Girls, their tarty appearance turning its back on the mosques now attended mostly by the few elderly survivors of the war, though in the Bihac Mosque we noticed a striking presence of young fundamentalist Muslim worshippers, hostile to strangers. In Orthodox Banja Luka there is not a single mosque for the Muslim minority there to worship in, and the only Orthodox church in Muslim Bihac is still in ruins, the walls daubed with graffiti announcing the triumph of the armies of Allah.

Everybody we met expressed a genuine willingness to live at peace with one another again, which surprised me. There did not seem to be any bitterness or resentment, not even from those who suffered most. Those who committed atrocities are judged to be criminals and murderers, and most people from all the different communities are recognized as being decent people who should not be blamed for the crimes of the few. However, there were a number of people we did not dare talk to, men in their thirties and forties who appeared to have enough money to drive expensive cars and eat in restaurants. They resented even being looked at, and I would not have dared to photograph them. Clearly SFOR, the peace-keeping force patrolling Bosnia, is still needed. The more we met and spoke with people, the more we realized how necessary and welcome our project was. Far from being interfering outsiders, we were seen as Europeans helping to bring Bosnia back into Europe. Each community hoped that we would rebuild their churches and help them in particular, as a priority. Most of all, everybody approved of our plans to include economic regeneration as a major part of the project, and everyone was touched by our willingness to visit their country. As for our plan to rebuild ruined churches in one particular place, given the situation I have described, this would need some radical reappraisal. However, our proposal to establish a centre for peacebuilding could not be more relevant and necessary.

Two impressions override all others: the beauty of the countryside and the large crowds of friendly, mostly young people everywhere, in towns, in villages, and on the road. They survived. In the rest of Europe young people are the future. In Bosnia the future is here and now.

Banja Luka

Our arrival began with an adventure. Lazar had decided to attend a lecture instead of greeting us at the hotel. He left instructions at reception, but the slender girl with model good looks could only point us roughly in the direction of the university, about half a mile away. "Across the bridge, and you're there," she said, smiling sweetly. Lazar had assumed we would communicate by mobile phone, but our phones did not function in the Srpska Republic. We walked apprehensively through the dark along a busy road which lead to the concrete tower blocks in the distance. We crossed the bridge and although we had evidently reached the university campus, we had no clue as to where Lazar might be. Fortunately two students took pity on us, and having consulted each other as to the location of an evening lecture, led us round several blocks, along dark alleys, and into an empty building. Eventually they opened a door into a lecture room and there sat Lazar, smiling and beckoning us in.

Exhausted after a long day's travel from Crediton to Banja Luka, we had little enthusiasm for attending a lecture in Serbo-Croat at nine in the evening, and so we waited for him to come out – which he did promptly. "You have to hear this lecturer," he insisted. "He is most important, a very good man." We would meet Professor Radovan Bigovic the next day, an eminent academic from Belgrade, an Orthodox priest and a noted critic of Milosevic. He supports our project wholeheartedly and intends to forge new links with the Anglican Church in Serbia, commissioning translations of Anglican theological books. He will also be an important ally and support to Lazar. So we crept back into the lecture hall. A hundred students, male and female in equal numbers, were paying close attention to the professor. None of them was studying theology and it astonished us that these secular youngsters, scientists and economists, had bothered to turn up. Imagine similar numbers of science students in England attending a lecture by an Anglican theologian late in the evening! Professor Bigovic spoke about the shared responsibility and guilt of all communities in the recent wars, particularly the Serbs. This sounded like dangerous insurrection here in the heartland of the Bosnian Serbs where the main aggression had been planned. We were quickly learning that assumptions about the people here needed reappraisal. I had expected most of them to be even more entrenched in their ethnic hatreds than ever, since the war had delivered no victory to either side and the Dayton Accord had forced everybody into an uneasy truce. The students applauded the young professor, a handsome priest with a melancholy martyr expression and clearly an inspiration to the next generation.

As the questions from the floor came to an end Lazar brought Donald forward to speak. The professor and his young assistant rose to their feet deferentially and smiled in welcome. "I am very happy to be in Bosnia," Donald began, at which point the students moved restlessly and I tried to hide under the bench. After some good humoured catcalling a student shouted from the back, "We are the Srpska Republic!" I felt nervous, but they were amused by Donald's gaffe. However, there is clearly a long way before Bosnia can be seen to be the shared homeland for Serbs as well as Muslims and Catholics. Despite the soothing words of peace and reconciliation by the professor, the divisions in the Federation of Bosnia remain hard and fast. Donald then spoke about the Bosnia Project, appealing to the students to be involved in the rebuilding of mosques as well as churches. Again I looked nervously for a place to hide, but the students welcomed the proposal. Perhaps the ground is ready for this project, even in fiercely Serb territory. They applauded loudly and voiced their readiness to help in any proposals which furthered reconciliation and peaceful collaboration.

As Lazar had already told us in Sweden, people in Bosnia know that they have no choice but to learn to coexist. They do not have to love one another, but fighting and killing one another is no longer an option. Working towards reconciliation and collaboration will not be easy, and I remembered the words of the ambassador from Bosnia in London telling Donald how necessary our project was, that the people here needed help from the outside to learn how to live together again.

We expected to have supper with the professor, but, its being past ten o'clock, he declined and agreed to meet us next morning. Lazar then led us through the darkness to the main road where students congregated in large numbers, enjoying the cool night air after a hot June day. A taxi took us to the castle restaurant overlooking the River Vrbas. Its waters gush from the depths of the hills nearby and so the river never warms up, even in the hottest summer. The cool air from below refreshes guests on the terrace and the view takes in the town on the opposite bank and the forested hills beyond.

The hotel in Banja Luka turned out to be so new that it had only been open four days and we were among the first guests. Despite the polished marble and high-quality furnishings, the important utilities had not been thought about, as though the place had been designed by men who were interested only in appearances and a well-stocked bar in the lobby, round which congregated the staff, their friends, and occasional guests. The showers worked inefficiently and leaked, having been inexpertly plumbed, and there was limited space in the rooms for luggage, with nowhere to hang towels and put toiletries. Some rooms provided access to the Internet, with a mass of equipment and a cat's cradle of flexes to negotiate in the middle of the floor. At breakfast the waitress smiled and poured glass after glass of orange juice, but the coffee arrived as an elegant espresso in a minute portion. A severe-looking chef rustled up omelettes in a tiny kitchen in response to any order for eggs, whether boiled or fried. The menu made no difference. Whatever we ordered, something else appeared: we just smiled and said thank you. The staff are uniformly polite, friendly, young, and strikingly attractive, as though the country had been scoured for the best-looking young men and women. The night porter in his chest-hugging vest and with his tanned muscles could have starred in any American soap, but had insufficient attitude, being far too polite and friendly. Nor did they appear bored, though most of the time they sat around doing nothing, waiting for the phone to ring. Life runs at a different tempo here and we have to forget our Western haste and impatience.

The Professor and the Deacon

After breakfast the professor arrived with his young assistant, a deacon, and we talked in the hotel lobby, the young staff looking on amazed at the rare sight of men in black cassocks.

Dialogue should continue on two levels, according to Professor Bigovic. The Christians have their specific problems (assuming these to be the unresolved conflicts between Catholics and Orthodox), but there should also be joint multi-faith dialogues, especially with Islam. Donald said that the project goes beyond dialogue, though dialogue must continue on the model of action and reflection, learning by doing. They agreed that now is the time for practical theology. "We must do whatever is real." "We must do something which is acceptable to people here, slowly and carefully, bringing people along."

The professor talked about organizing a theological symposium for 2001 which could be a dialogue leading to future dialogues about the Soul of Europe. Donald talked about funds and money. The Centre in Bihac is an important project. It will involve local communities so that the people who live there feel that it is theirs. "Nothing is real unless it is local."

The deacon runs an Orthodox Youth NGO which will cooperate with the project. If young people from all over Europe visit and help, the local people will not feel isolated. The professor stressed the importance of young people meeting one another, and that women should not be excluded, and that there could be exchanges with Anglicans. Donald asked whether women ordinands would be welcome and the professor answered, "Of course!"

Finally we spoke about the situation in Bosnia and recent history, the reasons for the atrocities and destruction. The professor talked of parts of the Serbian Orthodox Church being a mixture of pagan nationalism and petrified conservatism. He spoke quietly and earnestly, looking pale and ill. We were told later that he suffered from cancer and had already had two operations. He continues to criticise the government in Serbia and was therefore constantly in danger of being arrested. Until recently, opinions were still a matter of life and death in the Balkans.

The Mufti of Banja Luka

It was time to meet our first Muslim in Bosnia. Lazar took us to a patch of wasteland, a rectangular piece of ground with grass growing and beyond it a house where a man waited to take us upstairs to the mufti. As we entered he pointed at the charred doors and told us that people had set fire to the building only the week before. Fortunately a friendly neighbour alerted the authorities. There is still a hard core of ethnic cleansers who would like to eliminate every trace of Muslims in the town. But SFOR enforces peaceful relations and stamps down on these acts of vandalism.

The flat rectangular piece of ground is the site where the main mosque of Banja Luka once stood. Judging from photographs it had been a large, elegant, and beautiful building, a jewel of Muslim architecture dating from the sixteenth century. In 1979 it had already been vandalized and photos depict it with a broken minaret and rubble falling from the dome and roof. There had been no fighting in Banja Luka during the recent war but in a planned military action the mosque was systematically destroyed along with all fifteen others in the town, not a stone remaining to show what once stood there, all razed to the ground and cleared. As we walked through the entrance hall of the mufti's house we noticed a few remnants of the great building, the Ferhadija Mosque built by command of the Pasha Ferhad in 1579. The building was erected out of the ransom money paid by an Austrian general for the release of his son, in addition to the liberation of one hundred Turkish prisoners. Over the entrance had been written: "This sublime building was ordered by the Pasha Ferhad, friend of the faithful, in the name of God. This place was created in Allah's name for all the faithful." So, a war four centuries ago led to the building of a place of worship. Now, in the last decade, a war deliberately annihilated a place of worship. The surviving stones must have been rescued by devout Muslims before they fled the town. The few remnants show traces of delicate decorative symbols and patterns in pale blue. They resemble bits of bones left from a corpse that people have tried to burn without leaving a trace. Looking back at the empty rectangle of ground it was impossible to imagine the mosque ever being there. That was precisely what the Bosnian Serb militia intended when they destroyed it. A ruin reminds people of the vandalism and remains a remonstrance to all who see it. The empty space gives the illusion that nothing has been there in the first place. This is Banja Luka, a town which looks peaceful and ordinary with sixteen empty spaces and no explanation for them. But a few brave people remain to remind the rest of the world what happened, to remonstrate for these empty spaces.

In my book *The Road to Chartres*, I describe my visit to a town in eastern Germany from where Jewish families had been sent to be killed in Auschwitz, and how I experienced the strange, bleak sensation of empty spaces once occupied by these people. Their neighbours had tried to cleanse the town of these despised aliens, but the memory of their existence persists. The same sensation came to me as I looked at the flat grass-covered rectangle where the Ferhadija Mosque once stood.

The mufti, in a long black coat and fez, small in stature but vigorous and alert with the athletic build and rugged countenance of a farmer used to years of hard labour in the fields, stood in the middle of an elegantly but simply furnished room. He gestured us to sit round a table, a large bowl of apricots standing in the middle, and the man who had brought us upstairs served coffee and fruit juice. The mufti looked at us steadily, seriously, and questioningly while Donald spoke about the Soul of Europe and our project in Bosnia. The mufti was trying to judge our sincerity. His sad, haunted eyes were set in an expression resigned to extreme disappointment and never-ending problems. Occasionally he smiled bitterly at Donald's jokes. Thinking of the destroyed mosques or the fire started by fanatics to burn his residence and kill him inside only a week before, how could one begin to imagine what these last ten years must have been like for him?

We expected some hostility or at least defensiveness from our first Muslim in Bosnia, but he replied to Donald's presentation in the friendliest manner. He had visited England, at the time of the Islamic Exhibition in London in the 1970s, and told us a story about getting lost in Harrods, including a joke against himself. He intended to ask for help from some shoppers there and instead of excusing his lack of English the first words came out as, "*You* don't speak English!" For the first time his rugged face softened into a gentle laugh.

"As a man and a mufti I am glad you have come!" he announced with quiet solemnity. He then expressed his gratitude to the English who had saved his life in 1995 by releasing him from the Busovica concentration camp. He prayed every day for his liberators. He said nothing more about his experiences in the camp. He stressed that the war was over in Bosnia. SFOR helped a lot, and he was grateful also to the Pope who visited Bosnia during the worst period of the war, and to the Roman Catholic bishop of Banja Luka, Komarica, who had helped Muslims and Orthodox as well as his own flock. "Now we need peace, reconciliation and above all, forgiveness." I felt tears prickling in my eyes, astounded at this man's humanity in the face of all he had experienced. "This is why we welcome you," he added.

The mufti explained how he had thirty principalities in the district. There used to be eighty-six mosques and eighty-two imams. Every single mosque was completely destroyed. Four imams were killed. The rest fled as refugees. Only two remained. One died, but no one knows where and how: only one survived. There is no trace of the murderers and the mufti refused to say who might be responsible for burning the mosques. There had been no fighting in the town but all sixteen mosques there were destroyed. "Ask Komarica if he destroyed his own churches! Who mined his monastery?!" The mufti looked straight into Donald's eyes, adding, "But this is the past. We can't forget; but we try to forgive and reconcile, to build again."

The building is a problem. "We don't have permission yet. Mosques are a challenge to people. The authorities say, 'They will offend the religious feelings of Orthodox people.' " We thought of all the young people we had met and seen in the town so far and wondered whom the authorities might be referring to. I certainly hadn't come across any religious Orthodox people yet who might be offended by the sight of a mosque. The students we had met the night before had agreed to help with the rebuilding. But the local authorities were against it. They did not even permit a railing to protect the mufti's residence, which is why the arsonists were able to set fire to it a week earlier.

Regularly the mufti and the imam ask for permission to rebuild at least one mosque. Only ten days earlier he had been at the Prime Minister's office and got the same response as the previous year about offending the sensibilities of religious Orthodox people. So nothing happens. The mufti begged him, "As a friend, I implore you: it is against human rights!"

Donald spoke about the Soul of Europe being small. "We are European and Christian and we can put pressure on people to allow others to worship as they wish." He talked about the Sacred Land Project and the prospects of getting help from various sources. But he sounded chastened by the mufti's story. We were hearing the dark truth. Lazar, interpreting, looked nervous and began cracking his fingers. He resented the constant emphasis on Serbian bad behaviour, "as though only Serbs are the wrongdoers in Bosnia and everyone else is suffering". But even though he wanted to leave and take us to another part of Bosnia where the Serbs are an oppressed minority, he had to listen to the mufti quietly reminding him of the side to the story Lazar can't bear to hear.

Donald now spoke about the plan to rebuild ruined churches and a mosque in Bihac. The mufti alerted us to our ignorance of the situation in Bosnia. Not having yet been to Bihac, we were not to know that there are plentiful mosques there. He suggested we rebuild an Orthodox church in a Muslim area and a mosque in the Srpska Republic. There are already plans to rebuild an Orthodox Centre in Sarajevo and the bishop has been promised a sumptuous residence. In Mostar there will be a new Orthodox church, also one in Canski Most. The government is helping to finance these projects. There are Orthodox gains in the Federation of Bosnia and Herzegovina, but Muslims can't even get permission to pray in the Srpska Republic. "I am the only mufti without a mosque!"

The question of restitution is complicated by the history of the last century when Communists took land from all religious communities. It is not clear to whom the land belongs now, which is another reason for the total destruction of the mosques in Banja Luka. The ground, cleared of any buildings, could be made available for other projects. But the mufti courageously resists these alternatives. "Our intentions are honourable," he said, and suggested pitching a tent so that the three thousand or so

Muslims in Banja Luka could at least have a place to worship. "Tell the West," he smiled, "tell them about the mufti under the tent!" Then he added bitterly that the local authorities were not allowing people to be buried traditionally. There used to be thirty-one cemeteries before the war. One of these we had looked at earlier in the day, the ground recently churned up after a small earthquake and the graves neglected, the headstones broken and tilting, a piece of wasteland left untouched as though people feared to disturb the spirits of the dead.

Donald looked shattered. "A very shocking story," he said and spoke about changes needing to be forced through by young people, the next generation, that perhaps 'us' old people might not achieve this change of heart. But the mufti responded firmly, "*You* can help."

Though the mufti did not commit himself, he knew who was responsible for destroying the mosques in Banja Luka. A woman from Zagreb University in Croatia published a thesis on this subject. She is now in Sarajevo. A television crew interviewed the mufti with the Catholic bishop. They asked the mufti, "What is your cooperation with humanitarian organisations?" The mufti was about to reply when the secretary of the bishop interrupted saying, "There is no cooperation, just as there is none with the Catholics. There are only visits – only visits – only visits. Nothing gets done. There is no rebuilding of Catholic churches or mosques." The mufti looked at us and shrugged his shoulders implying what could he add to that? So he suggested to us that there would be more point rebuilding a mosque in the Srpska Republic rather than adding to all those apparently already being built in Western Bosnia where the Muslims are in the majority. The priority would be the Ferhadija Mosque.

Before the war, relations with the Orthodox bishop of Banja Luka were good, but during and after the war he never sent a greeting or visited them and now refuses cooperation. The previous Mufti Halilovic, who had been Mufti of Banja Luka during the war and until his death about eighteen months ago, personally witnessed the killing and expulsion of all but about three thousand of Banja Luka's forty-five thousand Bosnian Muslims. He also witnessed the destruction of his beloved Ferhadija, as well as Arnaudija and all the other mosques in Banja Luka. Well over two hundred mosques that fell within his jurisdiction in the area were destroyed, in fact every single mosque in his Muftiluk. Saba Risaluddin, our Muslim contact in Sarajevo, would later tell us more about Mufti Halilovic. "When I met him, in 1996 and several times subsequently, I never saw in him the slightest trace of bitterness or anger, only a deep pain – hands shaking, eyes often full of tears – and an equally deep compassion not only for his flock and for the Croats of Banja Luka, who also suffered, but also for the Serbs of that city. On my first meeting he said to me, 'We were killed and expelled and our mosques destroyed, it's true; but we are not the greatest victims of this evil, the Serbs are. They are living in a concentration camp of the mind, and they don't even yet know it.' It was just after the second brutal refusal of the Banja Luka authorities to grant permission for the rebuilding of Ferhadija that he suffered a fatal heart attack, still only in his early fifties. His wife said that his soul could no longer bear so much suffering. The authorities refused to allow him to be buried in the graveyard of the Ferhadija in Banja Luka."

Mufti Camdzic didn't want to speak about relations with the local authorities. But he announced darkly that if he didn't get permission soon to rebuild a mosque he would inform the United Nations about "this shame in Europe" and would tell countries everywhere. Donald quoted the Declaration of Human Rights, that all people should "have freedom to worship". Then he promised to be in touch with the Islamic communities in England and other western European countries and begin the process of pressuring the authorities in Banja Luka. "Tell our story," the mufti said.

Donald then asked how the mufti "carries on carrying on". The tough but broken man said he tries to protect himself from being killed. But he clearly didn't want to dwell on this disturbing subject. He smiled in adversity and spoke of his impatience, of being like a child, wanting changes to happen straight away. As we left he said he put great hope in the Soul of Europe, that he could rely on us to tell his story to the wider world. His despair came to haunt me when we returned to England, and only days later read a report in *The Tablet* about the improving situation in Bosnia, specifically in Banja Luka, where apparently permission is being granted to rebuild a number of mosques, and that people are living together peacefully with returning Muslims and Catholics who are starting businesses again, etc, etc. Not only is the mufti's story not being told, but a false picture is being circulated which will make people in the West feel that there are no problems in Bosnia and that there is no need for further help. Later we learned of reports about plans to rebuild the Ferhadija Mosque without waiting for permission from the authorities. The response came that any such unauthorised building would be immediately destroyed. The High Representative dismissed the leader of the Authorities but the new leader remains unavailable to comment on the situation "because he has scheduled meetings all the time".

The mufti's final words still resonate: "Don't let me die waiting."

Outside, the empty space looked even more desolate. "Fanatics, the shame of our people," muttered Lazar. "They ruined my life."

The Catholic Bishop of Banja Luka

A dark-haired young taxi driver charged us five pounds for driving the few hundred yards to the bishop's residence. He refused to negotiate, eyes darkening with determination. He heard us speaking in English and knew we would pay. He turned out to be the only unpleasant person we encountered in Banja Luka.

In contrast to the mufti's sparsely furnished and basic quarters behind the piece of empty ground where a young layabout lounged against a rusting old car and eyed us suspiciously, the Catholic headquarters of Banja Luka seemed luxuriously appointed with a new church, offices and apartments. These latter were decorated with numerous paintings, icons, sculptures, and artefacts. A nun took us into the spacious entrance hall, and moments later the modest, trim figure of Bishop Komarica came rapidly down the curving staircase to greet us. In his dark, worn suit and with his grey hair he resembled a timid, bookish Anglican vicar, someone tucked away in a distant country parish. It came as a surprise to discover in this unassuming, kindly, and gentle looking man a character with courage, resolve, and an acute mind

He took us upstairs to an elegantly furnished reception room with dozens of paintings and icons hanging on every inch of wall and sculptures of saints in every corner. Afterwards we learned that these had been rescued from destroyed churches throughout his diocese. We sat round a large table in the middle of the room while he ordered coffee and fruit juice. Donald immediately began his presentation and the bishop listened, head bowed, nodding emphatically at the proposal to rebuild churches and construct a centre of peace and reconciliation.

When Donald had finished the bishop responded with startling intensity and, like Mufti Camdzic, with a solemn sense of occasion: "I am deeply grateful, respected brother. This attempt will please God." He then launched into a series of presentations of his own, ones which he had clearly been refining for the last few years and which he had been longing to share with sympathetic listeners like ourselves. "But we must make it happen!" he continued. "I personally believe it is possible. We got used to suffering because of all the barriers, especially those difficulties which prevented reconciliation and peace building. Because of the war we experienced deeply inhuman qualities for the first time in our lives. Unfortunate people fell into the trap of hatred and spread the scent of death and destruction. When we read about the First World War we learn about communities being destroyed and places burnt, but churches were left undisturbed. Now it is churches which are destroyed and houses with people inside. Churches and mosques are places of transcendence: these are now deliberately destroyed. Bishop Ephraim said: 'Communism managed to kill the soul of people.' Now we can see the result. And these spiritually impoverished invalids now rule the country. This lack of spiritual qualities made possible the triumph of evil in the war."

Donald, stunned by the unexpected intensity of these observations coming from this mild-mannered man, paused, then passed greetings from the mufti and said how shocking was the denial of human rights to forbid people to worship. The bishop looked at Donald with warmth and said, "We are very grateful that people come from so far to bring medicine for our big wounds. Spiritual emptiness produces ruins – true to its essence. It expresses itself wherever constructive people are weakest. But we are positive. We bring constructive people together." His words came over as a distillation of a decade of trying to come to terms with the catastrophe in his country. The bishop spoke in potent aphorisms, having pared away all unnecessary words and wanting to reach the heart of the matter clearly, simply, irrefutably, and quickly.

He offered us fruit brandy, a local speciality which he kept in a decanter, and though he drank sparingly himself, kept filling our capacious glasses as soon as they emptied.

There used to be a hundred and twenty thousand Catholics in his diocese in forty-seven parishes with forty-three parish priests and sixty-seven monk-priests who do pastoral work. Now there are just a handful of Catholics. The bishop told us that planned ethnic cleansing took place on all sides. The first goal of the fanatics was to destroy churches. The bishop tried to intervene and appealed to the generals: "Why do you target the churches?" One general (could it have been Mladic?) replied, "We know that churches are the heart of your life and identity. If we destroy the heart, your community will be shattered." The bishop continued his flow of aphorisms: "It is more painful to lose your church than your house." But faithful people did remain wherever the priests stayed on, gathering in ruins and graveyards to keep their spirits up. The priests tried to help with humanitarian aid, clothes, food, and heating, helping all people in need, Muslims, Orthodox, and Catholic. Then six priests were murdered. "Because they delivered help to *all* people," explained the bishop. "It was forbidden to do good. This is the mystery of evil."

The Pope apparently appealed to the leaders to stop the

madness. The bishop himself went to Brussels and international conferences. He met Mr Hombach, from the Project for Stability and Peace, who spoke candidly about the type of war being waged. "The situation is what other people want; but of course we are also present in this discussion, and our voices should be heard."

Now, out of eighty thousand refugees only six hundred have returned. Even under the protection of SFOR their plight is inhuman. They are refused basic human rights. The bishop kept asking, "Why are we not treated as humans?" He had long been thinking about the reasons for Western apathy during the first years of the war, before concerted attempts were made to forge the Dayton Agreement. He came to the conclusion that it was a deliberate policy. My skin prickled as I remembered my own thoughtless and cynical attitude, keeping out of the conflict, putting barbed wire round the Balkans, and letting the Yugoslavs fight it out amongst themselves. "Let me tell you something," said the bishop, warming to his story. "I met an important politician, a guest from a powerful European nation, I will not tell you which. He told me, 'I don't understand why you were not liquidated. You were not meant to survive!' 'Oh, Your Excellency!' I responded, 'How could I welcome you if I were dead?' 'But your survival has messed up our plans!' I then said: 'I hope your government is not too upset about that.' He asked: 'What strategy did you have to survive?' 'No strategy,' I told him. 'God had the final word. I only had Christ's strategy.' "

Six times the Orthodox bishops, the muftis and Roman Catholic leaders met during 1992 appealing to everyone, local and international. Throughout the war they continued to meet. Unfortunately it was politics which played a dirty game and influenced religious attitudes.

Now relations between Church and State have stagnated. The Church tries to help people to reconstruct their homes and lives. Material assistance is filtered through the bishops to the people. The bishop considered our plans for rebuilding churches but pointed out more urgent priorities. People needed to be fed and cared for. Bricks, roofs, and power should come first.

He returned to the subject of Western apathy and interpreted the events of the last decade as being in his words a 'Stellvertreter Krieg' – German for a war by proxy – in which the Balkans could be kept weak by the West not interfering in the escalating violence. This turned out to be a successful policy. "Whatever we plan to build now, it is like an ant heap, something that boys can easily destroy."

The bishop then spoke about the legacy of Communism. 'Brotherhood without Fatherhood' was a state of affairs which led directly to the recent and present horrors. Most of the present leaders are former Communists, people who manipulated the system to achieve power, and at the collapse of Communism desperately searched for new means to hold on to their power. They found the simplest way was to play on the resentments of a disgruntled populace and appeal to their basest instincts, crude nationalism: "It is always someone else's fault." So each community blamed the other for their ills.

Donald spoke about our plans in Bihac. "That is a noble project," said the bishop, pouring more fruit brandy into our glasses. He would support us because there are Catholic parishioners there, suffering. But we might have difficulty with the mufti in Bihac, who might not agree. We should appeal to the General of SFOR and to the UK ambassador, then go to the local government for cooperation. There would be more chance of support from them than from the religious leaders. This turned out to be valuable advice. The bishop muttered darkly about religious people with evil in their hearts being worse than atheists. His supply of potent aphorisms seemed unending. "When politicians influence religious leaders only harm ensues."

The bishop echoed the sentiments of the mufti. We should speak the truth and tell the world what is going on in Bosnia. "Please don't give up!" Then he added in a tone of gentle appeal, "We expect every man of nobility to help in the reconstruction of spiritual and material values."

Our meeting drew to a close. "From darkness comes light," said Donald. "This is why we have come to the Balkans." The bishop responded, "This tragedy is the infection of one finger which has made the whole body ill." He then invited us into his private chapel to pray for the Soul of Europe. As we went out of the room he touched us personally by referring to the logo on our leaflet and saying, "There is a lot of darkness here. Even the smallest candle gives us hope."

We stood at the back of the chapel where the bishop asked Donald to say the Lord's Prayer after he too had said a prayer and crossed himself. I noticed the large quantity of statues which had been rescued from destroyed churches. A Virgin Mary had pride of place by the altar. Apparently the church from which she came had been completely demolished, and only she remained untouched, miraculously, standing undamaged in the middle of rubble.

After the intensity of the conversation earlier Donald felt choked, particularly when reciting the Lord's Prayer. The words: "Forgive them..." and "Deliver us from evil..." took on an acute poignancy and significance here, especially in the presence of this modest bishop with a mind and heart as it were 'purified by fire'.

Then, as we turned to leave, the bishop took us to a group of photographs on the wall of the chapel. These were the priests and a nun who had been murdered in the war: two of them had disappeared without trace and no one had yet come forward to say what happened to them. Looking at their fresh faces which reminded me of young soldiers in the First World War, I tried to imagine what their last moments might have been, the Serb Chetniks shooting them enthusiastically as though impatient to continue the depraved carnival of carnage of the Second World War. During that war it had been the Serbs' turn to suffer at the hands of Croat Catholics in particular. The notorious Ustashi, Croat Fascists, had tortured and killed hundreds of thousands of Serbs while the world was preoccupied with Nazi Germany and Japan. The Serbs are bitter at this ignorance of their past sufferings, particularly as now they are seen as the only criminals in the Balkans, the Croats and Muslims being the victims, when in the past all sides had committed atrocities and destruction. But looking at the faces of the young men and a woman, ordinary people we pass in the street everyday, it became clear that this vicious circle has to stop. The killing and destroying went further than before, as though wanting to plumb depths of depravity to warn and frighten future generations. The mass destruction of churches, which in the Balkans represented the total wealth of their culture, the equivalent of the West losing not only churches, but also its museums and galleries, meant that as well as people being killed and property destroyed, the heart and soul of the community had been snuffed out as well. Killing people in their prime is appalling enough, but to raze the best part of their culture to the ground, to wipe out centuries of what is most precious to them, what gives their lives meaning, sustenance, and nourishment, that does more than add insult to injury. The act wishes to wipe all trace of the hated people off the face of the earth. This is thorough ethnic cleansing, a continuation of the Holocaust, a purging not only of human beings, but of everything they gave to the world, their art, their spirit, their skills, their wisdom, and, most of all, their humanity. The Ferhadija Mosque, that used to be the most beautiful monument in Banja Luka and an outstanding example of Islamic art, is no more, as though it had never existed. And these young priests with most of their useful lives still ahead of them are also no more.

We visited Bosnia with open minds and hearts and therefore were unprotected to deal with the shock of what we saw and heard. Reading about it from a safe distance, though that is disturbing too, does not have quite the visceral impact of being there in Bosnia. In England the recent events in Bosnia seem incomprehensible, a bloodfest, a settling of ancient scores which have nothing to do with any other part of Europe. Being there, what was incomprehensible became excessively vicious and brutal, but also totally mad. In a way this insanity provides a flicker of hope, because now everyone is aware of the madness. No one, apart from the minority of resentful perpetrators and instigators of this violence, all crushed into submission by the Dayton Accord, wants to return to this cycle of retribution and destruction. As

Lazar told us, people have now to learn to live together: not necessarily to love one another just yet, but at least to cooperate and accept one another's differences, respect them, and simply coexist. Perhaps this is what the Soul of Europe can help to bring about. And if we succeed, then perhaps Bosnia can teach the rest of Europe how to live peacefully and tolerantly with all its minorities and different communities. The pace of western life and the size of its cities keep ethnic enmities at bay, though there are far too few signs of cooperation and collaboration. People prefer to live apart, despising and fearing one another; but in Bosnia in particular, where only recently these differences flared up to devastating effect, any sign of reconciliation and peaceful coexistence will be an example to the rest of the world.

The bishop took us downstairs, having presented us with two bottles of his special fruit brandy. An American army chaplain with two officers all in uniform were waiting to see him. They looked like extras from a Second World War film, the chaplain being tall, large, and authoritative like a colonel, the officers wide-eyed, straight-backed, and obedient. They listened to Donald's description of the Soul of Europe and looked even more bemused. "Good luck!" they wished politely, but their tone expressed doubts as to the success of our mission. Their job was to keep the peace, to show their presence yet not to provoke. They also did not seem too interested in our proposals, only in doing their job, protecting their backs, and not becoming involved in idealistic schemes. They looked out of place here in Bosnia, and as an occupying force, visibly foreign with their flak jackets and American manners, we could understand their reticence. They also have to deal with incidents and dangerous situations, clearing mines, sorting complaints, and following the line of least resistance, which often means appeasing those who caused trouble in the first place. The mufti and the bishop were ethnic Bosnians whose every word had to be interpreted, but neither of them felt as foreign to me as these army personnel, with whom we were nonetheless able to speak freely in our own language.

The Smooth Couple

Being in Bosnia felt different after these searching and comprehensive conversations with the mufti, the bishop and the Orthodox lecturer. The deceptive charm of Banja Luka with its predominantly young, attractive, and friendly population had now shifted to show us harsh realities and the desolation, pain, and conflicts which cried out for a resolution that was nowhere in sight.

Lazar, as usual, had packed the day with important meetings, and though we longed for a quiet evening to digest what we had learned, he announced that we were scheduled to go for supper with a couple from an American NGO who might support the Soul of Europe. We should put on a good face for them. They had access to "lots of money". After this day's lessons, money was not uppermost in my thoughts. The International Orthodox Christian Charities NGO is based in Banja Luka, which indicates that their concerns are not ecumenical and that they exist to protect the interests of the Orthodox in Bosnia.

The NGO's representative in Bosnia, Mark O'Hanian, came to pick us up from the hotel, and immediately I felt that we were an unwelcome obligation for him, that he had better things to do with his time, but that he had at least to check us out. Lazar had clearly charmed him over the phone into spending time with us. With Tom Cruise good looks, trim, smartly dressed and groomed, his cultivated beauty contrasted with the startling natural magnificence of the Bosnians working in the hotel. He politely offered to wait for us while we sent e-mails to England, but he could not hide the look of impatience in his eyes. Donald meanwhile explained the project and he suggested we meet his wife, waiting in the car, "she is the expert". Tina Wolfe, petite and sexy, reminded me of the attractive girls Woody Allen cunningly partners in his later films. She proved to be a tough interrogator behind her gleaming smile and immediately challenged us with questions about the feasibility of the project. Though they grilled us as thoroughly as the meat and fish we were eating in the restaurant that we drove several miles out of town to, they revealed as little as possible about themselves. They had assisted in setting up a creche for Orthodox mothers in Bihac, which underlined their priorities to support the Orthodox and not to encourage cooperation and collaboration between the communities.

They tucked into a number of authentic, powerfully flavoured, densely textured Bosnian dishes which defeated Donald's conservative palette and even stretched mine to its limit. I bit into a solid piece of corn bread but barely made an incision in its stale-tasting granite mass. The meat had been cooked earlier and came unheated with tepid vegetables swimming in oil – a health hazard made safe by the fortuitously copious servings of fruit brandy at the bishop's earlier. Perhaps the staff were punishing guests for the occupation of their country. After the meal Mark O'Hanian lit a cigarette with Tina Wolfe, crossed his sleek thighs, looked at us earnestly, and said he hoped we were not disappointed that they could not give us money. We were genuinely surprised, not realizing we had been under scrutiny for funding. This had been an exploratory meeting to find out more about one another. Donald had in fact regaled the couple with an honest and self-deprecatory response to Tina Wolfe about why he had become a priest. He hoped this might loosen them up to reveal something about themselves. But they avoided telling us more than that they had worked in Armenia and other places of the world where terrible wars and massacres had occurred, going from one disaster area to another. Tina Wolfe gave a storybook account of falling in love with handsome Mark O'Hanian in the Middle East during a delivery of humanitarian aid. It reminded me of a fifties Hollywood melodrama set in a remote, disease-infested part of the undeveloped world starring Audrey Hepburn as a sublime looking nun and dashing Peter Finch as a capable doctor battling against poor conditions and tropical infections. Mark O'Hanian did not comment or elaborate on his wife's confession but continued to look at us coolly, conscious of the effect his appearance has on everyone he meets, his eyes perfect ovals of amber and his skin glistening with silky smoothness. We tried to ascertain what made this wealthy and attractive young couple devote themselves to charity work in the toughest regions of the world, both of them groomed and dressed as though attending a fashionable New York soirée, but looking incongruous here in Bosnia where so many people still searched in vain for homes, jobs, and money. Momentarily they lost their cool and choked when asked why they had chosen this line of work, evidently a question rarely if ever put to them. Tina Wolfe coughed into her necklace and said that the work taught her so much: she learned new things every day. After this impressive show of modesty they both told us how life had become normal again in Bosnia, how people were finding homes and jobs, that we could trust local government officials and would find them helpful. The day before we might just have believed this optimistic view of Bosnia, but after our encounters with the mufti and the bishop the shallow attitudes and smugly optimistic opinions of this smooth couple were offensive. Could they be spies, representatives of the United States Government sent to investigate projects like ours, to see what we were up to in this politically sensitive region of the world? Everything else about them seemed to emanate from a glossy Hollywood film, so why not this outrageous scenario? They were non-committal and ill-informed despite their lengthy experience of the area; they gave us poor advice and asked us too many questions. Back home we conducted a post-mortem and agreed that the encounter had not been what it seemed and that we could not trust them.

The Journey into Western Bosnia

The Orthodox bishop had invited us to the Ascension Day service in the town of Shipovo where he stays in a hotel because he has no home of his own.

The day began early in the hotel in Banja Luka with a breakfast of pints of orange juice, a soft roll and portion of butter, and a slightly boiled egg, on its own, rolling about a large plate. Lazar turned up two hours later, having haggled for a car that turned out to have faulty brakes. We drove down the main street into Banja Luka, speeding alarmingly so that he could prove how bad the brakes were. We spent the next two hours in a car hire firm where we haggled for another car. The staff consisted of three men and two middle-aged women who sat at their tables in the office, smoking incessantly and looking generally negative about our prospects of finding a suitable car. Since they could not offer any insurance, this being Bosnia, we had to be careful about how much money we could afford. If we had an accident we would be bound to pay for the full cost of the car, and so a new one was out of the question. After an hour, having done no work and not having decided anything, they decided to take a coffee break and disappeared. As Lazar pointed out, there is no pressure on them from their bosses to do anything. So they spent their time having breaks, being slow and unhelpful, in order to have a stress-free working life. They also probably earned next to nothing. It is a tradition going back to Communism when people lacked incentive. The demands of a competitive market have not reached Bosnia yet. Eventually Lazar persuaded one of the men to unlock a car which turned out to be brand new, but for some reason they were prepared to hire out without demanding the full cost in case of accident. They had relented and were prepared to take a reasonable deposit of three hundred pounds. When we returned the car the deposit would be refunded. After another hour of signing papers, which depended on one of the women returning from a lengthy coffee break, and when we had checked the car and manoeuvred the staff into completing the procedure, we set off having missed the Ascension Day service by several hours and with a long drive ahead of us.

As we left Banja Luka and climbed the gorge leading into the hills, the River Vrbas snaking its azure path deep in the thickly forested valley below, we began to witness the spectacular scenery of Bosnia. Then the brand new car suddenly flashed a warning light at Lazar.

"We are finished!" he announced, in pessimistic tones. "We are dead!" We drove off the road and I walked in the hot afternoon sun, the dry grass crackling under foot, the wind rustling in the forest, but otherwise stillness and silence all round. In the distance I could make out the sound of rushing water. It might be hours before another car turned up to help us. Meanwhile Lazar tried to phone the car hire firm on his mobile, but could not find a signal. So we continued the journey fearfully, driving into the hills and hoping eventually to reach a town with a garage before breaking down.

Lazar was understandably nervous about leaving Bosnian Serb territory. He perpetually reminded us that beyond the hills lay Muslim Bosnia and he would no longer be safe. Only five years earlier both sides were massacring each other, on this very road. Whenever Donald asked whether the invisible border had been crossed, he told us to watch out for the signs. If they were in the Cyrillic alphabet, we would still be in Bosnian Serb territory. And we had not reached the last most western Bosnian Serb town in Bosnia, Mrkonjic Grad, which according to Lazar represents for all educated Serbs the epitome of uncouth provincialism, a place so remote from civilization that people there still live in the dark ages.

The town turned out to be attractive, lying in the folds of several hills and surrounded by fields, rivers, and forests. The streets and cafés teemed with people, mostly youngsters, sitting and idling, probably because there was no work for them. We drove up and down the narrow streets, observing a scattering of SFOR soldiers in flak jackets. We hunted for a garage but only came to the end of a street, which turned into a footpath leading into a meadow. A mile outside Mrkonjic Grad, on a hill with a panoramic view over the town and the valleys beyond, we came to a service station, where after half an hour some experienced mechanics, having first finished their leisurely lunch, looked under the bonnet of our new car, shook their heads, and informed us that we continued at our own risk. The car had a fault but this wouldn't affect us for the time being. And if it did, we had only to phone them and they would come and tow us back. Lazar felt better, particularly as the mechanics were Serbs. He would certainly not have trusted the opinion of Muslim mechanics.

Beyond Mrkonjic Grad we came across the first ruined buildings, remnants of the war when the armies of each ethnic group systematically torched villages belonging to the other side. Then the countryside turned wilder with thick forests covering whole mountainsides, peaks reaching six to seven thousand feet and no sign of human habitation. For miles to the south and west there were no towns or villages. Wolves and a few bears inhabited this wilderness. Rivers flowed down the numerous valleys where the lush meadows indicated the fertile quality of the land. The agricultural riches of the whole region of the Balkans mean that the people are spoilt for choice where to live. But this part of Europe is considered to be poor and isolated. Refugees pour into the West from Bosnia, yet people should be going there. It turned out that this wild countryside was only a foretaste of the splendours to come as we approached the region of Bihac Petrovac.

Suddenly in the middle of a wide vista of lower rolling hills and meadows a forest appeared shaped in the letters TITO. It looked particularly incongruous given the desolation of the region. Shortly afterwards we reached a narrow and stony mountain road which for the first time warned us of mines. So Tito's forest stands in the heart of the former Yugoslavia where the bitterest fighting took place, each community gaining ground from the other and shedding their blood there. In western minds, Communism under Tito, a benign autocrat, had controlled these opposing forces, suppressing them, so that when Communism collapsed, the simmering hatreds unleashed pandemonium. This is a simplistic interpretation of events. People used to live together more or less peaceably, and probably would have continued to do so if it had not been for opportunistic politicians, mostly old Communists, who stirred up ancient ethnic enmities the way Hitler managed to do in Germany, where Jews had for centuries been integrated into every part of society better than anywhere else in Europe. Considering the long tradition of coexistence between the different faiths in the Balkans, some other interpretation needs to be found to explain the degree and insanity of the violence.

The Poison Tree

The long journey through this wild region of Bosnia gave me time to ponder this issue, and as I looked at the trees growing large and plentifully all over the landscape I thought of two poems which deal with the intensity of humankind's hatred for neighbours who are different. Pushkin, in *Anchar*, describes a tree growing in the middle of a wilderness. The heat scorches the earth and concentrates the venom in its foliage. So poisonous is the tree that even passing breezes become polluted. A king sends a slave to collect the leaves of the tree, and the wretched man only just makes it back with the deadly cargo before dying at his master's feet. The king then dips his arrows in the poison and causes death and destruction in neighbouring lands. The poem is short and pithy, as potent as the poison in the Anchar tree, and is an unblinking look at human capacity for irrational violent hatred. William Blake, at around the same time as Pushkin, without either knowing of the other's existence, also wrote about a poison tree. Blake links this hatred to rankling malevolence.

> I was angry with my foe;
> I told it not, my wrath did grow.

Written subjectively, this poem provides a personal slant to Pushkin's political insight. The slave pours beads of sweat as he carries the poison to his master. Tears of fear water the roots of Blake's tree which will eventually produce poisonous fruit, "an apple bright".

> My foe beheld it shine, and he knew that it was mine,
> And into my garden stole
> When the night had veil'd the pole:
> In the morning glad I see
> My foe stretched lifeless beneath the tree.

The Bishop and the Waterfall

As the road ascended into the hills again, reaching a panoramic vista over the valleys below, we came across mounds of rubbish piled high on both sides. Croats use Serb territory to dump their waste. The sacks of tins, waste paper, and rotting matter interspersed with rusty machinery, old cars, and twisted metal provided an offensive contrast to the beauty of the surrounding scenery, a slap in the face.

The road continued along the high ridge, and sinister warnings of mines hung along both sides of the road, skull symbols flapping in between the white flags. Not only were past enemies defecating on each other's land, "If I can't have it, neither can you enjoy it," but they were also intending to leave a permanent legacy of death and destruction for future generations. The road itself became pitted and potholed, from bombs and mines detonated in the past few years.

Eventually, after many miles driving through deserted country, we descended into a verdant valley where we had been scheduled to meet the Orthodox Bishop of Bihac Petrovac several hours earlier. We entered the village of Martin Brod and crossed a river. A bright-eyed young monk with a trim beard, Brother Sophrone, waited for us at the door of a small Orthodox church standing in the middle of a meadow. He took us inside to glimpse a sparsely decorated cool space before leading us up the road to meet the bishop and the other monks. They lived temporarily in a house belonging to a Serb who had fled with many others to Belgrade during the War. The monks planned to rebuild the Rmanj monastery by the church, but while waiting for funds and permission they lived next door to the Serb's brother who cultivated a large garden stretching to the river. Beehives stood under the fruit trees of an orchard shading the rest of the garden which extended up the slope of a hill.

Bishop Chrysostom, a small stocky man with a bushy white beard, welcomed us with a broad smile and open arms. We were introduced to two other monks, Brothers Sergei and Seraphim. Sergei, a tall, broad shouldered, smooth-faced young man with long hair tied in a pony tail, appeared to be in charge of the kitchen and household; he bustled about in the background letting the others do the talking. Brother Seraphim's name described him perfectly, a seraphic looking young man with a trim black beard, dark eyes, rosy lips, and curly black hair. He was shy and withdrawn, but turned out to be determined and courageous, having decided to be a priest in a region of Bosnia where his life was still in danger. They told us about the recent attempt to mine the church and how a Canadian officer from SFOR saved their lives. To complete the party a young man from across the mountains had accompanied the bishop to meet us. He was a trainee priest and school teacher. The bishop had much to talk about and Lazar had prepared him for this meeting, and so we were treated as honoured guests. We were offered fruit brandy and sparkling water, and Brother Seraphim fetched two platters loaded with grilled trout caught that morning in the river. Brother Sergei produced plates of sliced tomatoes with chopped onions and some thick portions of cold pork. They had waited all day for our arrival and watched us eat, intently and with hope in their eyes because we were bringing them comfort and support from the outside world.

We sat round a long table outside in the pleasant shade of the cherry trees. The river gushed beyond the neighbour's garden, and bees foraging for honey in large numbers filled the air with urgent humming and crowded the entrances of their hives. Sunlight dappled the grass in between the trees. The song of thrushes, perched quite close, provided a sparkling accompaniment to the conversation. A predatory young cat prowled between the neat rows of beans and corn in the neighbour's vegetable garden before disappearing in a thicket of shrubs and brambles beyond.

The scene was timeless. Surrounded by fruit trees, birdsong, and the humming of nectar-sucking bees, we sat shaded from the blazing summer sun feeling the dreamlike suspension of time and space. It became a scene for painting, a moment to be recorded and made immortal. Enjoying the sensation of peace and natural harmony in this garden, I missed much of what the bishop had been eagerly telling Donald, but I gathered it was more along the lines of what we had heard from the mufti and Catholic bishop. Each gave their own slant on events. So Chrysostom interpreted the war as being about the existence and denial of Yugoslavia against which the Croats and Muslims fought. He asserted that extreme fanaticism was mostly among the Croats and Muslims. Each group would accuse the others of being fanatics. However, the bishop also admitted that during the last war Serbs definitely were responsible for the majority of the crimes and violence. He pointed out that in wartime national priorities intensify, they become atavistic, primitive. He also gave the practical reason why so many churches were demolished, in addition to the politics of destroying the heart and soul of each community, which Bishop Komarica had previously explained to us. The army had access to massive arsenals of explosives which they intended to deploy on property and churches.

However, now the priority is peace. The rest can follow later: justice, reconciliation. But peace must come first. The first projects of the Soul of Europe in Bosnia should reflect the communities of the first Christians, stressing what is common between people, not different. The three young monks and the jovial bishop sitting in this magical garden already provided a seductive image of what such a community might be like.

Most of the time the bishop joked and laughed, his face beaming and giving no impression of living in peril, homeless and trying to deal with the severe problems of his flock. Serbs were hesitating to return home, not because they feared for their lives but simply because there was no work for them. The main task would be to create business opportunities and the bishop already had a list of possibilities, farming projects, even a plan to start a local bus service round the villages and farms. Lack of transport here has made the economy of the region stagnate. Our project would help kick start the economy – it had to.

The bishop then observed Lazar refusing to eat the fish, just picking at the tomatoes. The bishop skilfully and neatly skinned and boned a trout then good humouredly ordered Lazar to eat it. "Obedience to your bishop!" he laughed, and Lazar cleverly pretended to be about to put some in his mouth but managed to avoid doing so by delaying the motion of his fork and talking incessantly to distract the bishop.

The afternoon became evening. "We must see the waterfall

before it is too late," the bishop announced, and we rose from the table and trooped across the garden and along a narrow lane which climbed a hill past several empty houses. We turned a corner to be suddenly astonished by a magnificent view of the river cascading over steep rocks into a dark cool pool below. There seemed to be dozens of separate waterfalls as the river negotiated a series of rocks and small precipices. All these cascades thundered and rushed, gurgled and foamed, spouted and tumbled in between trees, ferns and luxurious water plants, rainbows hovering in the spray mists below. A narrow wooden footbridge led to a vantage point where we stood surrounded by this natural spectacle, as it were bathed in the sound, cooled by the waters and suspended in space. Beyond lay a thick wood where more tributaries of the same river poured into the valley below. This was our first encounter with the River Una which flows on to Bihac and beyond.

Wherever we met this beautiful river with its clear blue waters and banks of lush meadows, flowing past forests, though gorges and landscapes of rolling hills, farmland and villages, the inspiration for our project grew stronger. The centre for peace and reconciliation would have to be named after the River Una.

By the waterfall stood a derelict house. It had belonged to a Serb family, now fled to Belgrade. Their home looted, mattresses still lay rotting across the threshold of the front door, furniture smashed as well as the plumbing and floorboards. Through the broken windowpanes we saw the waterfall cascading between trees and ferns. The reality of Bosnia could be summed up in this spot: a place of beauty and natural harmony, despoiled and desecrated. This house by a waterfall inspired in us a vision of a new community. After restoration it could become a studio for artists. People would come from all over Europe to restore their spirits in a paradise ready to be reclaimed.

Wild flowers and herbs grew abundantly along the path back to where the monks lived. Scarlet dots of wild strawberries peeped through the undergrowth.

Before continuing on our way to Bihac the bishop invited us to a shortened celebration of that morning's Ascension service. "The music is so beautiful," he said. "You must hear it." The brothers busied themselves with preparations. Brother Sergei the cook donned a black cassock, walked up and down the path leading to the church, and loudly banged two pieces of wood together, a ritual established centuries ago, when the Muslims forbade church bells to ring. The clacking sound echoed down the valley and up the hillsides. Brother Seraphim took on the role of priest dressed in freshly laundered robes, keeping his back to us but occasionally turning to bless us, blushing shyly and swinging a censer. The bishop stood at the side singing the responses, accompanied by the schoolteacher, a clear-voiced tenor, and Brother Sophrone who had occasional difficulty with the bottom lines. The Bishop conducted with his finger and sang in a powerful baritone, occasionally casting a severe look in the direction of the other two when they lost the harmonies.

Moments like this reveal the significance of religion. Normally the ritual of worship is experienced as a chore, a habit shared by members of the same club. The fragile and vulnerable circumstances of these three young monks gave the celebration poignancy. They braved hostility. They had chosen to live modestly and faithfully to their calling in a remote part of the country, far from assistance and support. They kept a small light burning in the darkness. Their voices sounded firm yet trembling with awareness of the perils around them. The world is now a secular place and religion has little meaning for most people. The singing of ancient chants followed seamlessly and smoothly one after the other. A few small reproductions of icons decorated otherwise blank walls. The intent and sincere observation of ritual, regardless of whether anyone else might be present, as though before God alone, provided a humane contrast to recent history, the massacres, atrocities, and destruction of homes and churches. Religion becomes light in the prevailing darkness.

Donald was asked to say the Lord's Prayer; then the bishop said, "Please sing one of your songs." Donald then sang the doxology: "Praise God from whom all blessings flow."

After the service the bishop explained that the church had been destroyed in the Second World War. Germans bombed it because it had become a shelter for refugees and was being used as a hospital. Only a single mosaic remained, a St Nicholas who looks down over the entrance outside. He led us across the meadow behind the building. A fish farm lay beyond and hills rose steeply around. The River Una flowed past, wide and placid after tumbling over waterfalls. Monks used to live in caves in these hills, and sent goats' and sheeps' milk down channels to the monastery below. A family sat on the terrace of their small house on the hillside beyond the river, enjoying the late afternoon sun and watching the monks and the bishop entertaining strangers.

Lazar chatted to the monks about our plans after the bishop had driven off with the schoolteacher, to return to his hotel in Shipovo, a lengthy drive across the mountains back along the road with mines on either side. Bees were still gathering nectar in the meadows full of flowers, wild clary, orchids, vipers bugloss, meadowsweet, vetches, and countless other plants, and we leaned over the bridge to watch the sun spangled waters of the Una flow over stones and rocks, weed floating like hair in the current.

Lazar relaxed with the monks, they were 'his' people, 'good' Orthodox and soon he would be taking us into enemy territory where he did not feel welcome. He felt nervous again and wanted to delay the final part of our journey.

The monks were clearly excited by our visit. Perhaps we would help them rebuild their monastery. They liked Lazar too, not wanting to let him go. Eventually they embraced us, and tall bustling Sergei gave me a wet kiss on both cheeks, awkward and blushing, while handsome shy Seraphim shook hands and Sophrone hugged me tightly. Then they watched us leave, before turning to walk home up the dusty road, across the vegetable patch with neat rows of sweet peppers, beans, tomatoes, and potatoes tended by Seraphim, the cat prowling through the orchard, the bees settling down for a hard night's fanning the nectar, turning it into honey, the thrushes still singing until nightfall. Behind the trees the waterfall thundered in the distance, a faint but perpetual roar. They would clear up the table, then finish their studies and prayers for the day before going to bed, each in his own room, the windows opening to the night and the harmonies of nature.

The Road to Bihac

A narrow dusty lane follows the River Una for about eight miles. We had to drive slowly over loose stones and thick dust which rose in clouds as we passed. The heady scent of meadowsweet wafted through the open windows and my hand stroked the grasses and flowers along the roadside. On the left the wide river flows peacefully, bounded on the other side by a thick forest with branches bending into the water as it murmured round islands with reeds, flowers, and bushes. Birds joined in vigorous evensong, and a solitary fisherman stood stock still, as though rooted in the shallows, blending with his surroundings. A mist began to rise from the surface of the water. Just once we encountered another vehicle, the road then suddenly hidden in a cloud of pale dust. On the right, meadows sloped down to the bank. A bewildering variety of wild flowers filled the fields. Fruit trees, branches hanging over the road, bordered the meadows, where now and then some cows grazed and a horse rested, waiting for night to fall. Behind, dark woods stretched into the hills. The meadowsweet reminded me of how in olden times people used to spread this herb over the floor so as to freshen the air. Variously coloured species of vetch twined up the banks, and the startling colours of golden arnica splashed vividly among the blues of columbines, clary, and bell flowers, also in varieties that I had never thought to see in the wild, from small delicate to large heavy blooms. Wild marjoram, dark patches of mint, and thick blankets of thyme covered the stones. The river kept the air cool along this dreamlike valley where the sun shone all day, moving from east to west and was now setting in a crimson haze.

The lane eventually emerged from the secluded valley and joined the road leading to Bihac. The landscape continued with far flung vistas over low rolling hills and woods. Massive spreading trees stood solitary in large unbounded fields. A notice by the wayside announced the presence of international charities involved in the rebuilding of communities, and we came across villages and ruined houses, one after the other, desolate in the placid beauty of the countryside. Though the signs looked rusty and weatherbeaten, the villages were still empty and derelict. Vigorous untended vines grew over the crumbling walls and through the gaping windows. These places looked forgotten. Ten years ago women turned the hay, men drove carts, animals grazed, chickens scratched, and children played. These memories haunted the eerily silent scene. Newsreels had shown burning houses along roads like this. Here was the aftermath.

Lazar warned us that we would soon come across a Muslim cemetery by the road. In a narrow gorge, where the woods were particularly thick, we saw on the lefthand side a field crowded with gravestones in the shape of miniature minarets, facing east to Mecca. During the war, Serb soldiers concealed themselves in the woods opposite and ambushed a group of Muslim soldiers marching up the road. They shot every one. The cemetery will remind future generations of the ruthless insane war that desecrated this otherwise peaceful and innocent-looking spot.

The road sped quickly through the deserted countryside and we came to the steep descent into Bihac. In the valley below we could see a string of derelict villages. As we reached the plain approaching Bihac, the ruins multiplied on both sides of the road, but already families were settling here and there, despite holes in the roof and general dereliction. One room seemed sufficient to gain a toehold on home. Women in kerchiefs stood at the door holding pots and jugs, men sawed planks of wood round the back, and children and animals ran around the front. The roof of one house had slid dramatically into the interior, beams pointing at the sky, gaps staring where windows used to be, slates and stones crumbled in a heap below. A family sat drinking on the terrace of a house opposite.

The first minaret appeared and though the people looked exactly like those we had left in Banja Luka, we felt as though we had entered another continent. Lazar told us that during the war soldiers could not be sure whom they were killing. When they came across men fleeing or hiding in the woods, they took down their trousers. Only by checking on whether they were circumcized could they tell whether they were Serbs or Muslims. But what of Croats and Serbs? This confusion only made the war even more insane.

As we approached the town, minarets sprouted in villages on either side in ever greater numbers. The region seemed to be well populated, with houses being repaired and rebuilt along the main road. We crossed the River Una to enter Bihac, and noticed children paddling and crowds of people strolling along the banks in the cool evening. A large mosque stands in the town centre.

Lazar worried about leaving the car untended overnight, and so we decided to find a hotel in the country. By the time we reached the Cedra Hotel, several miles along the River Una in the direction of Bosanski Novi to the north of Bosnia, night had fallen, and we only saw the magnificent scenery next day. But by now my eye had taken its fill, and the agonizing contrast of the beauty of nature with the horrifying relics of war had begun to blunt my capacity to react. Darkness came as a blessing.

The Cedra Hotel was a relic from communist times, large, solid, exclusive, and smart without unnecessary luxuries. Officials would probably have taken their vacation here or attended conferences. We appeared to be the only guests. The elegant dining room decked to host a banquet now stood empty, the staff not prepared for serving food. The kitchen opened in a panic and several ancient tins of mushrooms and cooked vegetables were tipped into a saucepan for reheating. Breakfast turned out to be as disastrous. Large dishes with greying slices of spam and cold omelettes resembling orange rubber mats lay in separate isolation on a massive table in the middle of the dining room. We ordered coffee from a polite and zealous elderly waiter who looked nervous at suddenly having to serve someone. He produced a small can of Turkish coffee, full of grains, and mixed it with cold milk to produce one of the most unpleasant concoctions we had ever tasted. Our stomachs churned and we satisfied ourselves with chewing on a soft roll, avoiding the pat of rancid butter on the side of the plate. When we start to bring tourists over from Europe, the Cedra Hotel would have to improve its cuisine. But its position could not be improved. The hotel overlooked the River Una, a lawn descending to the banks where children were already paddling and splashing in the shallows, their parents swimming in the deeper pools. Wooded hills rose steeply on both sides. A ruined castle looked down from a height behind. The River Una proceeded along this deep valley forty miles northwards to the Croatian border.

Bihac

We returned to Bihac for meetings with the mufti, a Catholic priest, and some government officials. Now in bright June sunlight we saw the magnificent scenery we had passed in darkness the night before. The river flowed over rapids, the foam glistening white against the azure blue of the water. Instead of the baroque churches we expected to see punctuating this temperate mid-European landscape of hills, woods, farms, and villages, minarets pointed slender fingers into the sky. Meadows bordered the river with allotments and gardens wherever houses stood near the edge, little rowing boats for fishing tethered to wooden piers on the bank.

Bihac is representative of part of the Balkans where all three ethnic groups once lived at peace together. Politics shattered that harmony. I began to learn rapidly that this was not an example of how fragile the harmony had been, a facile conclusion reached in western Europe which judges only from newspaper reports. On the contrary, this tradition of coexistence will eventually help heal the atrocious wounds of the last decade. The destruction of human bonds indicated the virulence of nationalist politics and the residual influence of a paternalistic totalitarianism which kept people ever more ignorant and unpoliticized, as the leaders became ever more corrupt and grasping, fearful of losing power to rivals, knowing that their lives, not just their careers were at stake.

Everyone we met and spoke to genuinely wanted to live at peace with their neighbours and welcomed reconciliation and future co-existence. The obstacle to this desired state of affairs was only too evident: economic stagnation. This devastated part of Europe lacked the basic infrastructure for businesses to flourish and for work to be available so that all the different communities can begin to move back together again. As it was, the dominant community became the overall majority – Serbs in the Srpska Republic, Muslims in the greater part of the Federation of Bosnia, and Croats in control of certain towns and small regions. There was not enough work even for the majorities, who of course claimed priority. So the minorities were not attempting to return – yet.

Considering the violence from all sides in the conflict in this Bosnian heartland of the Balkans where all communities fought for control, waves of destruction and massacres following one after the other, finally leaving the Muslims in charge of Bihac, it astonished us to hear conciliatory words and a readiness to support our project. We were right to emphasize the necessity of economic regeneration: roofs on houses and work for people are more pressing needs than the rebuilding of churches. Nevertheless our proposal for a centre for peace-building met with an immediate and enthusiastic response, particularly as it promised to bring people from all over Europe to this neglected region. The important issue was to bring Bosnia into Europe, to end its isolation, because only then will the economy start to grow. Our presence and the project promised this beginning, and so we received a wholehearted welcome where we expected at best a half-hearted response. Just the fact that we had bothered to come at all was in itself a sign of hope and a cue for the people we met to open their doors.

However, religion became an issue for us. We had not expected to find the Muslim society in Bihac to be so secularized. Though mosques were being built with Saudi money, regardless of the poor economy, the mostly young people of the area ignored religion, and from their dress and manners evidently want to devote their energies to the hedonistic and materialistic western European lifestyle. Boys dressed in fashionable sports gear and the girls, far from covering themselves in veils and long clothes, wore short skirts, and close-fitting blouses in imitation of the Spice Girls, and many bleached their hair. Nowhere in Europe could be seen such a large proportion of young people in a town which seemed to be on a perpetual school holiday even in early June. A few elderly people appeared occasionally, looking out of place in the crowds of confident youngsters, who evidently had no intention of carrying on the battles of their parents, who were themselves nowhere to be seen, presumably most of them killed and the few survivors keeping heads down and filling the few available work positions.

Elsewhere in the Balkans, church leaders had welcomed us and seemed to enjoy some influence in their constituencies, fulfilling a need for people to experience transcendence after years of pointless deprivation and suffering. In Bihac, for the first time, church leaders could not offer us the same unconditional welcome. With the harassed Catholic priest, Fra Anto, it was simply a case of his being completely overwhelmed by the demands of his dwindling flock. He listened impatiently to our long speeches about wanting to spend time on assessments before proceeding with the project and then told us that he had no time to wait. His people needed work and homes: unless we could provide immediate aid, he really didn't have time for us. He added bitterly that enough people like ourselves had come promising big schemes to help the situation, and had disappeared never to be heard from again. He looked at us as much as to say, "You're wasting my time too, building up my hopes for something that might happen, but I know you will soon be going back to England and will forget us." Fra Anto could only deliver band aid for the time being. Then he spoke about the history of the Catholics in Bosnia and how the Franciscans had been present here for many centuries. Catholics had even succeeded in keeping the Muslims at bay. History seemed so here and now, the thirteenth century only yesterday, that it came as a surprise to hear after so many victories and triumphs that only two

Franciscans remained in Bihac. There was in fact a tradition of good neighbourhood and working cooperatively in Bihac. The idea of rebuilding churches collaboratively would not be considered extraordinary, though Fra Anto looked momentarily stunned at the proposal. He explained pragmatically that people needed work. Full stop. Building a church or a school, it didn't matter what religion you were, the work was welcome. Fra Anto was a young priest, vigorous and muscular, reminding me of Anglican clergy who choose to minister in difficult inner-city parishes. For all his courage and resilience, his eyes stared with the frightened look of someone who has witnessed the extremes of human cruelty. As we left he pointed out the vandalization of his church where statues outside had been stoned out of their plinths and destroyed. It reminded us of the Reformation in England.

Two contrasting meetings brought our visit to Bosnia to a powerful close. Together they highlighted the importance of our work and the huge problems we would face. The first meeting, with the government officials, unexpectedly encouraged us unconditionally. The second, with the mufti, disturbed us, also unexpectedly and left an indelible impression of the extremity of the barbaric cruelties and suffering that had been inflicted so recently. The beauty of the countryside and the warm friendliness of the people, even the attractive girls and boys without attitude, made us forget that the war had ended only five years ago. It will take as yet unquantifiable time and energy to come to terms with the wounds inflicted, the scale of the atrocities, the numbers killed, and the destruction of homes and churches.

Lazar, a Serb, was also tested by these meetings. When we left him the following day we sensed the degree of stress he had endured, carrying the guilt of his community before the very people his community had tried to destroy.

Bosnia is divided into autonomously governed regions. The international peacekeeping force, whose job is to integrate the different communities, has the power to remove obstreperous authorities who refuse to implement this policy of integration. In the Srpska Republic the policy seems to be to allow the authorities a free hand, to avoid trouble. In Bihac we arrived to find a new authority in charge, the ministers having taken up their posts only that day. This may explain why the young doorman at the ministry refused to let us in. He did not know of Mr Sisic and for a while we thought we had hit our first brick wall. Perhaps no one wanted to see us. After Lazar had talked to various officials we were shown upstairs where Mr Sisic, a tall, friendly man in his thirties, had been waiting all along to greet us, having invited two other new ministers, a beaming elderly man called Mr Trgic, a mathematics professor who suddenly found himself in charge of education, and an athletic younger man, Mr Kunic, who took responsibility for small businesses and ecological projects. They had been looking forward to our arrival and conducted the whole meeting in the friendliest manner, with no obstacles that couldn't be immediately removed, and they expressed only encouragement for the future.

However, they expressed a reservation about our religious constituency, fearing that we might be a sect coming to convert young people. They also warned us about working too closely with religious groups in Bosnia, to avoid being sucked into sectarian politics. Mr Trgic, a devout Muslim, spoke about the need to "base religion rightly", that all truly faithful people live beyond the boundaries of their own faith. They appreciated in particular the way we brought together faith, dialogue, and discussion to include economic regeneration. "That is the beauty of your Project," Mr Sisic said – the word 'beauty' was again being used to describe our proposals. Rebuilding churches was less interesting to them than establishing a centre for peace-building and reconciliation. It should show the three symbols of the three faiths. They took to the idea of tourism, bringing people to this as yet unknown and beautiful part of Europe, Mr Sisic observing that they were still learning how to capitalize on their natural assets, particularly aware of preserving the natural ecological balance of the region. Donald offered to bring experts over from England to advise on these issues and we suggested calling ourselves the Una Project which delighted them even further. Our work would help bring Bosnia and Herzegovina into the rest of Europe as a new democracy. Employment and kick-starting the economy were crucial stepping stones not only to do that, but to developing integration of the communities within the country. "If a man has a job, he will learn to love other religions, other people," commented Mr Sisic, adding with potent simplicity, "But with no job, he is poor, he remains in prison, he becomes a criminal."

The meeting ended with a commitment to help each other. Mr Sisic considered our project which crosses the borders of different minorities to be significant enough for the President of Bosnia to be informed, which he would do. We should keep in touch regularly and not allow the impetus to wane.

Religious issues now faded into the background as the more urgent concerns of jobs and economy took a front seat. Gradually the project was becoming a practical reality. We could already imagine groups of people coming to stay at the Cedra Hotel, touring the region, learning about Bosnia, its history, its landscape, its culture and future. These visits might then encourage small businesses to develop. It would be a start and it was something we could do straight away. Then the process of rebuilding churches could be grounded in the communities, wherever the need was greatest. The centre for peace-building emerged as the crucial venture here in Bihac, country of the two rivers, the Una and Sana. At last the project was taking shape, moving beyond a vague idea. We were beginning to formulate a proposal that would inspire and be understood by people all over Europe. We had found our strongest allies, and these were the authorities themselves.

However, we needed to meet the Mufti of Bihac. We had written to him, faxed him, phoned him, and tried to arrange an appointment, with no luck. He seemed to be avoiding us. Perhaps as Muslims were dominant in Bihac he felt no need to talk to us. But without Muslim support we could not continue. As Lazar put it, "We can go home and forget about it." How to reach him? Fortunately we raised this question with Mr Trgic, who said he knew the mufti personally. He phoned him, and after a brief conversation the mufti agreed to meet with us, but only for ten minutes. He had another engagement.

Mr Trgic drove us to the mufti's office which had closed for the afternoon, and we waited for a while outside in the burning sun, Mr Trgic phoning the mufti again. Evidently we were a nuisance, though Mr Trgic himself could not have been friendlier and more helpful. But he gave us no indication of what to expect. Eventually the door opened and a young man showed us into Mufti Makic's office. Immediately we realized this would be the most difficult of all our meetings, but we had no idea how harrowing.

Mufti Makic sat with his back to the window in a dark room. Like Mufti Camdzic in Banja Luka, he had the robust frame of a farmer, but even bigger and burlier. Though his face was in shadow I noticed a pair of intensely burning eyes. He looked angry; probably Mr Trgic's phone call had compelled him to meet us against his will. He folded his hands on the desk table in front of him and indicated that we should proceed quickly and get the meeting over with as soon as possible. He motioned us to sit down. Mr Trgic listened without saying a word. He had stopped beaming, but he acted as a silent buffer to the onslaught that he probably did not want to warn us of in case we had decided not to meet the mufti.

For the first time we were not offered refreshment. The atmosphere became thick enough to slice. First Donald delivered his speech about the objectives of the Soul of Europe in Bosnia with particular reference to rebuilding a ruined mosque and establishing the centre of peace-building. The mufti heard him out politely but with barely concealed impatience. He looked sternly at us then began to speak. "Let me tell you something. Have you heard of Omarska?" "Who?" Donald asked, not catching the name but looking frightened, as we all were. I quickly explained to Donald about the most notorious of the Bosnian Serb concentration camps. This had been the place of some of the worst atrocities in the war, and the pictures of inmates who survived reminded everyone in Europe of Auschwitz. People were tortured and killed there in such appalling ways that even now it is impossible to believe the horrors perpetrated, just as we still find it hard to get our minds round the extent of the atrocities in Auschwitz, even over half a century after the event. Omarska became a hell in which psychopaths were able freely to indulge the most extreme tortures and brutalities. For example, men were forced to chew off one another's testicles before being crucified by having a pole rammed through their rectums and pushed through the shoulder blades. The brutalities that men perform on men are a rape, like that done to women: it is an act of humiliating violence that sets out successfully to negate the other person, if not killing them outright, making them feel not human and worthless. This is the nature of the trauma which victims carry for the rest of their lives. The link of sex with violence is the most important element in these tortures, since it negates absolutely any hint of emotion. It is feelings which make people human. Humiliating the victim with violent sex gives power to the rapist. Because of the shame of male sex, the violence has to be particularly atrocious. How do people survive the experience, even just witnessing it, as this mufti evidently had?

However the mufti did not dwell on his time in Omarska. As though that in itself were not terrible enough, he needed to tell us an even more disturbing story. His children had been forced to witness his arrest.

"I was there," the mufti said. "When they came to take me away, in front of my children, they put a knife against my throat and asked them, 'Would you like to see your father's throat cut or shall we take him to prison?' I was there for two months. They beat me every day. I was then an imam. I used to meet with a group of religious leaders. None of them visited me in the camp. I begged for help. One Orthodox priest said to my children when I sent them to inform him and ask him to help release me from the camp: "If the mufti is innocent nothing bad will happen to him. If he is innocent they will let him go.' "

We could not speak. Lazar, interpreting, looked pale and his voice trembled. How could we respond? Foolishly I had not prepared myself for such an encounter, though it must have been a likelihood. It had not occurred to me that religious leaders would be tortured, though I knew they had been shot. My mind was in turmoil, remembering stories, trying to come to grips with the situation, and horrified at the way history keeps repeating itself, one vengeance visited on another, only worse than before. The Serbs like to repeat the story of how fascist Ustashi Croats tortured an Orthodox bishop by slicing his nose and ears off, gouging out his eyes, and setting fire to him before throwing him into the river, the mutilated body found by his congregation in the mud on the banks of the River Vrbas in Banja Luka. That was in the Second World War, a couple of generations back. Now only five to six years ago the Serbs visited the same brutalities on their former enemies, the cycle of retribution and more violent terror continuing ad infinitum.

Donald tentatively pushed for the mufti's response on the project. The mufti shrugged as much as to indicate that nothing more needed to be said. He wouldn't block any proposals, but we mustn't expect him to be involved. On the other hand we could approach the Reis ul Ulema in Sarajevo, the leader of the Islamic community in the Balkans. Mufti Makic would go along with anything the Reis ul Ulema decided. We realized that our work had barely begun. The process of collaborating with Islam would be long and we needed to learn patience as well as persistence.

Donald could not leave without making a statement as well as a gesture, to hold out a hand to the mufti. Donald spoke about coming in penitence to Bosnia and, standing up, apologized for his Christian brothers who had betrayed and abandoned the mufti in his time of need. Donald spoke with utmost solemnity, rising to the occasion. Whatever happened, we could not leave the mufti without having at least started the process of reconciliation. The mufti had also risen, to see us out of the office, but began to realize the humane purpose of Donald's speech, Lazar interpreting with fervour. The mufti looked unblinkingly at Donald and I could see that a shaft of human light was penetrating his black, steely shell. No one had spoken like this to him before. No one had said sorry for what he had suffered. For a moment I thought the mufti would crumble, though his burly dignity prevented any sign of vulnerability. Donald rightly observed afterwards that the mufti had been waiting for this kind of support, understanding, and help. The man had suffered, and his children had been traumatized. Now he had been put in charge of the busy muftiluk of Bihac with all the responsibilities and stresses demanded of his position. Who was helping him deal with his trauma, anger, memories and nightmares? The mufti's face indicated that he hardly if ever slept. The man was haunted, and still in thrall to his all too recent sufferings. Donald determined to visit the mufti regularly on future visits to Bihac. When he had finished speaking, he presented the mufti with the gift we had prepared for all the religious leaders we met, a large glossy book about England. This gift enabled the mufti at last to extend a friendly hand. He would love to visit England, he told us, he had always dreamed of coming there. Donald then promised to invite him as part of the process of raising interest in the rebuilding of the Ferhadija Mosque in Banja Luka. The emotions now were bathing the meeting in an atmosphere of possibilities, rather than the hostility when we arrived. The mufti even shook hands with Lazar who trembled and apologized for the abominable behaviour of his compatriots, saying that most Serbs had always been against it. "Yes, I know that," said the mufti in a tone both conciliatory but also reserved. He could not yet forgive what had been done to him and above all to his children. He allowed us to take a photograph, and on it his staring black-rimmed eyes express the darkness of defiance and unappeased rage, the haunted gaze of a man who has literally been to hell.

Outside in the burning sun we spoke with the gentle Mr Trgic who promised us a welcome when we return to Bihac. We could even stay in his home and he wanted to help us in every way. He did not speak about the meeting, but his manner towards us indicated that he understood what we had achieved and that our behaviour with the mufti had proved that we could be trusted.

Now Lazar could not wait to show us the desecrated Orthodox church in Bihac. The meeting with the mufti had disturbed and angered him. "Those criminals!" he spat, referring to his Serb compatriots, "they ruined my life!" He could not bring himself to accept that they had also ruined the lives of others, including the mufti's. He needed to show us that the Orthodox had suffered too, that we get a balanced view of the Bosnian tragedy. Balanced? How can anyone be balanced about the extent of the atrocities and destruction, from whichever side it came? But through Lazar we learned that the Balkans have a long way to go when even educated and sensitive people like himself have such difficulties coming to terms with the enormity of the crimes committed. It no longer becomes a matter of weighing the scales, as though the quantity of crime committed by one side when equalled by that of another somehow negates the suffering and the consequences. The people in the Balkans are a long way from being able to forgive. They know how important it is for the present to put enmities in the past and learn at least to live together. But only when all sides face up to what they did, and admit to the crimes committed in their names, will there be an opportunity for each side to express forgiveness to the other. And without forgiveness there can be no reconciliation, and no foundations for lasting peace.

We stood by the unfinished Orthodox church standing in a piece of waste ground, the walls slashed with graffiti, "The Armies of Allah have triumphed!" Lazar clearly wanted to erase the impact of our meeting with the mufti with this visible sign of Muslim desecration. I could not equate the clumsy slogans with the physical and psychological traumas experienced by human beings. Lazar did not have to keep reminding me that the other sides committed violations too. All that needed to be said was, "We did wrong. I am sorry!"

Donald and I stood shattered by the last encounter, not ready to engage in more conversations with strangers, but Lazar tried to get us to speak to people on the street, to gauge their opinions, to talk, to take on the sufferings of the Serbs in Bihac, the abandoned ruined church, to hear an antidote to the mufti's disturbing story. A middle-aged man came round the corner beckoning to us enthusiastically, breathing hot fumes of garlic and only too happy to talk to us. Lazar eagerly translated every word of his experiences of being moved from house to house, now homeless, poor, and jobless. "We should take him to supper," Lazar said, looking at us accusingly, "See, he is lonely, he has no one to talk to!" "Another time," Donald said diplomatically, and we completed the conversation on the waste land. A young boy on a small bike listened solemnly, and then proceeded to play with a kitten who appeared from under a hedge. The boy grinned at me over his shoulder as he tickled the outstretched kitten's tummy. The gist of the conversation with the man was a reminder of the waves of violence that passed through Bihac, the Croats, Serbs, and Muslims in turn trying to clear the town of the other two groups. But now people just want to get on together. Blame is laid firmly at the feet of the politicians. He, as a Muslim, would be happy to live with Orthodox neighbours. Only one Serb family still lived in this part of town, the others having fled and left their homes which had either been occupied by Muslims or remained in ruins. This Serb family, mostly adolescent girls, could be seen enjoying a quiet drink in the garden but refused to be drawn into conversation with us despite Lazar's entreaties.

When the man left, looking at us disappointed that the conversation had been so short, we drove out of Bihac for a meal in a restaurant by the River Una. A pier and platform had been constructed so that the river flows under the guests, rushing over a weir and creating a deep pool into which boys dived from the trees and swam. Beyond the weir the river flowed smoothly and men in boats lurked among the forest of reeds and bulrushes, casting their lines quietly, moving slowly, paddling skilfully so that the oars just dipped in the water and created no disturbance. A large spit and barbecue had been rigged by the roadside and a whole lamb roasted slowly over hot charcoal. Large trees shaded the tables and a cool breeze from the surface of the river calmed the ferocity of the afternoon sun. Beyond the far bank of the river, meadows stretched to several villages on the hillsides beyond, each with a gleaming new minaret, and some with two. We concentrated on the positive encounter with the local government ministers and discussed the project. Lazar now wanted to drive immediately to Sarajevo to meet the Reis ul Ulema. "If we don't, we are finished!" he said. Taking all our recent conversations into consideration, we decided it would be better to visit Sarajevo separately on our next visit and try to arrange meetings with not only the principle Muslim religious leader but some government officials as well. Meanwhile we made plans for the next day, taking photographs of ruins and investigating accommodation for the Soul of Europe, to establish a base in Bihac.

The River Una gushed under our feet, children splashed in the shallows, and older boys made a series of spectacular dives into the deep pool. A fisherman moved his boat stealthily through the reeds as the evening wore on. Meanwhile an attentive waiter served local wine, grilled fish from the river, and several plates of fried potatoes and salads for Lazar. Three men in their late twenties and early thirties sat at a neighbouring table, thuggish and quietly menacing. "Don't look at them," advised Lazar, "they will kill you!" Later he added, "They probably killed many Serbs." We observed them drinking several bottles of wine and sharing a platter of grilled lamb from the roadside barbecue, eating with their knives. One of them cast warning glances, and we turned our attention to a fisherman slowly paddling his way downstream along the River Una. The hills rolled on either side into the distance, minarets delicately fingering the sky. Then evening began to steal across the landscape and we decided to return to the Cedra Hotel.

On the way Lazar took us on a detour into the high mountains which provide a natural border between Bosnia and Croatia. He hoped I might organize a visa to enable him to drive us to Zagreb the next day. It was more difficult for a Serb to gain a visa to Croatia than for any other nationality. The Croatian embassy in Belgrade had already played cat and mouse with him. They were aware of the dates for which he needed the visa and took his money. Then they kept him waiting and issued the visa too late. The officials probably smiled with satisfaction. Such was the continuing conflict in the Balkans, petty and persistent. But maybe an Englishman could sort the problem out at the border. We arrived at the highest pass where the border guards look out on desolate moorland. The Bosnians treated me politely and allowed me to walk across no man's land. Mines stretched in every direction and no cars passed, so remote was this crossing. Here the war continued, a gesture of menace from both sides. The Croats looked at my passport and, though friendly, declined to help me with Lazar's visa. We should approach the Croatian embassy in Bihac. So I walked back along the empty road, the white warning flags fluttering over the invisible mines and felt the sadness of this region of political games and hate. But a soft wind blew from the mountains from one country to the other, and I also sensed the provisional nature of these gestures.

The Last Day

The medieval castle on the hill behind the hotel turned out to be a Muslim ruin. Serb soldiers had sacked the interior and tried to demolish it, but though the pock-marked walls indicated where grenades had landed, the solid structure withstood the pounding. Since it had once housed a mosque, according to Muslim law the building could not be used for any other purpose than worship. So what might be renovated and turned into a luxurious residence, conference centre, or hotel with spectacular views down the valley cannot be touched. Weeds grew over the threshold, empty windows stared out onto miles of forested hills, mouldy floors gave way to gaping holes opening onto rooms below, the interior crumbled into further ruin day by day. The delicate craftsmanship of carvings and mouldings were turning to dust and rubble. Outside, a series of massive stone sculptures commissioned by Tito as a celebration of communist art sank into the ground, gradually being covered by grass and trees. The statues depicted beefy figures of men and women sitting, crouching, and falling into stupor as though giving up on life.

A wizened elderly porter opened the gates for us. He told us there were no plans to renovate the castle. A shining new mosque stood in the middle of the village nearby. A marble arch covered the path to the entrance with the names of local Muslims killed in the war carved on the walls. No expense had been spared. Most of the houses around the mosque still stood derelict; a few elderly peasants sat on carts piled with hay and were scratching an evidently poor living. Though money had been found to rebuild their mosque, none had been made available to improve their lives. The people looked at us with tired curiosity.

We spent the rest of the day driving around the countryside choosing ruins to photograph. However dramatic the sight of caved-in roofs, scorched and crumbled walls, weeds growing in gaping doorways, even a tree branching through an empty window frame, ruins look like incomplete, derelict, neglected buildings anywhere, even in England. Their history makes the difference, and that history exists only in newsreel footage of these very houses blazing along the roadside. The ruined mosque in one village made an attractive picture, covered in moss and tilting slightly. The gleaming new mosque next to it looked incongruous and out of place in the poverty-stricken village, the houses still needing repair. Heavily made up young girls with bleached hair, exposed midriffs and short skirts, watched us drive past. They were the only signs of life in these villages, and the newness of the empty mosques only emphasized the sad condition of the homes waiting to be repaired.

Before catching the bus to Zagreb we visited two houses for rent where we might base the project offices. A young Muslim owned one of them, which stood on the road leading out of Bihac in the direction of Sarajevo. His mother with a kerchief wrapped around her head smiled proudly at the gate of their home next door. He was a gastarbeiter, guest worker, who lived mostly in Germany and now owned several houses in Bihac, aiming to let them out. This one had been decorated in western style, furnished simply but comfortably with carpets and a fitted kitchen. The neat garden with an orchard stretched into a large meadow behind, at the far side of which we could see more houses belonging to this young entrepreneur.

The other house stood in the middle of the town. A dejected-looking elderly couple sat outside in the shade of a large cherry tree heavy with crimson fruit. They refused to look at us, continuing uninterrupted in the task of separating lime flowers from their stalks, and laying them in large piles on sheets of newspaper. The garden beyond was well tended, with a substantial vegetable patch, beans growing, more fruit trees, and a row of beehives thundering with activity. The agent whispered to us that the couple were refugees, probably Serb, and were being moved from home to home. We hoped to look inside the attractive though neglected small house, but the man refused. He did not want us to see "the wretched way we live" so we left the beautiful garden with roses growing along the front. The couple persisted in turning their faces away from us, and their posture expressed both shame and misery as well as injured pride. Why should they have to suffer these indignities? They were entitled to their home, but where was it, who had destroyed it? Why couldn't they have it back? Here they sat and had to endure strangers disturbing their privacy. They wanted to set down roots, but had always to be ready for the next move to yet another temporary place.

The bus to Zagreb crossed the border high in the hills where I had walked through no man's land the day before. A group of young Kosovar passengers, teenage boys, tried to cross over. They managed to satisfy the Bosnian guards, but the Croats detained them. "Goodbye!" they waved at us smiling, having anticipated this obstacle, but evidently confident of continuing their journey later. They sat by the guardhouse on a few small bags, which held all their belongings, and watched the bus continue into Croatia. Would they be sent back to Kosovo, be held in Bosnia, or find some way of carrying on their journey to seek asylum in western Europe? They could not stay the night in this bleak spot, surely? Then I remembered a wretched-looking figure from the night before, sitting with his back against the guardhouse, a young man so thin that I almost missed seeing him. His long dirty hair hung matted round his face as he glanced sorrowfully at me passing, another refugee seizing any chance to leave Bosnia, preparing to sleep without shelter in the cold night air high in the mountains, waiting and hoping.

Beyond lay the bleak landscape of Croatia. Behind us the verdant and sun-drenched hills of Bosnia fell away in folds of untilled meadows and thick forests down to the glistening azure waters of the River Una. Like gaping wounds in the lush countryside, ruined and deserted villages stretched in a chain up the distant valleys.

NO FUTURE WITHOUT FORGIVENESS[1]

DONALD REEVES

Radovan, a twenty-five-year-old lawyer from Banja Luka learned about the work of the Soul of Europe and what we were trying to achieve in Bosnia. We conversed on the Internet. At first he was cynical about our presence in the Srpska Republic. "You are taking other people's money and just playing around," he said. He refused to meet us because he despises and mistrusts foreigners whom he describes as being arrogant, dispensing advice and opinions without deeper knowledge of the history and traditions of his culture. However, he admitted that his country needed our help, and he appreciated the seriousness of our intent and our readiness to listen and learn.

Radovan had grown up witnessing his parents' generation killing and destroying. His father had been killed in the war. "Don't speak to me about fathers!" he said. "We were brought up to respect older people. Look what they have done. What kind of life is there for me in Banja Luka? There is no future for us here. For our politicians, the peace has just been an excuse to continue the war by other means. Young people, our lives, our work and our future do not matter to them."

In a survey completed by the United Nations Programme in 2000, sixty-two per cent of people between fourteen and twenty-five would leave Bosnia if they could. In a country where fifty-six per cent of the population is unemployed such a percentage is not surprising.

Radovan works as a legal advisor to workers who suffer discrimination and harassment in the workplace. He does not intend to emigrate, despite the fact that his work scarcely earns him a basic wage. Throughout our long conversation he unburdened himself of years of pain, resentment, and grief. Towards the end he said: "Old people who should have been an example to us have destroyed my country. But what upsets me more than anything is that not one of them, not one, has said sorry." He then excused himself abruptly: "I am tired and must go to bed." And signed off. He was still traumatized by the destruction and massacres that had ruined his country, but what disturbed him most was that no one had yet been prepared to take responsibility and apologize. If we cannot acknowledge our guilt, how can we say sorry and how can we then ask forgiveness? Without forgiveness there is no future.

The Dayton Peace Agreement brought the war to an end. The killing and the destruction stopped. The attempted genocide of the Muslim population failed. One hundred and fifty thousand people died, men, women and children. Two million people were forced to flee their homes. Towns and villages were devastated.

President Milosevic of Serbia and President Tudjman of Croatia had agreed between themselves to turn Bosnia into a Christian state to be divided between Orthodox and Catholics. Every trace of Islam was to be removed. Men were sent to killing camps. Women were raped, not only to defile them but to ensure that they would no longer bear Muslim children. People were destroyed on the basis of their religious identity, even those who were not active adherents of their religion. Christian leaders sanctioned and blessed this slaughter. As Metropolitan Nikolaj of Sarajevo said at the beginning of the war: "To follow General Mladic and Radovan Karadjic is to follow the path of Christ." The extermination of Muslims was perceived as a sacred act, endorsed by a manipulated version of religious mythology which regarded Muslims as Christ-haters. Despite the fact that Bosnian Muslims have lived in the Balkans for five hundred years and have always been as native to the region as the other ethnic groups, the aversion and deep suspicion of Islam fuelled the policy of genocide.

Now Bosnia is divided into ethnic communities. Only a substantial international presence holds the united but weak country together. Billions of dollars of aid assist the reconstruction of

Bosnia, but the future of such a divided country remains uncertain and perilous. Only the minimum demands of the three communities were met by Dayton. The Bosnian Serbs did not get their independence, nor union with Serbia. A semi-autonomous state was created, the Srpska Republic, which, though part of Bosnia and Herzegovina, keeps itself separate from the Federation. The Muslims did not achieve independence from their aggressors. They remain a majority in the Federation of Bosnia and Herzegovina, but endure the continued hostility and menace of Croat separatists who regret failing to merge with Croatia and wish to carve out a Republic for themselves in Western and Southern Bosnia.

Despite the insecurity of these arrangements and the shadow of unfinished business concerning the failure of genocide and the continued Muslim presence in Bosnia, peace is now taken for granted. No one wants a return to war. Serb and Croat nationalists are said to be biding their time until the international presence is lessened or removed. Bosnia meanwhile remains dependent on foreign aid. It has an unsustainably large trade deficit. Unrealistic budgets are produced. There are few domestic investments. There is massive unemployment, inefficient institutions, and corruption. Political agendas are still dominated by old nationalist issues to the detriment of the pressing social and economic problems from which all Bosnia suffers – in particular the young generation.

For the foreseeable future the international community will need to assist Bosnia in establishing institutions that will strengthen the rule of law and the observance of human rights. A framework for regional and European integration will have to be created. This means abandoning the nineteenth-century notion of the nation state, and integrating Bosnia and the rest of the Balkans into a transnational Europe. Unless there are speedy positive movements in this direction, nationalist issues centred round the ownership of land will flourish, political conflicts will continue to fester, the younger generation will leave, and the forces of disintegration will plunge Bosnia once again into despair and war.

This is the routine analysis of many commentators, academics, and historians about Bosnia and its future.[2] It evokes that negative melancholy which perceives history as tragic. It predicts that, in spite of all the best intentions – let alone the massive financial and human resources poured into Bosnia – the enemies of Bosnia's welfare and ours too are waiting to undo whatever good has been achieved. It is therefore easy to understand and sympathise with the anger, disillusion, and grief of young people like Radovan.

This gloomy prognosis need not have the last word. In future conversations with Radovan the mood lightened. He appreciated our interest in his country and in his future. He valued the human contact in itself. No situation is intractable or utterly without hope. He agreed that we are all made to live in harmony one with another and with the earth. We are invited to see and to experience our enemies as potential friends, simply because we belong on this small planet together. This is a generous vision of reconciliation and it is expressed in the hope which, like faith and love, is a gift from God. There is nothing easy, sentimental, or trivial about this hope and never in this life will such a vision be fully realized. But it is possible for everyone to take some steps along the way.

A significant step is to engage in the process of forgiveness.[3] This process is not the same as political negotiation which rightly and inevitably leads to compromise. But these endeavours can create the conditions through which forgiveness is mediated.

The experience of contrition, remorse, shame, admission of guilt, and reparation, leading some way to a reconciliation that signals a new start, are among the most difficult and painful elements of human experience. Too much of our language about forgiveness is static and tidy. As in politics there are no conclusions.

The setting up of the International War Crimes Tribunal in The Hague has been the most public way in which those accused of ordering and supervising the attempted genocide of Muslims in Bosnia is being addressed. As I write there are fifteen people named in the Srpska Republic who have yet to be handed over to the tribunal. The Soul of Europe is not concerned with the fate of these public figures.

But there are others. There are those who abused, tortured, raped, and murdered. In the region of Banja Luka the perpetrators of these crimes were mostly urban gangsters from Serbia. They are no longer in Bosnia. These men are those who 'obeyed orders' (given by some of those summoned to appear before the tribunal), those who supported the bureaucracy of genocide in Banja Luka. There are those who knew and did not want to know. There are those who looked on and did not know what to do and were fearful of doing anything. There are those who live in fear in case they will be found out. There are those who taunted Muslims and Croats and made the daily lives of these non-Serbs intolerable. In Banja Luka the fear and mistrust many people still have for one another is palpable. Unless these fears are acknowledged and addressed (which involves some sort of amnesty) the future looks bleak, simply because the past will return to haunt everyone.

Any process of forgiveness has to begin with establishing the facts. What happened to whom, by whom, and why? Those who have suffered should have the opportunity to tell their stories. Being forgiven is not like an acquittal, where the past is wiped out and a new start can be made. In the story-telling the past is remembered, but the evil that has happened no longer sets the agenda. Remembering will involve anger at what the victim has suffered. It is an abuse of justice to move through this anger too quickly – even if that were possible.

Remembering may provide some sort of release, but it is not always possible to make sense of atrocities. Most of us are fascinated, repelled, and disturbed by the way in which we can so easily abuse and destroy one another. It is a blasphemy to attempt to explain and find meaning in atrocities because such attempts tend to reduce and normalize the suffering. The arbitrary character of this type of suffering can easily be lost. There are some actions which defy explanations, but it is important to remember them: "O Earth, cover not their blood." As George Santayana puts it: "Those who cannot remember the past are condemned to repeat it."

It is often the victim who will initiate the process of forgiveness. A story is told of a woman whose daughter had been murdered. The murderer had been caught and was put on death row. The daughter's mother was consumed with bitterness and hatred for what this man had done. She determined to confront him and witness his death. Eventually she met him and began to speak. Suddenly she began to weep. She found herself forgiving him and a great burden fell from her. She continued to visit him and after a while the man confessed his guilt and asked for her forgiveness. He had, in fact, already received it. He was executed and the woman now campaigns vigorously against capital punishment. Her life has been given back to her. [4]

There are many who remain unforgiven. The people who could offer an open hand, their victims, are dead. No one speaks for them. So the killers are forever locked in a prison of their own making.

It is impossible for forgiveness to happen in such circumstances because forgiveness is about making connection. "Only connect," says E. M. Forster. Sometimes the connections are irretrievably lost. Sometimes they can be restored, slowly and painfully, and when that happens it is as if the victim and offender receive a gift – light and warmth penetrates the cold darkness of their lives. Those who offend then come to know what it means to be powerless and vulnerable. They begin to recognize their arrogance and the limited view of the world they had constructed for themselves. They begin to see themselves through the eyes of the other and in the light of this larger world discover hope and new possibilities for the future. These involve acknowledging their offence, admitting their guilt, and desiring to make reparation.

What is certain is that when the fluid process of forgiveness begins there will be no retaliation, no revenge, and no victimization.

I have described some of the elements of the process of forgiveness. How this process should happen is another matter. The offenders should hear the stories of the victims. There has to be some kind of amnesty, the criteria for which require careful discussion. There needs to be the possibility of reparation for victims. The management of these hearings – which are not a court of law – demands the experience and wisdom of those from all over the world who have been involved in this process. It is clear that in every town and city throughout Bosnia such a forgiveness process needs to happen to ensure a stable and peaceful future. There are also many people with experience and wisdom who have worked in Northern Ireland, South Africa, and the Middle East to help with this process.

The Soul of Europe's work in Banja Luka offers just one way of developing such a process of peace and forgiveness. Between April and September 1993 fifteen mosques in Banja Luka were destroyed. This was part of a programme of the attempted extermination of all traces of Islam in the city, including the presence of thirty thousand Muslims who were forcibly removed from their homes. Banja Luka had not been in the war zone, but the authorities made no efforts to stop the destruction of the mosques including the Ferhadija Mosque, a jewel of Ottoman architecture, which was a UNESCO listed building and reckoned to be most important.

Since the mosque's destruction and up to the granting of permission in March 2001 for reconstructing it, there has been a consistent policy of humiliating the Muslim community, those still living in Banja Luka and those attempting to return to their homes. Letters requesting the rebuilding have neither been acknowledged nor answered. Poplar trees in the grounds of the mosque were cut down, the mufti's apartment destroyed, worship in the remaining offices was disrupted and attempts made to burn them down. The police did not investigate these offences. When the Chamber of Human Rights of Bosnia and Herzegovina tried to find a place for meetings to debate the issues concerning the destroyed mosques in Banja Luka, obstacles were put in the way of where these meetings should take place.

Now permission has been granted for the reconstruction of the mosque. But this does not mean that attitudes have changed.

No compensation has been offered, no apology given. There is no sign of regret nor any desire to make reparation. The mosque will be rebuilt, but nothing will change until an occasion is created for the people of Banja Luka to consider a future shared by all its citizens from all ethnic communities. The main religious and secular leaders of Banja Luka have now agreed to meet in Coventry in September 2001 and take some steps along the path to peace and reconciliation. Such a consultation will involve the exchange of painful memories. But there is already a shared desire to look forward to the future and develop practical and agreed outcomes.

The reconstruction of the Ferhadija Mosque will be an international and European project. The aim is to establish a Centre for Economic Development and a Centre for Reconciliation from among all religions and none. But whatever emerges will be of no use unless the community of Banja Luka welcomes the newly reconstructed Ferhadija Mosque. This means a seismic shift of attitudes not only towards the Muslim community but also between the Orthodox and Catholic communities whose mutual hostility still blights the politics of the country. The Soul of Europe, by setting up the consultation in Coventry, hopes to initiate a peace and forgiveness process.

This is a tricky process. It means working with every sort of agency to create a normal life in Banja Luka, and create a stability for which young people like Radovan crave. The process involves more than aid and advice. It creates those conditions in which the gift of light and warmth can begin to flood into the cold darkness. Whenever hands are shaken and fresh beginnings celebrated, however small, these symbolic acts and gestures need to be acknowledged so that they can provide evidence of how the perceptions of adversaries and former enemies are beginning to change. There is no instant forgiveness, peace, or reconciliation. As John Milton put it: "Long is the way and hard, that out of hell leads up to light."

If the people of Bosnia, who took mutual hatred to such extremes, can show the rest of the world this light and warmth, they will also be providing inspiration for future generations, and far beyond their own frontiers.

There is considerable theological reflection in these words, a vibrant, eschatological hope and a vision of the Kingdom of God in which everyone and everything can flourish.

The Passion narratives disclose the crucified victim as our hope: the powerless and vulnerable are those with whom God identifies. Those words from the Cross: "Father, forgive them for they know not what they do", remind us time and again that ultimately no one is completely monstrous. That may be easy for me to say for I am not one of those who have seen their family and home destroyed. But there are a few who have managed to do just that and these people have taken justice, which often seems mechanistic, to a different arena of healing, transformation, and hope.

In the midst of fear, distrust, and anger I can come to believe, through the courage and laughter of those who witnessed pain and sorrow, something of the vulnerable and precarious and limitless love, the Divine Love, which is there unconditionally for us all.[5] I also recognize, in the necessary, difficult, and painful process of bringing enemies together, the possibilities of that love expressing itself with freedom and generosity.

The Resurrection, for me the special, unique, mysterious sign at the first Easter, subsequently vouchsafed and glimpsed in so many different ways, is a promise that the faith, hope, and love of which I have written, does have the last word. That is why the Soul of Europe is working in Bosnia.

FURTHER READING

The numbers relate to the references in the previous section.

1. *No Future Without Forgiveness* by Desmond Tutu (Publisher: Rider). The title of this chapter is taken from Desmond Tutu's book of that name – largely an account of the South African Truth and Reconciliation Commission of which he was Chairman.
2. Much of the preceding analysis is taken from Carl Bildt's 'The Balkan's Second Chance', published in *Foreign Affairs* (January/February 2001). Carl Bildt is Special Envoy of the UN Secretary General to the Balkans. A former Prime Minister of Sweden, he served as European Co-Chair of the 1995 Dayton Peace Conference and as the international community's first High Representative in Bosnia and Herzegovina.
   Bosnia: A Short History by Noel Malcolm, published by Macmillan, is indispensable for learning about Bosnia. It sells well in Sarajevo's bookshops, and his views are acceptable to just about everyone, except hardline nationalists.
   The Bridge Betrayed – Religion and Genocide in Bosnia by Michael Sells, published by the California University Press, is essential reading to understand the attempted genocide of Muslims during the Bosnian War.
   The Denial of Bosnia by Rusmir Mahmutcehajic, published by Pennsylvania State University Press, is an analysis of Bosnia's complex history and of its potential role in a multi-faith Europe.
3. I have been greatly helped by Archbishop Rowan Williams' insights into forgiveness. It is a constant theme in his writings, particularly the essay on 'Remorse' in *Lost Icons*, published by T&T Clark, Edinburgh, and *Resurrection*, published by Darton, Longman and Todd.

4. I discovered this story written in an address Bishop Richard Holloway gave at Gresham College, London on 'What's the use of Jesus?'. But I have heard it told by others.
5. Theological sleuths will recognize my source: W. H. Vanstone's *Love's Endeavour, Love's Expense*, published by Darton, Longman and Todd – a marvellous description of the phenomenology of Love.

AFTERWORD

A Tender Bridge ended with our first visit to Bosnia in June 2000. Since then the Soul of Europe has returned to Bosnia six times. As a result of our visit, two projects are emerging: one in Bihac and the other in Banja Luka.

In May 2000 a resource centre was established in Bihac. Its aim is to promote a cross-sector partnership approach to development and to promote a spirit of entrepreneurship – the latter is central to the promotion of stability, economic growth, and reconciliation in the region. The centre will assist in setting up small business enterprises. In June 2001 the centre together with the Union of Small Businesses established the Una Sana Partnership Forum, committed to a partnership approach to the economic development of the region. This is a Soul of Europe project but technical and management assistance is provided by the Resource Centre for the Social Dimension of Business Practice based in London and managed by the Prince of Wales International Business Leaders Forum.

In Banja Luka a unique model of peace making is developing. As this book goes to print, the Soul of Europe is preparing for a consultation at Coventry Cathedral to which key religious and political leaders from Banja Luka are coming, together with teachers, local government officials, and business people. We are developing a type of peace making which recognizes different but complementary objectives in the overall aim of helping to make Banja Luka a flourishing European city where Serbs and non-Serbs will find a home.

Such bald descriptions of our intentions do not convey the difficulties and excitement of this work. Peter Pelz has written a sequel to *A Tender Bridge* which we hope to publish in 2002.

DONALD REEVES

THE SOUL OF EUROPE

Extracts from the website

Beyond conflict – towards peace, prosperity and reconciliation

The building of a new Europe is not just a matter for polticians and businessmen. Other voices need to be heard: women, poets and artists, theologians and philosophers, those who speak for the poor and on behalf of the environment. These voices together with Christian, Muslim, Jewish and other communities express the soul of Europe.

1. The Soul of Europe is clear-eyed about the evils that have been perpetrated in Bosnia. Our work is informed by a deep realism.
2. But we do not believe that continuing injustice is inevitable, that the issues are so intractable, or that people are so intransigent that nothing or little can be done. In this respect we part company with those observers, academics, historians and journalists who believe that there is some invisible indestinctible thread of fate woven into the fabric of Bosnia. We create our problems. We can unmake them.
3. The Soul of Europe is driven by a strong hope – Christian teaching expresses an eschatological hope – that in the case of Banja Luka, for example, steps can be taken towards developing a more peaceful, just, and prosperous region of the Balkans.
4. The Soul of Europe is European. We believe the future of all Bosnia lies in its full integration into the European Union, although recognizing this is a long way off.

5. The Soul of Europe is a guest in Bosnia. We are visitors and regard it as privilege to be there.
6. William Blake, the English poet, said that everything begins with the imagination. Alongside our realism and our hope, we want to see the world as it could be, in which everybody and everything in it flourishes. Therefore we approach our work with what the philosopher Paul Ricoeur calls a second naivety' – but coupled with intellectual rigour and integrity.

If you would like to keep in touch with the work of the Soul of Europe, this is our address:

The Coach House
Church Street
Crediton
Devon
EX17 2AQ
United Kingdom

or see the website:

www.soulofeurope.com

A NOTE ON TREES

How many trees have been used to publish this book? Well, only the pulp is used, which comes from the trimmings: the trunks are used for furniture. A commercially grown softwood tree produces, on average, about one-sixth of a ton of pulp. Since this book has used about one ton, it has needed the pulp of six trees to produce it. But by weight it has needed only three-quarters of one tree. So Cairns Publications is donating the wherewithal for the planting of two trees, in gratitude and recompense.